P9-AOS-304

Nutshell Series

of

WEST PUBLISHING COMPANY

P.O. Box 43526

St. Paul, Minnesota 55164

June, 1984

Accounting—Law and, 1984, 377 pages, by E. McGruder Faris, Professor of Law, Stetson University.

Administrative Law and Process, 2nd Ed., 1981, 445 pages, by Ernest Gellhorn, Dean and Professor of Law, Case Western Reserve University and Barry B. Boyer, Professor of Law, SUNY, Buffalo.

Admiralty, 1983, 390 pages, by Frank L. Maraist, Professor of Law, Louisiana State University.

Agency-Partnership, 1977, 364 pages, by Roscoe T. Steffen, Late Professor of Law, University of Chicago.

American Indian Law, 1981, 288 pages, by William C. Canby, Jr., Adjunct Professor of Law, Arizona State University.

Antitrust Law and Economics, 2nd Ed., 1981, 425 pages, by Ernest Gellhorn, Dean and Professor of Law, Case Western Reserve University.

Appellate Advocacy, 1984, 325 pages, by Alan D. Hornstein, Professor of Law, University of Maryland.

Art Law, 1984, 335 pages, by Leonard D. DuBoff, Professor of Law, Lewis and Clark College, Northwestern School of Law.

Banking and Financial Institutions, 1984, 409 pages, by William A. Lovett, Professor of Law, Tulane University.

Church-State Relations—Law of, 1981, 305 pages, by Leonard F. Manning, Late Professor of Law, Fordham University.

I

Criminal Law, 1975, 302 pages, by Arnold H. Loewy, Professor of Law, University of North Carolina.

Criminal Procedure—Constitutional Limitations, 3rd Ed., 1980, 438 pages, by Jerold H. Israel, Professor of Law, University of Michigan and Wayne R. LaFave, Professor of Law, University of Illinois.

Debtor-Creditor Law, 2nd Ed., 1980, 324 pages, by David G. Epstein, Professor of Law, University of Texas.

Employment Discrimination—Federal Law of, 2nd Ed., 1981, 402 pages, by Mack A. Player, Professor of Law, University of Georgia.

Energy Law, 1981, 338 pages, by Joseph P. Tomain, Professor of Law, University of Cincinnatti.

Environmental Law, 1983, 343 pages by Roger W. Findley, Professor of Law, University of Illinois and Daniel A. Farber, Professor of Law, University of Minnesota.

Estate Planning—Introduction to, 3rd Ed., 1983, 370 pages, by Robert J. Lynn, Professor of Law, Ohio State University.

Evidence, Federal Rules of, 1981, 428 pages, by Michael H. Graham, Professor of Law, University of Illinois.

Evidence, State and Federal Rules, 2nd Ed., 1981, 514 pages, by Paul F. Rothstein, Professor of Law, Georgetown University.

Family Law, 1977, 400 pages, by Harry D. Krause, Professor of Law, University of Illinois.

Federal Estate and Gift Taxation, 3rd Ed., 1983, 509 pages, by John K. McNulty, Professor of Law, University of California, Berkeley.

Federal Income Taxation of Individuals, 3rd Ed., 1983, 487 pages, by John K. McNulty, Professor of Law, University of California, Berkeley.

Federal Income Taxation of Corporations and Stockholders, 2nd Ed., 1981, 362 pages, by Jonathan Sobeloff, Late Professor of Law, Georgetown University and Peter P. Weidenbruch, Jr., Professor of Law, Georgetown University.

Federal Jurisdiction, 2nd Ed., 1981, 258 pages, by David P. Currie, Professor of Law, University of Chicago.

Future Interests, 1981, 361 pages, by Lawrence W. Waggoner, Professor of Law, University of Michigan.

Government Contracts, 1979, 423 pages, by W. Noel Keyes, Professor of Law, Pepperdine University.

Historical Introduction to Anglo-American Law, 2nd Ed., 1973, 280 pages, by Frederick G. Kempin, Jr., Professor of Business Law, Wharton School of Finance and Commerce, University of Pennsylvania.

Immigration Law and Procedure, 1984, 345 pages, by David Weissbrodt, Professor of Law, University of Minnesota.

Injunctions, 1974, 264 pages, by John F. Dobbyn, Professor of Law, Villanova University.

Insurance Law, 1981, 281 pages, by John F. Dobbyn, Professor of Law, Villanova University.

Intellectual Property—Patents, Trademarks and Copyright, 1983, 428 pages, by Arthur R. Miller, Professor of Law, Harvard University, and Michael H. Davis, Professor of Law, Cleveland State University, Cleveland-Marshall College of Law.

International Business Transactions, 2nd Ed., 1984, 476 pages, by Donald T. Wilson, Professor of Law, Loyola University, Los Angeles.

Introduction to the Study and Practice of Law, 1983, 418 pages, by Kenney F. Hegland, Professor of Law, University of Arizona.

Judicial Process, 1980, 292 pages, by William L. Reynolds, Professor of Law, University of Maryland.

Jurisdiction, 4th Ed., 1980, 232 pages, by Albert A. Ehrenzweig, Late Professor of Law, University of California, Berkeley, David W. Louisell, Late Professor of Law, University of California, Berkeley and Geoffrey C. Hazard, Jr., Professor of Law, Yale Law School.

Juvenile Courts, 3rd Ed., 1984, 291 pages, by Sanford J. Fox, Professor of Law, Boston College.

Labor Arbitration Law and Practice, 1979, 358 pages, by Dennis R. Nolan, Professor of Law, University of South Carolina.

Labor Law, 1979, 403 pages, by Douglas L. Leslie, Professor of Law, University of Virginia.

Land Use, 1978, 316 pages, by Robert R. Wright, Professor of Law, University of Arkansas, Little Rock and Susan Webber, Professor of Law, University of Arkansas, Little Rock.

Landlord and Tenant Law, 1979, 319 pages, by David S. Hill, Professor of Law, University of Colorado.

Law Study and Law Examinations—Introduction to, 1971, 389 pages, by Stanley V. Kinyon, Late Professor of Law, University of Minnesota.

Legal Interviewing and Counseling, 1976, 353 pages, by Thomas L. Shaffer, Professor of Law, Washington and Lee University.

Legal Research, 4th Ed., 1984, approximately 425 pages, by Morris L. Cohen, Professor of Law and Law Librarian, Yale University.

Legal Writing, 1982, 294 pages, by Dr. Lynn B. Squires and Marjorie Dick Rombauer, Professor of Law, University of Washington.

Legislative Law and Process, 1975, 279 pages, by Jack Davies, Professor of Law, William Mitchell College of Law.

Local Government Law, 2nd Ed., 1983, 404 pages, by David J. McCarthy, Jr., Professor of Law, Georgetown University.

Mass Communications Law, 2nd Ed., 1983, 473 pages, by Harvey L. Zuckman, Professor of Law, Catholic University and Martin J. Gaynes, Lecturer in Law, Temple University.

Medical Malpractice—The Law of, 1977, 340 pages, by Joseph H. King, Professor of Law, University of Tennessee.

Military Law, 1980, 378 pages, by Charles A. Shanor, Professor of Law, Emory University and Timothy P. Terrell, Professor of Law, Emory University.

Oil and Gas, 1983, 443 pages, by John S. Lowe, Professor of Law, University of Tulsa.

Personal Property, 1983, 322 pages, by Barlow Burke, Jr., Professor of Law, American University.

NUTSHELL SERIES

Post-Conviction Remedies, 1978, 360 pages, by Robert Popper, Professor of Law, University of Missouri, Kansas City.

Presidential Power, 1977, 328 pages, by Arthur Selwyn Miller, Professor of Law Emeritus, George Washington University.

Procedure Before Trial, 1972, 258 pages, by Delmar Karlen, Professor of Law Emeritus, New York University.

Products Liability, 2nd Ed., 1981, 341 pages, by Dix W. Noel, Late Professor of Law, University of Tennessee and Jerry J. Phillips, Professor of Law, University of Tennessee.

Professional Responsibility, 1980, 399 pages, by Robert H. Aronson, Professor of Law, University of Washington, and Donald T. Weckstein, Professor of Law, University of San Diego.

Real Estate Finance, 2nd Ed., 1985, approximately 300 pages, by Jon W. Bruce, Professor of Law, Vanderbilt University.

Real Property, 2nd Ed., 1981, 448 pages, by Roger H. Bernhardt, Professor of Law, Golden Gate University.

Regulated Industries, 1982, 394 pages, by Ernest Gellhorn, Dean and Professor of Law, Case Western Reserve University, and Richard J. Pierce, Professor of Law, Tulane University.

Remedies, 2nd Ed., 1984, approximately 325 pages, by John F. O'Connell, Professor of Law, Western State University College of Law, Fullerton.

Res Judicata, 1976, 310 pages, by Robert C. Casad, Professor of Law, University of Kansas.

Sales, 2nd Ed., 1981, 370 pages, by John M. Stockton, Professor of Business Law, Wharton School of Finance and Commerce, University of Pennsylvania.

Schools, Students and Teachers—Law of, 1984, 409 pages, by Kern Alexander, Professor of Education, University of Florida and M. David Alexander, Professor, Virginia Tech University.

Sea—Law of, 1984, approximately 250 pages, by Louis B. Sohn, Professor of Law, Harvard University and Kristen Gustafson.

NUTSHELL SERIES

Wills and Trusts, 1979, 392 pages, by Robert L. Mennell, Professor of Law, Hamline University.

Workers' Compensation and Employee Protection Laws, 1984, 248 pages, by Jack B. Hood, Professor of Law, Cumberland School of Law, Samford University and Benjamin A. Hardy, Professor of Law, Cumberland School of Law, Samford University.

Hornbook Series

and

Basic Legal Texts

of

WEST PUBLISHING COMPANY

P.O. Box 43526

St. Paul, Minnesota 55164

June, 1984

Administrative Law, Davis' Text on, 3rd Ed., 1972, 617 pages, by Kenneth Culp Davis, Professor of Law, University of San Diego.

Agency and Partnership, Reuschlein & Gregory's Hornbook on the Law of, 1979 with 1981 Pocket Part, 625 pages, by Harold Gill Reuschlein, Professor of Law Emeritus, Villanova University and William A. Gregory, Professor of Law, Georgia State University.

Antitrust, Sullivan's Hornbook on the Law of, 1977, 886 pages, by Lawrence A. Sullivan, Professor of Law, University of California, Berkeley.

Common Law Pleading, Koffler and Reppy's Hornbook on, 1969, 663 pages, by Joseph H. Koffler, Professor of Law, New York Law School and Alison Reppy, Late Dean and Professor of Law, New York Law School.

Conflict of Laws, Scoles and Hay's Hornbook on, Student Ed., 1982, 1085 pages, by Eugene F. Scoles, Professor of Law, University of Illinois and Peter Hay, Dean and Professor of Law, University of Illinois.

Constitutional Law, Nowak, Rotunda and Young's Hornbook on, 2nd Ed., Student Ed., 1983, 1172 pages, by John E. Nowak, Professor of Law, University of Illinois, Ronald D. Rotunda, Professor of Law, University of Illinois, and J. Nelson Young, Professor of Law, University of North Carolina.

Contracts, Calamari and Perillo's Hornbook on, 2nd Ed., 1977, 878 pages, by John D. Calamari, Professor of Law, Fordham University and Joseph M. Perillo, Professor of Law, Fordham University.

Contracts, Corbin's One Volume Student Ed., 1952, 1224 pages, by Arthur L. Corbin, Late Professor of Law, Yale University.

Corporate Taxation, Kahn's Handbook on, 3rd Ed., Student Ed., Soft cover, 1981 with 1983 Supplement, 614 pages, by Douglas A. Kahn, Professor of Law, University of Michigan.

Corporations, Henn and Alexander's Hornbook on, 3rd Ed., Student Ed., 1983, 1371 pages, by Harry G. Henn, Professor of Law, Cornell University and John R. Alexander, Member, New York and Hawaii Bars.

Criminal Law, LaFave and Scott's Hornbook on, 1972, 763 pages, by Wayne R. LaFave, Professor of Law, University of Illinois, and Austin Scott, Jr., Late Professor of Law, University of Colorado.

Criminal Procedure, LaFave and Israel's Hornbook on, Student Ed., 1985, approximately 1300 pages, by Wayne R. LaFave, Professor of Law, University of Illinois and Jerold H. Israel, Professor of Law University of Michigan.

Damages, McCormick's Hornbook on, 1935, 811 pages, by Charles T. McCormick, Late Dean and Professor of Law, University of Texas.

Domestic Relations, Clark's Hornbook on, 1968, 754 pages, by Homer H. Clark, Jr., Professor of Law, University of Colorado.

Economics and Federal Antitrust Law, Hovenkamp's Hornbook on, Student Ed., 1985, approximately 375 pages, by Herbert Hovenkamp, Professor of Law, University of California, Hastings College of the Law.

Environmental Law, Rodgers' Hornbook on, 1977 with 1984 Pocket Part, 956 pages, by William H. Rodgers, Jr., Professor of Law, University of Washington.

HORNBOOKS & BASIC TEXTS

Evidence, Lilly's Introduction to, 1978, 486 pages, by Graham C. Lilly, Professor of Law, University of Virginia.

Evidence, McCormick's Hornbook on, 3rd Ed., Student Ed., 1984, 1155 pages, General Editor, Edward W. Cleary, Professor of Law Emeritus, Arizona State University.

Federal Courts, Wright's Hornbook on, 4th Ed., Student Ed., 1983, 870 pages, by Charles Alan Wright, Professor of Law, University of Texas.

Federal Income Taxation of Individuals, Posin's Hornbook on, Student Ed., 1983, 491 pages, by Daniel Q. Posin, Jr., Professor of Law, Southern Methodist University.

Future Interest, Simes' Hornbook on, 2nd Ed., 1966, 355 pages, by Lewis M. Simes, Late Professor of Law, University of Michigan.

Insurance, Keeton's Basic Text on, 1971, 712 pages, by Robert E. Keeton, Professor of Law Emeritus, Harvard University.

Labor Law, Gorman's Basic Text on, 1976, 914 pages, by Robert A. Gorman, Professor of Law, University of Pennsylvania.

Law Problems, Ballentine's, 5th Ed., 1975, 767 pages, General Editor, William E. Burby, Late Professor of Law, University of Southern California.

Legal Writing Style, Weihofen's, 2nd Ed., 1980, 332 pages, by Henry Weihofen, Professor of Law Emeritus, University of New Mexico.

Local Government Law, Reynolds' Hornbook on, 1982, 860 pages, by Osborne M. Reynolds, Professor of Law, University of Oklahoma.

New York Practice, Siegel's Hornbook on, 1978, with 1981–82 Pocket Part, 1011 pages, by David D. Siegel, Professor of Law, Albany Law School of Union University.

Oil and Gas, Hemingway's Hornbook on, 2nd Ed., Student Ed., 1983, 543 pages, by Richard W. Hemingway, Professor of Law, University of Oklahoma.

Poor, Law of the, LaFrance, Schroeder, Bennett and Boyd's Hornbook on, 1973, 558 pages, by Arthur B. LaFrance, Dean and Professor of Law, Lewis and Clark College, Northwestern School of Law, Milton R. Schroeder, Professor of Law, Arizona State University, Robert W. Bennett, Professor of Law, Northwestern University and William E. Boyd, Professor of Law, University of Arizona.

Property, Boyer's Survey of, 3rd Ed., 1981, 766 pages, by Ralph E. Boyer, Professor of Law, University of Miami.

Property, Law of, Cunningham, Whitman and Stoebuck's Hornbook on, Student Ed., 1984, approximately 808 pages, by Roger A. Cunningham, Professor of Law, University of Michigan, Dale A. Whitman, Dean and Professor of Law, University of Missouri–Columbia and William B. Stoebuck, Professor of Law, University of Washington.

Real Estate Finance Law, Osborne, Nelson and Whitman's Hornbook on, (successor to Hornbook on Mortgages), 1979, 885 pages, by George E. Osborne, Late Professor of Law, Stanford University, Grant S. Nelson, Professor of Law, University of Missouri, Columbia and Dale A. Whitman, Dean and Professor of Law, University of Missouri, Columbia.

Real Property, Burby's Hornbook on, 3rd Ed., 1965, 490 pages, by William E. Burby, Late Professor of Law, University of Southern California.

Real Property, Moynihan's Introduction to, 1962, 254 pages, by Cornelius J. Moynihan, Professor of Law, Suffolk University.

Remedies, Dobb's Hornbook on, 1973, 1067 pages, by Dan B. Dobbs, Professor of Law, University of Arizona.

Sales, Nordstrom's Hornbook on, 1970, 600 pages, by Robert J. Nordstrom, former Professor of Law, Ohio State University.

Secured Transactions under the U.C.C., Henson's Hornbook on, 2nd Ed., 1979, with 1979 Pocket Part, 504 pages, by Ray D. Henson, Professor of Law, University of California, Hastings College of the Law.

Securities Regulation, Hazen's Hornbook on the Law of, Student Ed., 1985, approximately 550 pages, by Thomas Lee Hazen, Professor of Law, University of North Carolina.

Torts, Prosser and Keeton's Hornbook on, 5th Ed., Student Ed., 1984, 1286 pages, by William L. Prosser, Late Dean and Professor of Law, University of California, Berkeley, Page Keeton, Professor of Law Emeritus, University of Texas, Dan B. Dobbs, Professor of Law University of Arizona, Robert E. Keeton, Professor of Law Emeritus, Harvard University and David G. Owen, Professor of Law, University of South Carolina.

Trial Advocacy, Jeans' Handbook on, Student Ed., Soft cover, 1975, by James W. Jeans, Professor of Law, University of Missouri, Kansas City.

Trusts, Bogert's Hornbook on, 5th Ed., 1973, 726 pages, by George G. Bogert, Late Professor of Law, University of Chicago and George T. Bogert, Attorney, Chicago, Illinois.

Urban Planning and Land Development Control, Hagman's Hornbook on, 1971, 706 pages, by Donald G. Hagman, Late Professor of Law, University of California, Los Angeles.

Uniform Commercial Code, White and Summers' Hornbook on, 2nd Ed., 1980, 1250 pages, by James J. White, Professor of Law, University of Michigan and Robert S. Summers, Professor of Law, Cornell University.

Wills, Atkinson's Hornbook on, 2nd Ed., 1953, 975 pages, by Thomas E. Atkinson, Late Professor of Law, New York University.

Advisory Board

DEBTOR-CREDITOR LAW
IN A NUTSHELL

By

DAVID G. EPSTEIN
**Dean, University of Arkansas
School of Law**

SECOND EDITION

ST. PAUL, MINN.
WEST PUBLISHING CO.
1980

Library of Congress Cataloging in Publication Data

Epstein, David G   1943–
    Debtor-creditor law in a nutshell.

    (Nutshell series)
    Includes bibliographical references and index.
  1. Debtor and creditor—United States. I. Title.
KF1501.Z9E67 1980   346'.73'077   79–25091

ISBN 0–8299–2072–2

Epstein Debt.–Cred.Law 2d
4th Reprint—1984

TO DANNY

*

PREFACE

Late in 1978, Congress enacted a new bankruptcy law which applies to all bankruptcy proceedings filed on or after October 1, 1979. The Bankruptcy Reform Act of 1978 changes the language of bankruptcy law so that instead of a "bankrupt" being "adjudicated" there will be an "order for relief" for a "debtor." It also changes the numbering system for the chapters of the bankruptcy law from Roman numerals to arabic numbers so that a business will file for relief under Chapter 11, not Chapter XI. More important, the Bankruptcy Reform Act of 1978 makes a number of significant substantive changes in bankruptcy law.

Because of these changes and recent developments in state creditors' rights law (and because my wife and I bought a large, old house in Fayetteville which we are remodelling), I have prepared a second edition of the debtor-creditor nutshell.

It was necessary to write completely new material explaining the new Bankruptcy Code. It was also necessary to revise the non-bankruptcy part of the nutshell significantly. Fortunately, the preface from the first edition was still usable with only minor changes:

> "This book attempts to summarize the law of debtor-creditor relations, a/k/a creditors'

rights. It sets out the rules, the problems, and the answers to those problems that I can answer. It does not attempt to develop the history of the law, to evaluate the law critically or to propose reform of the law. In short, I have attempted to follow West Publishing Company's suggestion that a nutshell 'be a succinct exposition of the law usually covered in one law school course to which a troubled student can turn for reliable guidance.' This, of course, does not preclude beneficial use of this nutshell by people studying for a bar examination, lawyers unfamiliar with debtor-creditor law, or even *untroubled* students taking a course in debtor-creditor relations (if any such creatures exist.)

"Relatively few cases are mentioned by name. Essentially, this book contains citations only to leading, recent or illustrative cases. Virtually no secondary sources are cited. There are, however, numerous references to statutory provisions—particularly the Uniform Commercial Code and the Bankruptcy Reform Act of 1978. In reading Chapter IV, A, 1 it will be helpful to keep a copy of the Uniform Commercial Code handy; in reading Chapters VI through XII, it will be helpful to have the Bankruptcy Reform Act of 1978 on hand. Provisions in both the Bankruptcy Reform Act of 1978 and the Uniform Commercial Code are generally referred to as 'section ____'; however, the different numbering schemes of the two acts should prevent your confusing the two.

"I hope this book will prove helpful in reviewing or learning debtor-creditor law. Debtor-creditor relations is not a very easy course, and this is not a very easy book. However, a course in debtor-creditor relations is—or at least should be—challenging, interesting and even enjoyable. Writing this nutshell has been all of these things. I hope that, to at least some extent, reading it is."

D. G. E.

Fayetteville, Arkansas
October, 1979

*

OUTLINE

I. Introductory Material

II. Extrajudicial Collection Devices

III. Judicial Debt Collection

OUTLINE

IX. Chapter 7 and Secured Claims

X. Chapter 7 and General Claims

XI. Chapter 11

XII. Chapter 13

OUTLINE

*

TABLE OF CASES

References are to Pages

TABLE OF CASES

CITATIONS
OF THE
BANKRUPTCY CODE

BANKRUPTCY ACT

BANKRUPTCY ACT

BANKRUPTCY ACT

BANKRUPTCY ACT

BANKRUPTCY ACT

DEBTOR — CREDITOR LAW

I. INTRODUCTORY MATERIAL

A. DISCLAIMER OF ANY IMPLIED WARRANTIES AS TO "FITNESS OF TITLE"

First, it should be noted that the order of appearance of the words "debtor" and "creditor" in the title is of no legal significance. It does not mean that debtors are more important than creditors. It does not mean that this book can not be used as a study aid in a course in creditors' rights. All that it does mean is that I find it easier to say "debtor-creditor" than "creditor-debtor."

Secondly, it must be confessed that the title is probably doubly misleading. It is misleading in the sense that use of the term "nutshell" implies that a complex and confusing area of the law is completely synthesized and translated into a few pages of relatively readable everyday English. I have attempted to discuss as succinctly and clearly as possible the topics covered in most law school debtor-creditor or creditors' rights courses, to consider the questions that are most commonly raised, and to answer those questions that are answerable. Nevertheless, this brief text should not be viewed as a substitute for study of the cases and the statutes in this area. Particularly the statutes. Particularly the Bankruptcy Code.

B. LIENS AND PRIORITIES *

The title is also misleading in that it indicates that there are only two separate identifiable interests to consider: the debtor's and the creditor's. There are at least three identifiable categories of creditors: (1) creditors with a "lien," (2) creditors with a "priority" and (3) creditors with neither a lien nor a priority. While each of these three classes of creditors has the same basic interest—prompt and complete payment of all

---

* Unfortunately, the word "priority" has two different meanings in debtor-creditor law:

1. rights of a lien creditor *vis-a-vis* another creditor with a lien on the same property

E. g., on January 10, S lends D $10,000 and obtains and perfects a security interest in D's equipment;

February 2, X lends D $20,000 and obtains and perfects a security interest in D's equipment;

March 3, D defaults on both loans. The equipment is only worth $8,000. Both S and X are lien creditors. The property subject to the two liens is not sufficient to satisfy both liens. It is necessary to determine which lien has PRIORITY.

2. rights of a creditor without a lien in an insolvency proceeding.

debts—the law affords each distinctive rights and remedies.

A "lien" is a charge on the debtor's property that must be satisfied before the property or its proceeds is available for satisfaction of the claims of general creditors. A lien thus affects not only the lienor and the debtor but other creditors as well, because it withdraws some of the debtor's resources that would otherwise be available for distribution to other creditors.

The lienor may resort to the encumbered property for the purpose of collecting its claim by means of its appropriation or sale in preference to other creditors and subsequent purchasers, yielding only to certain creditors with competing liens. To illustrate, assume that *D* has property worth $1,000 and owes *A* $300, *B* $400 and *C* $500. Assume further that *D*'s property includes a 1951 Henry J worth $400 on which *B* has a lien. In the event that *D* defaulted on his debts, *B* would have first right to the Henry J or the proceeds from the sale thereof. If, however, *D*'s Henry J was worth only $300, *B*'s claim for the other $100 would be treated no differently from the claims of *A* and *C*. A creditor is a lien creditor only to the extent of the value of its collateral.

A lien may be created by agreement, common law, statute, or judicial proceeding.* Consensual

* The term "lien creditor" is given an artificial meaning by the Uniform Commercial Code. Section 9–301(3) limits

liens on personalty are governed by Article 9 of the Uniform Commercial Code and are commonly referred to as security interests; consensual liens on realty are generally called mortgages. The creation and perfection of consensual liens is treated in the commercial law course in most law schools and is beyond the scope of this nutshell. Judicial liens result from prejudgment collection efforts such as attachment or garnishment, from the judgment itself or recordation thereof, and from post-judgment efforts to enforce the judgment such as execution and garnishment. Statutory liens are more difficult to describe and more difficult to identify. Common statutory liens include landlords' liens, mechanics' liens and tax liens.

Not all devices that are called liens are liens, however. Some are merely "priorities."

The major distinction between liens and priorities is drawn on the basis of when the interest arises. A priority does not arise until distribution of a debtor's assets on insolvency. Liens normally arise before and are enforceable without

---

"lien creditor" to a creditor who has obtained through judicial proceedings a lien that reaches the same property as the unperfected security interest in question. If the creditor obtained his lien by reason of statute or through agreement, he is not a "lien creditor" as the term is used in the UCC, and section 9–301(3) does not apply. Cf. section 9–310 (statutory liens); section 9–312 (consensual liens).

regard to insolvency of the debtor. There are, as the following chart indicates, other differences.

Liens	Priorities
1. Consensual, judicial or statutory	1. Almost always created by statute
2. Interest in particular property of the debtor	2. Satisfied from the general assets of the debtor
3. In a distribution governed by state law, lien creditors are paid first. Some lien creditors have "priority" over other lien creditors	3. Priorities generally affect only the rights of one general creditor (or group of general creditors) *vis-a-vis* other general creditors. Accordingly, in a distribution governed by state law, creditors with a priority usually are paid after lien creditors and before general creditors without any priority
4. In a distribution governed by the Bankruptcy Act, liens that meet certain statutory standards are paid first	4. All state-created priorities are invalid in a bankruptcy proceeding. Bankruptcy law contains its own priority provision, section 507

[C511]

C. SOURCES OF DEBTOR–CREDITOR LAW

This nutshell considers both bankruptcy and nonbankruptcy debtor-creditor law. The non-bankruptcy part of debtor-creditor law is primarily state collection law. Much of the state law is codification of early English common law doctrine. These codifications and the judicial interpretations thereof vary considerably from state to state. Rather than attempting to set out a fifty-state survey on each topic, I have tried to explore the principal issues and the common resolutions of such issues. There is no recent treatise dealing with state debtor-creditor law.

Bankruptcy law is federal law. The Constitution in article 1, section 8, clause 4 empowers Congress to establish "uniform laws on the subject of Bankruptcies throughout the United States." Congress has acted pursuant to this grant of power and so states are preempted from enacting bankruptcy laws.

Bankruptcy laws can be found in Title 11 of the United States Code. If you look at a copy of Title 11 published prior to 1979, you will find the Bankruptcy Act of 1898, as amended.

In 1970, Congress established the Commission on the Bankruptcy Laws of the United States to evaluate the Bankruptcy Act of 1898 and propose a concrete statutory alternative. The Commission issued a report in 1973 that contained a statutory proposal entitled the Bankruptcy Act of 1973. After five years of delay and debate, bankruptcy legislation was passed by Congress and sent to the President. On November 6, 1978, the President signed the Bankruptcy Reform Act of 1978. With few exceptions, its substantive provisions apply to all bankruptcy proceedings initiated on or after October 1, 1979. Bankruptcy proceedings pending as of October 1, 1979, will be governed by the earlier bankruptcy law, the Bankruptcy Act of 1898 (as amended).

Most of the case law interpreting these bankruptcy statutes is decisions of bankruptcy judges. In response to the passage of the Bankruptcy Reform Act of 1978, West Publishing Company has added a new unit to the National Reporter System—the Bankruptcy Reporter. There are, also, two loose-leaf services that reproduce a number of bankruptcy judge decisions: Bankruptcy Court Decisions and Collier Bankruptcy Cases.

The bankruptcy portion of this book will focus on the provisions of the Bankruptcy Reform Act of 1978. There are a number of helpful texts on the Bankruptcy Act of 1898: Collier on Bankruptcy (14th edition) (15 volumes); D. Cowans, Bankruptcy Law and Practice (2d edition) (3 volumes); D. Epstein, Debtor-Creditor Relations in a Nutshell (1st edition).

II. EXTRAJUDICIAL COLLECTION DEVICES

As long as the debtor is making payments when due, debtor-creditor law is of little practical significance. The debtor, of course, does not always make the required payments. The ready availability of consumer credit often leads to over-extension in debt and, subsequently, default. The creditor can proceed to collect the debt by using either extrajudicial or judicial methods. Because of the delay and expense involved in litigation, the creditor is likely initially to employ extrajudicial tactics to obtain payment.

The extrajudicial collection method most generally used is the dunning letter. This letter, containing a request for payment, can be either cordial or hostile depending on the policy of the creditor and the length of time that the debt is outstanding. Debtors often do not respond to a polite request for payment. Consequently, creditors seek other methods to recover the money due and owing, including telephone calls, personal visits, threats of law suit, and communications with the debtor's employer. Occasionally the creditor or his agent becomes overzealous, particularly when the debtor is weak and vulnerable.

A. COMMON LAW LIMITATIONS

Courts have sought to moderate the conduct of creditors by allowing debtors to recover for unreasonable collection activities under the following common law tort concepts: defamation, invasion of the right to privacy, and intentional infliction of mental anguish. Recoveries on these theories, however, are relatively rare. It is difficult to match the facts of debt collection with the elements of these torts.

Defamation is aimed at publication of false material. Truth is thus a defense—in most jurisdictions, an absolute defense. A statement truthfully disclosing that a debt is due, owing and unpaid is not actionable. A statement that falsely imputes a general unwillingness to pay debts or unworthiness to obtain credit may be the basis of a defamation action.

Another defense to defamation is privilege. A communication will be privileged if it pertains to a matter in which the recipient of the communication has a legitimate interest. Informing an employer that his employee has not paid his debts is a common collection tactic to induce payment through indirect pressure on the employee. Employers want to avoid the bother and costs of wage garnishment. Courts are divided as to whether employers have a sufficient interest to cause the communication to be privileged.

Debtors have also sued on invasion of privacy for injuries resulting from creditors' communications with employers—generally with little success. Public disclosure of private facts is one form of invasion of the right to privacy. However, as a general rule, reasonable oral or written communications to an employer have not been viewed as a sufficient disclosure of private facts; as with defamation, the communication is privileged based on the employer's interest in his employee's debts.

Some courts have granted recovery where the creditor has done more than inform the employer that a debt is overdue—for example, contacting the employer on numerous occasions. Additionally, there are cases finding an invasion of privacy by communications such as calls to the debtor's neighbors, publication of the debtor's name and amount of debt in a newspaper, and posting a notice of the indebtedness at the creditor's place of business.

A second form of violation of the right to privacy is a wrongful intrusion on the solitude of the debtor. Obviously, every creditor contact, every intrusion, is not actionable. The creditor has the right to contact the debtor—has the right to try and collect the debt. The problem is one of balancing the respective interests. Only unreasonable intrusions are actionable. In determining reasonableness, courts generally consider factors such as the content, nature, number and time of communications.

Where these communications are "extreme and outrageous" and result in emotional distress, the debtor may be able to recover on a theory of intentional infliction of mental distress. Several difficulties inhere in such an action. First, the creditor's actions must be beyond all bounds of decency; as the Restatement puts it, "recitation of the facts to an average member of the community would arouse his resentment against the actor and lead him to exclaim 'Outrageous'." Restatement of Torts 461 (supp. 1948). Another difficulty attending this cause of action is the requirement that the emotional stress be severe. The normal strain caused by contact with a collection agency is not sufficient. The debtor has to establish serious mental stress. Most courts also have been hesitant to impose liability for mental distress alone, and have insisted on some form of physical injury.

The following paragraph from an excellent student note summarizes the shortcomings of present judicial remedies for debt collection abuses.

"In short, relief available through present common law remedies is not sufficient for several reasons. Not all conduct that one might wish forbidden affords a basis for relief in court. The economic and social class most in need of protection is precisely the class most alienated from the legal system and therefore least likely to attempt to vindicate its rights through litigation. Relief to one debtor does not necessarily provide any protection to other members of that class. Finally, a judicial sanction can be somewhat indefinite because of difficulties inherent in the translation of adjudicated results into generalized rules. These shortcomings contrast sharply with the capacity of legislative prohibition and regulation."

Note, Debt Collection Practices: Remedies for Abuse, 10 B.C.Ind. & Com.L.Rev. 698, 702–3 (1969).

B. FAIR DEBT COLLECTION PRACTICES ACT

A number of states statutorily regulate the collection of consumer debts. The Federal Trade Commission has published a *proposed* trade regulation rule relating to the collection of consumer debts. And, in 1977, Congress enacted the Fair Debt Collection Practices Act, FDCPA.

FDCPA does *not* apply to all consumer credit collection efforts. It governs the conduct of "debt collectors," i. e., persons who regularly collect debts owed to someone else. FDCPA does not apply to the lender or credit seller that is attempting to collect its own debts.*

The Act severely limits "debt collector" contacts with third parties. A "debt collector" may contact a person other than a consumer, the con-

---

* It does apply to a creditor who "in the process of collecting his own debts, uses any name other than his own which would indicate that a third person is collecting or attempting to collect the debts," section 803(6).

sumer's spouse (or the consumer's parents if the consumer is a minor) and the consumer's attorney only for the purpose of finding the debtor. Section 804 sets out specific guidelines which a "debt collector" must follow when contacting third parties to learn a debtor's whereabouts. The "debtor collector" may not volunteer that s/he is a "debt collector"; such information may be furnished only if "expressly requested." Even if expressly requested, a "debt collector" may not tell a third party that the debtor owes a debt.

Once the debtor has been located and contacted, the "debt collector" must give the debtor the opportunity to require verification of the debt. No later than five days after first communicating with the debtor, the "debt collector" must send the debtor a written notice setting out the amount of the debt, the name of the creditor, the debtor's right to dispute the accuracy or existence of the debt, and the debt collector's duty to obtain verification of the debt if it is disputed by the debtor within thirty days.

FDCPA does not expressly limit the number of times that a "debt collector" may contact a debtor in attempting to collect a debt. Section 805, however, governs such contacts. The contact must not be at a time or place "which should be known to be inconvenient." All "debt collector" contact with the debtor must cease when the debt collector learns that the debtor is represented by an attorney, receives a written refusal to pay, or receives a written communication from the debtor requesting that such contacts end.

In addition to the above rules limiting contacts by "debt collectors," FDCPA also generally forbids any conduct by "debt collectors" which is abusive, deceptive, misleading, or unfair. Sections 806 through 808 contain "laundry lists" of illustrative practices which are specifically forbidden.

Section 811 governs venue of collection suits filed by "debt collectors." Actions brought to enforce a lien on real property may be brought only in the county in which the real property is located. Other collection actions may be brought by "debt collectors" only where the debtor resides or where the contract is signed.

A "debt collector" who violates the FDCPA is civilly liable for (1) actual damages, (2) "additional damages" up to $1,000 [In assessing "additional damages," the court is to look to the frequency, persistence and nature of the violations as well as the extent to which the violations were intentional], and (3) attorneys' fees and costs. The court may grant attorneys' fees *to* the "debt collector" if the action against the "debt collector" was brought in "bad faith and for the purpose of harassment."

A violation of FDCPA is also considered an unfair or deceptive act or practice, in violation of the Federal Trade Commission Act, section 814. The Federal Trade Commission may thus seek a variety of remedies against a "debt collector" that violates the FDCPA, including a fine of up to $10,000 per violation.

III. JUDICIAL DEBT COLLECTION

A. EXEMPT PROPERTY

Today all states constitutionally or statutorily restrict creditor recourse to certain property. Property designated in these exemption provisions can *not* be reached by creditors through judicial collection efforts. A three-pronged purpose is commonly attributed to exemption statutes: protection of the debtor, protection of the family of the debtor, and protection of society. By allowing the debtor to retain certain property free from appropriation by creditors, exemption statutes extend to a debtor an opportunity for self-support so that s/he will not become a burden upon the public.

There are two notable characteristics of state exemption statutes: (1) obsolescence and (2) extreme variety.* Nevertheless, certain generalizations are possible. All states exempt certain personal property from creditor process. In some jurisdictions, the exempt property is identified by type (e. g., the family bible, the family rifle); in others, by value (e. g., personal property of a val-

---

* In 1976, the National Conference of Commissioners on Uniform State Laws promulgated a Uniform Exemption Statute. To date, no state has adopted this uniform act. Section 522 of the Bankruptcy Reform Act of 1978, considered infra at page 164 is markedly similar to the Uniform Exemption Statute.

ue of $5,000); in still others, by both type and value (e. g., an automobile with a value of not more than $1,500). In most states, some specific provision is made for the exemption of life insurance (both the proceeds of the policy and the cash surrender value thereof) and wages.

The procedure for asserting rights under an exemption statute also varies from state to state. The burden usually is on the debtor to claim the exemption, and usually the statute sets a time limit on assertion of an exemption. Where the statute is of a "value" type—e. g., personal property of a value of $5,000—the statute generally provides for the appointment of appraisers who value property selected as exempt by the debtor. Where the statute specifies items of property that are exempt, courts are often confronted with the problem of applying a 19th century statute to 20th century property—e. g., whether a television set is a "musical instrument" or whether an automobile is a salesman's "tool of trade."

Almost all states also have homestead laws designed to protect the family home from the reach of certain classes of creditors. Homestead laws only protect real property interests of the debtor and so are of no aid to the urban apartment dweller. Moreover, not all real property interests of the debtor may be the subject of a homestead claim. Common statutory limitations include the requirements that the debtor have a family, that the property be occupied and used as a residence (an almost universal limitation), that the owner have a specified (usually present, possessory) interest in the property, and (in a few states) that there be a formal declaration that the property is a homestead.

The protection afforded by an exemption statute is not absolute. The federal tax lien reaches and may be satisfied from "exempt property." A number of states make similar exceptions for state taxes, claims for alimony and child support, materialmen and mechanics' liens. By statute in most states, case law in others, purchase money mortgages and security interests are generally not affected by an exemption statute. Thus, the bank that finances the purchase of a home or car will be able to seize and sell the property notwithstanding the fact that the property is covered by an exemption statute. And, most states treat nonpurchase money mortgages and security interests similarly. So, if D gives C a second lien on her car to secure a Christmas loan, C can, on D's default, foreclose on D's car. On the other hand, an executory agreement to waive the benefit of an exemption has generally been held to be invalid as against the public policy, notwithstanding some obvious similarities between such a waiver and a nonpurchase money mortgage.

There are also federal statutes that exempt property from the reach of creditors in either federal court or state court. Most of the federal provisions relate to the benefits of federal social legislation such as money paid under social security and veterans' benefits. The most significant federal exemption provision is Title III of the Consumer Credit Protection Act which provides a statutory minimum exemption of wages from garnishments.* Under Title III, creditors may garnish in the aggregate only 25% of a person's weekly "disposable earnings" or the amount by which his disposable earnings exceed thirty times the minimum hourly wage, whichever is less.

"Disposable earnings" is statutorily defined as salary less deductions "required by law." The following hypothetical illustrates the operation of Title III. X's salary is $10,800 a year. X does not, however, receive $900 a month. Rather, X's "take-home pay" is only $700 a month because of the following deductions: $130 for taxes, $50 for social security, $20 for Blue Cross. Only the $130 for taxes and the $50 for social security are

* Title III of the Consumer Credit Protection Act also affords protection to a debtor from discharge because of garnishment. The Act prohibits the discharge of any employee "by reason of the fact that his earnings have been subjected to garnishment for any *one indebtedness*." Thus if D is indebted to C, and C garnishes D's wages several times in an attempt to satisfy his claim, D's employer cannot discharge him because of these garnishments. Only "one indebtedness." On the other hand, if D is indebted to both C and E and both garnish D's wages, D's employer can discharge him because of the garnishments. More than "one indebtedness." The prohibition against discharge is probably of limited practical significance in light of the difficulty of establishing the reason for dismissal and the absence of any express private remedy for wrongful discharge. The Act provides for enforcement by the Secretary of Labor. Courts are divided as to whether to imply a private right of action.

deductions "required by law." X's "disposable earning" is thus $720 a month or $180 a week. Title III limits the amount that X's creditors can garnish to $45.

Title III does not preempt state statutes "prohibiting garnishments or providing for more limited garnishments than are allowed under [Title III]." Where state restrictions are stronger, it will be state law which regulates. Title III also makes provision for state law to apply in lieu of the wage garnishment provisions of Title III where the Secretary of Labor determines that the laws of that state provide restrictions on garnishment which are "substantially similar" to those provided in the Act.

B. PREJUDGMENT REMEDIES

A creditor trying to collect a claim through the judicial process is not always going to be able to obtain a judgment immediately. Litigation is costly and time-consuming. While the collection law suit is pending, the debtor may dispose of his assets or other creditors may seize the debtor's property to satisfy their claims. While the collection action is pending, the creditor may want to try to pressure the debtor to settle. Accordingly, it is necessary to consider prejudgment remedies.

1. ATTACHMENT

At early common law, attachment was a form of process to compel the defendant to appear and answer if he failed to appear in response to the summons or original writ. The writ commanded the sheriff to attach the property of the defendant to compel his appearance. If he appeared the property was returned to him; if he failed to appear, the property was forfeited. In the 17th century, the nature of attachment changed from a means of compelling the defendant's appearance to a prejudgment (provisional) collection remedy: attached property was no longer released upon the appearance of the defendant but remained attached until after judgment and collection of same. No longer is the main objective of attachment to coerce the defendant debtor to appear by seizure of his property; today the writ of attachment seizes the debtor's property in order to secure the debt or claim of the creditor in the event that a judgment is obtained.

Today attachment is purely statutory. The statutes vary considerably as to when attachment is available. [Federal courts follow the local rules relating to attachment, Fed.Civ.Proc. Rule 64.]

In no state is attachment available to every creditor in every collection action. Rather, the use of attachment is generally limited in the following ways:

(1) The statutes providing for attachment commonly spell out specific kinds of actions that may be the basis for the issuance of an attach-

ment. Attachment statutes in many states distinguish between claims *ex contractu* and claims *ex delicto,* sometimes establishing different requirements with respect to attachment for each type of claim, and sometimes providing for attachment only upon claims *ex contractu.*

(2) Attachment is usually to be had only on a showing of special statutory grounds. In general the statutory grounds deal with one of three situations: (i) where the plaintiff is unable to obtain personal service upon a defendant because the defendant is absent from the state, concealing himself or a nonresident; (ii) where the nature of the plaintiff's underlying claim entitles it to special treatment such as a claim based on fraud or a claim for "the necessaries of life"; (iii) where the defendant has assigned, disposed of, or secreted, or is about to assign, dispose of, or secrete property with the intent to defraud creditors.

(3) A bond is commonly required. The usual condition of the bond is that the plaintiff shall pay all costs that may be awarded to the defendant and all damages that defendant may sustain by reason of the attachment, if the order of attachment is dissolved or if the plaintiff fails to obtain judgment against the defendant.

(4) As a result of *Sniadach v. Family Finance Corp., Fuentes v. Shevin,* and *North Georgia Finishing, Inc. v. Di-Chem, Inc.* (all of which are dis-

cussed infra on pages 37–41,) an increasing number of states now require that the debtor be provided notice and an opportunity for a hearing before the debtor's property may be attached.

Attachment procedure varies considerably from state to state. In most states, a creditor seeking attachment must first file a complaint. The creditor then files an affidavit stating that a ground for attachment exists, a bond, and a writ of attachment.

Originally, the clerk of the court in which the action had been or was being commenced was authorized to issue writs of attachment ex parte. Since *Sniadach* and its progeny, most states require the opportunity for some form of hearing before a judge. If the judge orders attachment, the order of attachment is directed to the sheriff of a county in which property of the defendant is located. The order instructs the sheriff to attach and safely keep all non-exempt property of the defendant within the sheriff's county, or so much thereof as is sufficient to satisfy the plaintiff's demand together with costs and expenses. It also directs the sheriff to make a written return to the clerk of the court in which the action is pending showing all property attached and the date of seizure.

The act of the sheriff in taking custody over the property of the defendant is commonly referred to as "levy." What "levy" entails depends on the nature of the property. Levy on real property generally involves some act giving notice to the defendant of the lien and some act giving public notice that the debtor's realty is encumbered, such as filing in the real estate record system. A levy of attachment upon tangible personal property generally requires a seizure or taking possession or control of the property. If the chattels are capable of manual delivery, most jurisdictions require the sheriff to take the chattels into his actual custody by either removing them or appointing an independent keeper. Where the property to be attached is of a bulky or cumbersome nature and removal would be very difficult and expensive, levy does not require removal or seizure. For example, in Brunswick Corp. v. Haerter, 182 N.W.2d 852 (N.D.1971), removing a part from each pinsetter making the bowling alley inoperative constituted an effective levy.

Levy on property creates a lien thereon. In most states this lien of attachment dates from the time of the levy although in some states the date of the lien relates back to the date of the issuance of the writ.

A creditor with an attachment lien enjoys a number of advantages:

(1) *Security*

While a collection action is pending, a debtor may try to dispose of his assets. An attachment lien is effective against subsequent purchasers from the debtor. To illustrate, D is in default on its loan obligations to C. C files a law suit and obtains an attachment lien on D's collection of Franklin Mint coins by having the sheriff seize the coins pursuant to a writ of attachment. While C's law suit against D is pending, D sells the coins to B. C then obtains its judgment against D. C will be able to sell the Franklin Mint coins to satisfy its judgment. C's attachment lien is effective against B, a subsequent purchaser from the debtor, D.

To obtain its attachment lien, C had to levy on, i. e., seize, the Franklin Mint coins. D's lack of possession put third parties such as B on notice of possible creditor's claims.

(2) *Priority*

Often, a debtor lacks sufficient assets to pay all of his creditors. In such instances, state law does *not* provide for pro rata distributions. Rather, state law provides a series of priority rules. Most of the rules are "first-in-time" rules: the earlier the creditor obtains its lien, the greater its priority. For example, a creditor with an attachment lien takes priority over a creditor who subsequently obtains a judgment lien on the same property. To illustrate, D owes A $10,000 and B $20,000. D is in default on both debts, and D's only significant non-exempt asset is Greenacre. A sues D and obtains an attachment lien on Greenacre. Subsequently, B sues D, obtains a $20,000 judgment against D, and obtains a judgment lien on Greenacre. Then, A obtains $10,000 judgment against D. If a sale of Greenacre only yields $17,000, A will receive $10,000 of the sale proceeds and B will receive the remaining $7,000.

(3) *Jurisdiction*

The priority and security afforded by the lien are not the only advantages to a creditor of obtaining a writ of attachment. Attachment can also be used as a basis for jurisdiction. State courts can take jurisdiction over nonresidents who have property in the state if that property is brought within the court's jurisdiction by attachment and if substituted service (such as service by publication) is made. Such jurisdiction, called "quasi-in-rem" jurisdiction is generally less valuable to plaintiffs than personal jurisdiction: a judgment quasi-in-rem binds only the parties to the action and not the entire world, and it imposes no personal liability on the defendant, the award being limited to the property seized.

The importance of quasi-in-rem jurisdiction—and hence of attachment as a jurisdictional mechanism—has declined over the years.

Long-arm statutes have increased the availability of in personam jurisdiction. Shaffer v. Heitner, 433 U.S. 186 (1977), has decreased the availability of quasi-in-rem jurisdiction.

Prior to *Shaffer*, presence of property in a state was itself sufficient basis for quasi-in-rem jurisdiction of the courts of that state. In *Shaffer*, however, the Court held that the "minimum contacts" standard of International Shoe Co. v. Washington, 326 U.S. 310 (1945), governs not only *in personam* jurisdiction but also *in rem* jurisdiction.

(4) *Leverage*

A more important advantage of attachment is the leverage that it gives the plaintiff. By directing the sheriff to levy on property essential to the defendant/debtor, the creditor greatly strengthens its bargaining position. Deprivation of property used daily or essential to a business may induce the debtor to pay even if the claim is of questionable validity.

Notwithstanding the advantages of attachment discussed above, plaintiff/creditors do not always and should not always obtain a writ of attachment.* There are at least three distinct hazards in attachment:

(a) *Fees*

As indicated above, a bond is generally required of the creditor. And, the sheriff will usually require an indemnity bond before levying

---

* Remember, attachment is not always available to a creditor. Limitations on the availability of attachment are discussed on pages 21–22 supra.

on property to protect him from liability should he attach the wrong property and incur liability for conversion. The sheriff is also entitled to reimbursement of expenses incurred in levying on the property and in preserving the attached property. Last, but not least, an attaching creditor must pay its attorney for the legal work involved in obtaining an attachment lien.

(b) *Liability for wrongful attachment*

Attachment of personal property deprives the debtor of the use of the property for the duration of the litigation. Attachment of real property makes it difficult if not impossible for the debtor to sell the property for the duration of the litigation. If the debt collection action ends in a judgment for the debtor, the debtor can recover any actual damages s/he has suffered as a result of the attachment. Additionally, if the creditor attached the debtor's property maliciously and without probable cause, the debtor can recover punitive damages.

Tort liability has even been imposed on a creditor who prevails in the debt collection action. If the creditor has directed the sheriff as to which property to seize, the creditor is liable to the debtor if excessive property is seized, and is liable to third parties if their property is wrongfully seized.

(c) *Bankruptcy of the debtor*

Attachment benefits a single creditor at the expense of the debtor and other creditors. A debtor deprived by attachment of the use of important property, may decide to file a bankruptcy petition. Moreover, attachment may motivate the debtor's other creditors to initiate involuntary bankruptcy proceedings. See page 146 infra. Under section 547 of the Bankruptcy Code, an attachment lien obtained within 90 days of the filing of the bankruptcy petition is invalid if the debtor was insolvent when the lien was obtained.

Failure to obtain a judgment will result in the attachment being dissolved. A debtor may also terminate the attachment and obtain the attached property by posting a "discharging" or "dissolution" bond; these bonds are conditioned that the defendant in the attachment suit will perform whatever judgment will be entered against him and that, in the event of his default thereof, the surety will pay the amount of the judgment. A second class of bond available in most jurisdictions are "forthcoming" or "delivery" bonds. These are conditioned that if judgment in the attachment suit is rendered against the defendant, the property shall be forthcoming to satisfy such judgment, otherwise the surety will be liable to the extent of the value of the property. Such bonds release the property only from the custody of the levying officer; they do not release the attached property from the lien of attachment.

2. PREJUDGMENT GARNISHMENT

Garnishment (or, in most New England states, trustee process) is a collection remedy directed not at the defendant but rather at some third person, the garnishee, who owes a debt to the principal debtor, has property of the principal debtor, or has property in which the principal debtor has an interest. Prejudgment garnishment is a warning or notice to the garnishee that the plaintiff/creditor claims the right to have such debt or property applied in satisfaction of his claim, and that the garnishee should hold such property until the creditor's suit has been tried and any judgment satisfied. For example, if C brought an action against D to collect a debt that was due and owing and C learned that G held property of D, C might garnish this property. Then, if C was successful in her action against D, C's judgment could be satisfied by the property of D held by G, and, if G no longer had such property, C could recover from G personally. The most common examples of garnishees are the employer of the principal debtor and the bank in which the principal debtor has a savings or checking account.

Garnishment is frequently referred to as a form of attachment. The two remedies are similar in many respects. In a number of states, garnishment is not an independent remedy but rather is a proceeding ancillary to attachment. In other states, however, garnishment is an independent action available for grounds other than those required for the issuance of an attachment and subject to different provisions for bond. In all states, there are some differences between attachment and garnishment. The following chart compares attachment and garnishment.

ATTACHMENT	GARNISHMENT
1. Statutory	1. Statutory
2. Federal courts follow state rules as to availability Fed.Civ.Proc. Rule 64	2. Federal courts follow state rules as to availability Fed.Civ.Proc. Rule 64
3. Device for obtaining quasi-in-rem jurisdiction over a nonresident *	3. Device for obtaining quasi-in-rem jurisdiction over a nonresident *
4. Directed to property in the possession of the principal debtor	4. Directed to property of the debtor held by the garnishee
5. Prejudgment remedy	5. Both a prejudgment and a post-judgment remedy
6. Seizure of the property pending judgment	6. Property left in the care and custody of the garnishee
7. Lien on attached property, generally dating from time of levy	7. In a few states, no lien; generally held to create a lien that dates from the service of process on the garnishee

* Remember that Shaffer v. Heitner, supra at page 27, limits the availability of quasi-in-rem jurisdiction.

[C512]

3. REPLEVIN

At early common law, a landlord could enforce his rights to rent by the self-help remedy of distraint, i. e., seizing the personal property of the tenant. If the tenant disputed the landlord's claim of unpaid rent, s/he could, upon giving the sheriff security, obtain a writ of replevin directing the sheriff to recover possession of the seized personal property, pending litigation of the tenant's rent liability.

In this country, replevin has developed into a more general remedy. Today replevin (and sequestration and claim and delivery) is a proceeding to recover possession of any personal property. At the commencement of the action, the sheriff seizes, i. e., replevies the property and turns it over to the plaintiff, pending outcome of the litigation over possession. If the defendant wishes to regain possession of the goods replevied, s/he may give a delivery or forthcoming bond.

Replevin may not be used by all creditors. Replevin can only be maintained by one who has title or the right to possession of the property sought to be recovered. Unpaid unsecured creditors do not have a right to possession of their debtors' property. Unpaid secured creditors do have a right to possession of the property encumbered by their liens.

To illustrate, assume that Pizza Inc. owes U $1,000 and S $2,000. U is a general creditor. S has a security interest in Pizza Inc.'s oven. Pizza Inc. defaults on both debts. The remedy of replevin is not available to U; S can *possibly replevy* the pizza oven. Either U or S *possibly* can *attach* the pizza oven and/or other property of Pizza Inc.

The following chart compares attachment and replevin.

ATTACHMENT	REPLEVIN
1. Statutory	1. Statutory
2. Federal courts follow state rules as to availability Fed.Civ.Proc. Rule 64	2. Federal courts follow state rules as to availability Fed.Civ.Proc. Rule 64
3. Any non-exempt property in the possession of the debtor	3. Limited to personal property which the creditor has a lien on and/or the right to possess
4. Prejudgment remedy	4. Both a prejudgment remedy and a form of action
5. Seizure of the property by sheriff who retains custody thereof pending judgment	5. Seizure of property by sheriff who turns property over to plaintiff pending judgment
6. Lien on attached property, generally dating from the time of levy	6. Generally thought to create a lien that dates from the time of seizure

[C513]

[*33*]

4. RECEIVERSHIP

Receivership, like garnishment, is both a pre-judgment and a post-judgment collection remedy. A prejudgment receiver is a disinterested party, appointed by the court to administer, care for, collect and dispose of the property or the fruits of the property of another brought under the orders of the court by litigation.

The power to appoint a receiver is inherent in a court of equity. The appointment of a receiver is to a considerable extent a matter resting in the discretion of the court to which the application is made. Courts are very reluctant to appoint receivers prior to judgment, i. e., receivers *pendente lite*. There is a wealth of dictum to the effect that the appointment of a receiver is a harsh remedy and is to be used sparingly—only when the securing of ultimate justice seems to require it. And, since receivership is an equitable remedy, a court will not appoint a receiver when there is an adequate legal remedy such as attachment. Reported cases in which a receiver *pendente lite* has been appointed generally involve allegations of danger of loss, deterioration, or other impairment of the value of property that is the subject matter of the action or that will be necessary to satisfy any judgment in the action.

In 1844 New York adopted a civil code uniting the practice of law and equity; the Field Code provided in what cases a receiver should be appointed. Numerous other jurisdictions have followed New York's lead. Most such provisions are little more than a codification of the rules of equity except with regard to corporations. Many states have provisions for the appointment of receivers of corporations both before and after dissolution.

The receiver has only such powers as are specifically conferred upon him by the court or by the statute under which he was appointed. Absent a statutory provision to the contrary, the appointment of a receiver works a change in possession of, but not title to, the property over which the receiver is appointed; statutes governing the appointment of a receiver prior to judgment generally contain no provision to the contrary. The powers of receivers *pendente lite* are generally quite limited. The receiver is usually required to take possession of the property as soon as possible after the order appointing him has been entered. The order may contemplate the mere holding of the property for the purpose of preserving it or it may direct some active duties such as the continuance of a business, collecting rents and profits, or the sale of property.

The preceding paragraphs indicate one of the primary reasons that a creditor petitions for the appointment of a receiver *pendente lite*—preservation of property of the defendant/debtor pending determination of the creditor's claim. Receivership is similar to provisional remedies already discussed in that it is also used as leverage to obtain a favorable settlement. Receivership, however, differs from attachment and garnishment in that no advantage *vis-a-vis* other creditors accrues to the creditor who secures the appointment of a receiver. The petitioning creditor does not gain a lien on the property over which the receiver is appointed. And, since the appointment of a receiver *pendente lite* generally does not affect title to the property, existing liens on the property remain valid, and creditors can continue to obtain liens on property held by a receiver *pendente lite*. To illustrate, C sues D; prior to judgment C obtains the appointment of a receiver to hold and manage Greenacre Farms, a tract of land owned by D in Orange County. Prior to C's obtaining a judgment, E obtains a judgment against D. E dockets this judgment in the county in which Greenacre Farms is located. Under the applicable state law, the docketing of a judgment creates a lien on all real property held by the judgment debtor in the county of docketing. [Judgment liens are considered infra at pages 46–50]. This judgment lien would reach Greenacre Farms.

The appointment of a receiver does in a limited way affect the rights of other creditors. While the appointment does not divest existing liens or prevent the creation of new liens, lien creditors cannot enforce their claims and thus disturb the receiver's possession without the permission of the court. Consent of the court that appointed the receiver is also generally regarded as necessary in order to garnish property held by a receiver.

5. LIMITATIONS ON PREJUDGMENT REMEDIES

In the last ten years, prejudgment remedies have come under attack by both the courts and the legislatures. In Sniadach v. Family Finance Corp., 395 U.S. 337 (1969) the Court held that the Wisconsin statute providing for prejudgment garnishment of wages was unconstitutional. Justice Douglas' opinion emphasizes the hardship that results from wage garnishment and suggests that due process requires notice and hearing prior to the issuance of a writ, except in "extraordinary situations."

Sniadach, however, gives little guidance as to what constitutes "extraordinary situations" or whether "extraordinary situations" coincide with the typical statutory grounds for prejudgment garnishment. Justice Douglas cites four cases as instances where summary procedure may be used: three involve summary seizure or impounding of property by a governmental agency to protect the public welfare. The only "creditors' rights" case cited involves attachment of property by a nonresident debtor. [Remember that Shaffer v. Heitner, supra at page 27, limited the use of prejudgment remedies to obtain quasi-in-rem jurisdiction. |

Fuentes v. Shevin, 407 U.S. 67 (1972), expands the due process limitations first recognized in *Sniadach* to property other than wages, to prejudgment remedies other than garnishment. *Fuentes* involved replevin of consumer goods. The Court held the Florida and Pennsylvania replevin statutes unconstitutional; the opinion suggests that except in "extraordinary situations", notice and hearing must precede the seizure.

In discussing what constitutes "extraordinary situations", the *Fuentes* decision cites the same decisions as the *Sniadach* opinion cited. In *Sniadach,* the Court spoke of situations "requiring special protection to a state or *creditor* interest." In *Fuentes*, the Court referred to seizures "directly necessary to secure an important governmental or *general public* interest." While *Fuentes* seems to impose a more restrictive "extraordinary situations" test, there is dictum in *Fuentes* that indicates that "a showing of immediate danger that a debtor will destroy or conceal disputed goods" is an "extraordinary situation."

In Mitchell v. W. T. Grant Co., 416 U.S. 600 (1974), the Court held that a Louisiana statute permitting a judge to issue, without prior notice and hearing, a writ of sequestration based on a vendor's lien adequately balanced the property interests of the creditor and the debtor and satisfied due process.

The opinion distinguishes this Louisiana statute from the Florida and Pennsylvania replevin provisions involved in *Fuentes*. The Louisiana statute requires the creditor to allege specific facts supporting its claim, rather than the conclusory allegations of right that were sufficient under the Florida and Pennsylvania provisions. In *Mitchell*, the application for prejudgment relief was made to a judge, not a clerk. And, the Louisiana statute at issue in *Mitchell* gives the debtor the right to an immediate post-seizure hearing.

The majority opinion in *Mitchell* generated confusion (even among the Justices of the Supreme Court) as to whether *Fuentes* had been overruled. The *Mitchell* decision has also created uncertainty as to whether (1) *Mitchell* applies to all prejudgment remedies or is limited to prejudgment remedies such as sequestration that are available only to creditors with an interest in the property to be seized, and (2) whether *all* of the safeguards present in the Louisiana statute are necessary in the absence of a pre-seizure adversary hearing.

North Georgia Finishing, Inc. v. Di-Chem, Inc., 419 U.S. 601 (1975), provides some answers. In finding the Georgia prejudgment garnishment statute in violation of procedural due process, the Court cites and relies on *Fuentes*. The *North*

Georgia opinion also relies on *Mitchell* even though the creditor in *North Georgia* had no property interest in the bank account it was trying to garnish. "The Georgia garnishment statute has *none* of the saving characteristics of the Louisiana statute." The Georgia garnishment statute did not require specific factual allegations of entitlement, judicial participation, or provide the opportunity for a prompt post-seizure hearing.

North Georgia's use of both *Fuentes* and *Mitchell* makes it necessary (and difficult) to reconcile these two opinions. Some commentators have suggested that the unusual procedural safeguards in *Mitchell* come within *Fuentes'* "extraordinary situation" exception. (Remember, the *Fuentes* opinion suggests that notice and hearing must precede the seizure except in "extraordinary situations.")

While the relationship between the various cases is somewhat unclear, the following basic propositions seem clear:

1. Prejudgment remedies are not unconstitutional per se.

2. The use of prejudgment remedies is subject to due process limitations.

3. Due process requires notice and an opportunity for an adversary proceeding.

4. In at least some situations, a pre-seizure ex parte hearing coupled with the opportunity for a

prompt post-seizure adversary proceeding will satisfy due process.

Since *Sniadach* a number of state legislatures have eliminated prejudgment wage garnishment and restricted the availability of other prejudgment remedies. Congress by Title III of the Consumer Credit Protection Act has restricted both prejudgment and postjudgment garnishment of wages. The Act exempts a minimum of 75% of the debtor's wages from garnishment, and it prohibits an employer from discharging an employee because of garnishment for a single debt. The statute is considered in more detail at pages 19–21.

C. OBTAINING A JUDGMENT

The prejudgment remedies considered in the preceding sections afford a creditor less than complete relief. At best, such remedies pressure the debtor to pay and provide some security of payment. Accordingly, where the debtor does not capitulate after the use of available provisional remedies, it is necessary for the creditor to obtain a judgment.

A creditor, of course, wants to obtain the judgment as quickly and as inexpensively as possible. A default judgment is thus preferable to a judgment resulting from prolonged litigation. Most collection actions result in a default judgment for the creditor. Some creditors increase the chances for judgment by default by never delivering the summons and complaint and executing a false and fraudulent affidavit of personal service. [This is commonly called "sewer service" to indicate the probable resting place of the process papers.] No formal consideration of the legal implications of "sewer service" is necessary; anything labeled "sewer service" has to be illegal.*

Filing a collection action in a distant forum also significantly increases the chances of a default judgment. For example, an Arkansas debtor is more likely to default if the collection action is filed in King of Prussia, Pennsylvania, instead of Little Rock, Arkansas.

Spiegel, Inc. v. FTC, 540 F.2d 287 (7th Cir. 1976), held that the Federal Trade Commission has the power to prevent creditors from suing consumers in inconvenient forums. Spiegel, a catalog retailer with its principal place of business in Chicago, regularly sued in Illinois courts to collect delinquent accounts of out-of-state consumer customers. The Illinois long-arm statute granted jurisdiction for such suits. Nevertheless, the FTC issued a "cease and desist order." The Seventh Circuit held that the "unfair practice" language of section 5 of the Federal Trade Commission Act empowers the FTC to enjoin distant forum abuse of consumer debtors.

---

* For a discussion of the efforts to eliminate "sewer service", see Tuerkheimer, *Service of Process in New York City: A Proposed End to Unregulated Criminality*, 72 Colum.L.Rev. 847 (1972).

Section 811 of the 1977 Fair Debt Collection Practices Act protects consumers from suits by *"debt collectors"* * in inconvenient forums. Actions by "debt collectors" to enforce a lien on real property may be filed only in the county in which the real property is located. Other "debt collector" collection actions may be brought only where the debtor resides or where the contract is signed.

Even cheaper and quicker than a default judgment is a cognovit judgment. In cognovit judgments (a/k/a judgments by confession), the parties agree at the time that the debtor-creditor relationship is created that if the debtor defaults on his/her obligations, the creditor can obtain a judgment against the debtor without any notice to the debtor, without any hearing. An attorney chosen by the creditor appears in court to confess judgment against the debtor for any unpaid portion of the debt along with various fees and charges without the necessity of even service of process on the debtor. A debtor generally does not know when the cognovit judgment is entered. After learning that a judgment has been entered, a debtor is limited to two avenues of relief. The first available remedy is a petition to strike the judgment. This petition is only available in cases where irregularities constituting fatal defects are apparent on the face of the record. The other

* Remember the limited scope of the term "debt collector." See page 12 supra.

available remedy is the petition to open judgment; its main disadvantage is that the burden of proof is placed on the debtor.

Most states have enacted legislation eliminating confession of judgment or severely restricting its use.

The Supreme Court considered due process attacks on confession of judgments; in D. H. Overmyer Co., Inc. v. Frick Co., 405 U.S. 174 (1972), the Court held that a confession of judgment provision is not per se violative of due process. *Overmyer* presented the most appealing possible fact situation for upholding the constitutionality of cognovit judgments: both the debtor and the creditor were substantial business entities, and the facts revealed that the cognovit provision was included in the contract as a result of good faith bargaining between the parties. The Court in *Overmyer*, indicated by way of dictum that a confession by judgment may well violate due process "where the contract is one of adhesion, where there is great disparity in bargaining power, and where the debtor receives nothing for the cognovit provision. * * * "

In a case decided the same day as *Overmyer*, Swarb v. Lennox, 404 U.S. 191 (1972), the Court held the Pennsylvania cognovit provisions not unconstitutional on their face. In *Swarb*, a three judge district court had held *inter alia* that (1) the action challenging the constitutionality of the

Pennsylvania provisions could not be maintained as a class action on behalf of all Pennsylvania residents who signed cognovit notes; (2) the action, however, could be maintained as a class action on behalf of natural persons residing in Pennsylvania who earned less than $10,000 annually and signed such instruments; (3) the Pennsylvania practice of confessing judgment was unconstitutional as applied to the designated class. Swarb v. Lennox, 314 F.Supp. 1091 (E.D. Pa.1970). Only the plaintiffs appealed, claiming that the court should have declared the Pennsylvania rules and statutes unconstitutional on their face. In rejecting this contention and affirming the district court's opinion, the Court said: "*Overmyer* necessarily reveals some discomforture on our part with respect to the present case. However that may be, the impact and effect of *Overmyer* upon the Pennsylvania system are not to be so delineated in the one-sided appeal in this case and we make no attempt to do so." In light of the facts of both *Overmyer* and *Swarb*, the constitutionality of cognovit notes in a *consumer* credit transaction is still in question.

D. POST–JUDGMENT COLLECTION CONCERNS

1. JUDGMENT LIENS *

In most states, a judgment has been statutorily endowed with lien status, i. e., a judgment creates a lien on property of the judgment debtor. The mechanics of obtaining a judgment lien, the scope of the lien and the means of enforcing the lien vary from state to state.

Many states provide that the rendition of the judgment itself creates a lien. Others provide that a lien arises only after docketing of the judgment by the clerk of the county in which the property is located. [The act of docketing is usually accomplished by the county clerk's making an entry of judgment under the last name of the judgment debtor in the appropriate docket book.] In such states, a judgment rendered in County *X* cannot create a lien on property in County *Y* until the judgment is docketed in the latter county.

A federal court judgment does not create a lien until docketed in states that provide for docketing of the judgments of federal courts in local of-

---

* Do not confuse the term "judgment lien" with the term "judicial lien." "Judicial lien" describes any lien obtained through use of a court-related action. A "judgment lien" is one form of "judicial lien." Attachment lien, garnishment lien, and execution lien are other common examples of "judicial liens."

fices in the same manner as provided for judgments of state courts. 28 U.S.C.A. § 1962. Judgments of other state courts generally do not so easily give rise to a lien. A creditor with a judgment rendered by a state court in state *1* usually must bring an action in state *2* based on the debt created by the judgment in state *1*, obtain a judgment in state *2*, and docket this judgment in order to have a judgment lien on property of the debtor in state *2*.

The Conference of Commissioners on Uniform State Laws has recommended a Uniform Enforcement of Foreign Judgments Act that provides a summary procedure for proving a foreign judgment; to date, it has only been adopted in a handful of states.

The judgment lien operates as a general lien on all of the debtor's property subject thereto, not as a specific lien upon particular property. In Alabama, Georgia, and Mississippi, the judgment lien reaches both real and personal property; in all other states that recognize the judgment lien, it is limited to real property—not a specific piece of real property, but all real property of the debtor or, in states that require docketing, all real property of the debtor in counties in which the judgment has been docketed. What constitutes "real property" for judgment lien purposes varies somewhat from state to state. For example, there is disagreement as to whether the judgment lien reaches contingent remainders, leasehold estates, or timber that has been severed from the land. A division also exists as to whether equitable interests are subject to a judgment lien.

In most jurisdictions in which a judgment gives rise to a lien, the lien reaches property obtained subsequently thereto. There is a conflict of authority as to the relative priority of judgment liens on after-acquired property. To illustrate, in January, A obtains a judgment against D and dockets his judgment in Orange County; in May, B obtains a judgment against D and she also dockets her judgment in Orange County. It is not, however, until November that D owns any real property in Orange County. Does A's judgment lien on the real property acquired by D in November have priority over B's judgment lien on the same property? Some courts would answer in the affirmative—priority is governed by the order of docketing. A great majority of courts, however, would respond in the negative— while priority of judgment liens is generally determined by date of docketing, judgments attach simultaneously to after-acquired property, and thus the liens are of equal standing.

A judgment, or even a judgment lien, is not the final step in the collection process. As was stated by Justice Story in Conard v. Atlantic Ins. Co., 26 U.S. 386 (1828), a judgment lien "only creates a right to levy on the * * * [property of the judgment debtor], to the exclusion of other adverse interests subsequent to the judgment; and when the levy is actually made on the same, the title of the creditor for this purpose relates back to the time of his judgment so as to cut out intermediate encumbrances. * * * If the debtor should sell the estate, he [the judgment creditor] has no right to follow the proceeds of the sale. * * * The only remedy of the judgment creditor is against the thing itself by making that a specific title which was before a general lien."

To illustrate, C obtains a judgment against D and dockets the judgment in Orange County in the manner statutorily prescribed. D subsequently transfers Orange County real property that she owns—real property that is subject to C's judgment lien—to T for $10,000. C's judgment lien gives it no rights as to the $10,000; the lien only reaches the real property now owned by T, and C's remedy is to enforce the lien as to such property.

The jurisdictions vary considerably with respect to the proper method of enforcement of judgment liens. In some jurisdictions, foreclosure proceedings is the only method; in other states, levy and sale under a writ of execution is required; and some states permit a choice between foreclosure actions and a writ of execution.

At common law a judgment was presumed paid and became dormant so as not to support an execution if the judgment creditor failed to take out a writ of execution within a year and a day. The dormant judgment lien could be revived by (1) *scire facias* or (2) an action in debt on the old judgment resulting in a new judgment and a new lien. [This new judgment would encumber only property owned by the judgment debtor at or after the time of docketing the new judgment, with priority determined as of that date.]

Today most states statutorily limit the duration of judgment liens and limit revival of judgment liens to the second alternative described above. To illustrate, A obtains a judgment against D on January 5, 1979, and properly dockets the judgment in Orange County; six months later B obtains a judgment against D and also dockets the judgment. As to real property in Orange County acquired by D prior to January 5, 1979, it would seem that A's lien would have priority over B's. Assume, however, the lifespan of a judgment lien is statutorily limited to five years and A fails to enforce his judgment by January 1984. Prior to January 5, 1984, A can bring an action in debt based on the 1979 judgment and obtain a new judgment and a new lien. This new lien would, however, date from 1984 so that B's lien would have priority. Moreover, if D has sold property to T in the interim between 1979 and 1984, A's new lien would not reach such property.

2. EXECUTION LIENS

By way of review, what is the practical significance of a judgment lien? Does it give a creditor an interest in the debtor's chattels? In his real property? If so, what is the interest? Can the creditor lawfully seize the property? Can the creditor cause the property to be sold in satisfaction of his claim?

The generally negative answers to the above questions reveal the need for some further creditor remedy. At early common law, the "further" remedy generally took one of four permissible forms: *elegit, capias ad satisfaciendum, fieri facias* and *levari facias*. A writ of *elegit* resulted in the transfer of the debtor's personal property to his creditor at an appraised price, and, if this was not sufficient, the assignment of the use of one half of the debtor's land to the creditor as tenant by *elegit* for a term based on an appraisal of its value. *Elegit* is mainly of historical interest today.

Capias ad satisfaciendum required the local sheriff to arrest a judgment debtor and keep him imprisoned until the debt was paid. Today, a majority of states have constitutional provisions prohibiting imprisonment for debt. In most states, however, the prescription is limited to contract debts; many of these states statutorily provide for imprisonment for failure to satisfy liability resulting from tortious conduct, fraud, and breach of fiduciary relationship. Even in the states that absolutely prohibit imprisonment of debtors a judgment debtor may be imprisoned for civil or criminal contempt of court if s/he fails to satisfy a judgment.

By the writ of *fieri facias* (fi-fa), a creditor with a judgment could have the sheriff seize and sell the debtor's personal property in satisfaction of his claim; by means of *levari facias,* the judgment creditor could similarly reach the debtor's realty.

Today, the law of execution is statutory. Most statutes provide for a single writ of execution by which a judgment creditor can have the judgment debtor's property seized and sold in satisfaction of the judgment. In most states a writ of execution can reach both personalty and realty; in a very few states a writ of execution does not reach realty; in still others, the judgment creditor is statutorily required to look first to the personal property of the debtor.

As execution is statutory, the exact procedure varies somewhat from state to state. A writ of execution is issued by the clerk of the court in which the judgment was rendered. Issuance of the writ is a ministerial act and involves neither a hearing nor discretion on the part of the clerk. The writ is directed to the sheriff or some other statutorily authorized official; it orders the official to levy on the property described in the writ and, usually after appraisal and due notice, to sell such property at public sale. As with attachment, there are problems as to what constitutes an effective levy and problems of liability for an improper levy. The writ specifies a "return date"; by that date, the sheriff or other official must return the writ to the issuing clerk with an endorsement stating the property seized and sold or the impossibility of finding leviable assets. The latter form of return is often referred to as return *nulla bona*. If the return is *nulla bona*, a second (*alias*) and further (*pluries*) writs may issue.

Execution is also similar to attachment in that it creates a lien on the property seized by the sheriff. Most states date the execution lien from the time of levy. In a few states, the execution lien relates back to the date of issuance of the writ by the clerk or delivery of the writ to the sheriff.*

Execution is different from attachment in that the property seized pursuant to a writ of execution is to be sold by the sheriff to satisfy the creditor's judgment while property seized pursuant to a writ of attachment is to be held by the sheriff to secure payment of any judgment obtained by the creditor. Delays in holding an exe-

---

* These minority rules create problems as to the rights of third parties who obtain liens on or purchase property of the debtor after the writ has been issued but before the property has been levied on by the sheriff. Assume, for example, that C obtains a writ of execution on January 10 and delivers the writ to the sheriff. On January 11, B, a bona fide purchaser, buys a boat from the judgment debtor. Can the sheriff now levy on the boat? Under the minority rules, C's execution lien predates B's purchase. Most jurisdictions that date execution liens from issuance or delivery of the writ statutorily protect "gap purchasers" such as B.

cution sale may result in the loss of the execution lien. There are statutory limitations on the life-span of an execution lien. Additionally, a creditor will lose its execution lien if the lien becomes "dormant."

The classic statement of the judicial doctrine of dormancy is Excelsior Needle Co. v. Globe Cycle Works, 48 App.Div. 304, 309–310, 62 N.Y.S. 538, 540–41 (1900):

> "The law is quite clear that the object of the execution is to enforce the judgment, and not to convert it into a security upon the property, and still allow the judgment debtor to prosecute his business regardless of the lien of the execution. As was said in Freeman Executions, § 206: 'In other words, it is not the mere issuing or delivery of the writ which creates a lien, but an issuing and delivery for the purpose of execution. The execution of a writ for the purpose of making or keeping it effective as a lien cannot stop with a mere levy upon the property. If the officer is instructed by the plaintiff not to sell till further orders, the lien of the execution and levy becomes subordinate to that of any subsequent writ placed in the officers' hands for service.' * * * The law, therefore, seems to be settled that any direction by the execution creditor to the sheriff which suspends the lien or delays the en-

forcement of the levy renders the execution dormant against subsequent creditors or bona fide purchasers. However veiled may be the direction, however much it may be founded on a humane desire to protect the debtor, if it is tantamount to a mandate or instruction to the sheriff to withhold the execution of his process, during the interim that he accedes to this demand the levy ceases to be effective."

3. CREDITOR'S BILL

At early common law, writs of execution were issued by courts of law and so were confined to those estates and interests of the debtor recognized at law. If the debtor had title to land, the writ of *levari facias* could be levied, giving the creditor the right to collect rents and the property. Similarly, if the debtor owned tangible personal property, the writ of *fieri facias* could be levied, giving the creditor the right to have such property seized and sold. But if the debtor had something which was property in a practical sense, something on which he could realize at anytime but which was not capable of being the subject matter of a common law possessory action, no writ of execution was available. Thus at early common law the creditor could not reach the debtor's equitable interests such as beneficial interests in property held in trust or the debtor's intangible property such as choses in action.

To provide a remedy for reaching such property, the Court of Chancery developed an equitable counterpart to execution—the creditor's bill (sometimes referred to as creditor's suit). A creditor unable to satisfy its judgment completely through execution could file a bill in the Court of Chancery asking that court to compel the debtor to turn over his equitable assets to be sold to satisfy the creditor's judgment.

By use of a creditor's bill, a judgment creditor can reach any nonexempt property interest of the debtor that is alienable or assignable under state law. While, as with other judicially created liens, there is some division in the case law as to the time the lien arises, "The general rule is that the filing of a judgment creditor's bill and the service of process creates a lien in equity on the judgment debtor's equitable assets." Metcalf v. Barker, 187 U.S. 165 (1902).

The flexibility of equitable procedure allows the creditor's bill to be used in a variety of ways. A creditor's bill can be used as a liquidation device—a substitute for bankruptcy. A judgment creditor can file a bill not only for himself but also on behalf of such other judgment creditors as may choose to join the action. Under this general creditors' bill, the petitioning creditor does not obtain priority over other participating creditors; rather the court makes a *pro rata* distribution to all such creditors. Despite equity's preference for equality, a creditor may file a bill on his behalf alone and thus obtain priority over other creditors. Such judgment creditor's bills are far more common than the general creditors' bill described above. Usually the judgment creditor's bill includes a prayer for discovery of all of the debtor's property; the debtor and third parties holding property of the debtor are then examined in court to locate the assets. A common step after discovery is the issuance of an injunction to prevent the debtor from disposing of or encumbering the property. Sometimes a receiver is appointed for collecting money due to the debtor or taking charge of property requiring management.

The creditor's bill has not only the advantages but also the limitations of an equitable remedy. For example, the notion that jurisdiction in equity will not be entertained where there is an adequate remedy at law requires exhaustion of legal remedies. There is some confusion as to what constitutes exhaustion of legal remedies in this context. There is uniformity of opinion that, subject to limited exceptions, a judgment must be obtained before a party is entitled to institute a suit by creditor's bill. The difficulty arises in determining exactly how far a plaintiff must proceed after he has obtained a judgment. Most authorities indicate that a creditor must have (1) a judgment, (2) execution issued and (3) return unsatisfied before obtaining a creditor's bill.

Other courts merely require judgment and the issuance of execution. The question of which rule is preferable would seem to be academic today in federal court and in states that have adopted rules of procedure modeled after the Federal Rules. Rule 2 abolishes the distinction between law and equity; Rule 18(a) authorizes joinder of legal and equitable claims; Rule 18(b) states that "whenever a claim is one heretofore cognizable only after another claim has been prosecuted to a conclusion, the two claims may be joined in a single action."

4. SUPPLEMENTARY PROCEEDINGS

Several statutory developments have limited the need for and use of the creditor's bill. In most states, the writ of execution has been extended to equitable interests in property and intangible property. Garnishment is now available in many states for the collection of judgments from property of the debtor held by third parties. And, a number of states have enacted an additional remedy: as part of his procedural reform in the middle of the nineteenth century, Field created a new remedy—proceedings supplementary to execution (also called supplemental proceedings)—designed to achieve the purposes of a creditor's bill by a more simple and summary process; a number of states followed New York's example. As the name of the remedy implies, supplementary proceedings could be used only

after execution had been issued and returned unsatisfied. Subsequently, in a number of jurisdictions the title of the procedure was changed to
proceedings supplementary to judgment, and the
requirement of return of execution unsatisfied
was eliminated.

While a creditor's bill is an independent, quasi-
in-rem action, governed by equitable rules, and a
supplementary proceeding is a summary, in personam action, administered by the court in which
the judgment was obtained and governed by the
provisions of the applicable state law, the reach
of supplementary proceedings is very similar to
that of the creditor's bill. Most supplementary
proceedings statutes provide for (1) discovery of
assets through the right of examination of the
debtor and others; (2) issuance of injunctions to
prevent disposition of property; (3) discretion-
ary power to appoint receivers; and (4) orders
for the sale of property.

In a few states, the supplementary proceedings
provisions expressly abolish the creditor's bill.
Absent any such express provision, the existence
of supplementary proceedings in other states neither abolishes creditor's bills by implication nor
limits the availability of creditor's bills. Supplementary proceedings need not be tried first and
found wanting before a creditor's bill action can
be brought. This is in accordance with the well-
established equitable principle that where new
power is conferred upon the law courts by statu-

tory legislation, the former jurisdiction of equity is unaffected unless the statute contains negative words or other language expressly taking away the pre-existing equity jurisdiction, or unless the whole scope of the statute, by its reasonable construction and its operation, shows a clear legislative intent to abolish that jurisdiction.

While supplementary proceedings usually afford a more expeditious remedy than the creditor's bill, there is at least one situation in which the creditor's bill is still used: recovery of property of the debtor that has been transferred to some third party in fraud of creditors. [The concept and elements of a transfer in fraud of creditors are considered infra at Ch. ——]. As noted above, supplementary proceedings are summary in nature without the usual requirements as to pleadings or jury trial. Thus supplementary proceedings generally can not be employed where a third party asserts an interest in the property. A few states have amended supplementary proceedings statutes so that the court can adjudicate rights and interests in the debt or property which is the subject of the proceeding.

5. EXECUTION SALES

While obtaining a lien, through execution or otherwise, is important to a creditor for reasons previously stated, it is not tantamount to satisfaction of the claim. Execution, like the provisional remedies and judgment, is but one of the steps that a creditor must take to obtain payment. The final step is the sale of the property levied on; the proceeds of the sale, after deduction for fees and costs of the sale and payment to creditors with priority, are distributed to the levying creditor, with any excess going to the judgment debtor.

Most states have detailed statutory provisions governing the sale of property pursuant to execution. These statutes vary from jurisdiction to jurisdiction as to matters such as property subject to sale, notice, mechanics of the sale and safeguards as to inadequate price.

Most states also have statutory provisions designed to prevent the sale of property at execution sales for unfair prices. One such statutory device is appraisal statutes. Such statutes, generally provide (1) that an appraisal of the subject property must be made before the sale and (2) either that an execution sale must bring not less than a stated percentage of the appraised value or a stated percentage of the appraised value must be credited on the debt.

Another statutory device providing some protection against inadequate bidding is redemption. Generally, the right of redemption is limited to the repurchase by the execution debtor, within a stated time and at a stated price, of real property sold at execution. Some states permit redemption of personal property; some states have extended the right of redemption to junior lienors of the debtor.

An execution sale differs from a judicial sale in that the writ does not designate any specific property to be sold and the court gives no directions and imposes no conditions with respect to an execution sale, as it may do in its order for a judicial sale of specific property. While most statutes do not provide for judicial confirmation of an execution sale, the court from which the execution issued may, for sufficient cause shown, vacate a sale. Courts usually state that mere inadequacy of price is not sufficient to vacate an execution sale. There are cases to the contrary; additionally, a number of decisions have stated that where the price is inadequate, slight additional circumstances justify setting aside the sale.

One reason for the generally low prices realized at execution sales is the limited protection afforded purchasers at such sales. *Caveat emptor* is the answer customarily given to the unhappy execution purchaser who learns that there are other existing liens prior to that of the judgment creditor or that the judgment debtor had defective title to the property sold by the sheriff. The execution purchaser acquires only such interest as the execution debtor has and generally cannot recover for defects in title. Execution sales are made without implied warranties, either on the part of the sheriff or the execution creditor or debtor.

Most courts likewise hold that the doctrine of *caveat emptor* is applicable even where the levy and sale is made on property to which the judgment debtor has no title: a majority of the cases have denied recovery in actions by the purchaser against the sheriff or the judgment creditor for the price paid at the execution sale, where the debtor had no title to the property so sold. The purchaser's only remedy in such cases is usually by way of subrogation to the creditor's claim against the debtor.

The doctrine of *caveat emptor* is generally not applicable where the sale is rendered void because of irregularities in procedure; while the execution purchaser is not entitled to assume that he will obtain good title, he is entitled to assume that he will obtain such interest as the execution debtor has. Thus, where the sale is set aside, the execution purchaser has been given a variety of remedies—recovery from the person benefitted by the sale price, subrogation to the plaintiff's rights under the judgment including any judgment lien, a lien on the property for all amounts paid, and injunctions to protect possession of the property until reimbursement. The execution purchaser, may, however, be required to account to the execution debtor for rents and profits from the use of the property.

6. GARNISHMENT

Many of the comparisons of attachment and prejudgment garnishment in Ch. III, B, supra, are applicable to execution and post-judgment garnishments. Here again garnishment has more of the attributes of a full-fledged lawsuit. The judgment creditor files an affidavit stating that there is a judgment, that the judgment is wholly or partially unsatisfied and that the garnishee holds property of the judgment debtor. The court then issues a writ of garnishment that is served upon the garnishee; many states [more after *Sniadach*] serve the principal debtor with a copy of the writ.

As with prejudgment garnishment, the service of the summons creates a lien, and there is a division in the authorities as to the property subject to the lien. In some states, the lien reaches only property of the principal debtor and debts owed to the principal debtor as of the time of service of the summons. In others, the lien also reaches property of the principal debtor which comes into the possession of the garnishee and debts of the garnishee which accrue in the interim between service on the garnishee and answer by the garnishee; and, in a few states, the date of determination of the garnishment proceeding is the relevant date, if the garnishee's answer is controverted.

The garnishee is required to answer within a stated time. Failure to answer may result in a default judgment or contempt proceedings. In its answer, the garnishee must set out what, if any, funds, property or earnings of the principal debtor it holds. Along with this disclosure, the garnishee may set up any defense to the garnishment action that it might have. Since the judgment creditor in effect represents the principal debtor as against the garnishee and is entitled to whatever the principal debtor might recover, the garnishee may make any defense which it might make if sued by the principal debtor. For example, the garnishee might assert that it has already paid over the funds or turned over the property to the principal debtor before it was served with the notice of garnishment. The garnishee may also plead as a defense to the garnishment the exemptions [exempt property is discussed at pages 16–20] of the principal debtor. And, in most states, the garnishee may set off any of its claims against the principal debtor.

If the garnishee's answer is controverted by the plaintiff, the controverted issue is tried as other civil cases. If the answer is not controverted, the answer is taken as true. If the answer admits indebtedness to the principal debtor, the court will render judgment against the garnishee for the admitted amount. Similarly, any property of the principal debtor acknowledged to be held by the garnishee will be ordered turned over to the court for sale to satisfy the creditor's judgment.

The garnishee is protected by statute in some states, case law in others, from double liability.* Payment by the garnishee to the judgment creditor of the amount owed by the garnishee to the principal debtor liberates the garnishee *vis-a-vis* the principal debtor. On the other hand, a judgment in the garnishment proceeding limiting or negating the garnishee's liability to the principal debtor is generally held not to bar an action by the principal debtor for the debt. To illustrate:

(1) C brings an action against D and obtains a judgment for $500. C, believing that G is indebted to D in the amount of $500, garnishes G. G acknowledges the $500 debt to D and pays this sum to C. D could not subsequently maintain an action against G to collect the $500.

(2) Same facts as #1 except that G denies any liability to D and prevails in the garnishment proceeding. D would not be bound by the judgment in favor of G from bringing an action against G to collect the debt.

---

* Protection from double liability is not absolute. A garnishee who fails to disclose that property held by him or the indebtedness owed by him is exempt may be subject to double liability. Also, dictum in Harris v. Balk, 198 U.S. 215 (1905), and numerous subsequent decisions indicate that where the garnishment was prior to judgment in a state other than that of the principal debtor's residence, notice of the garnishment proceeding to the principal debtor is required to protect the garnishee from double liability.

(3) Same facts as #1 except that G acknowledges a debt of only $300 and pays that amount to C. D could maintain an action against G to collect any amounts owed by G in excess of $300 so that if the court in the second proceeding found that G did owe D $500, D could collect $200.

7. FRAUDULENT CONVEYANCES

a. WHAT CONSTITUTES A FRAUDULENT CONVEYANCE

A not untypical reaction of a debtor confronted with the possibility of seizure of property to satisfy the claims of creditors is to convey away his property to friends or relatives for little or no consideration or with the understanding that the debtor shall continue to enjoy the use and benefit of the property. Since Roman law, such attempts to defraud creditors have been ineffective; creditors have been permitted to recover property so conveyed.

The basis of the modern law of fraudulent conveyances is the Statute of 13 Elizabeth, enacted in 1570. It provides that "covinous and fraudulent feoffments, gifts, grants, alienations, conveyances, bonds, suits, judgments and executions, as well of lands and of tenements as of goods and chattels, * * * devised and contrived of malice, fraud, covin, collusion or guile, to the end, purpose and intent, to delay, hinder or defraud creditors and others   *   *   *   shall be utterly void, frustrate and of no effect.   *   *   * "

The law of fraudulent conveyances soon became something other than the language of the statute. The Statute of Elizabeth says that fraudulent conveyances are "void", but void only as to persons "hindered, delayed or defrauded." In other words, a fraudulent conveyance is valid as between the grantor and the grantee; in other words, a fraudulent conveyance is not void but rather is voidable by certain creditors of the grantor. The language of the Statute also indicates that it is a penal statute with the remedy being the delivery of half the fraudulently transferred property to the crown and the other half to the defrauded creditor. Courts, however, since Mannocke's Case, 3 Dyer 293b (1571), have taken the position that the judgment creditor need not rely on the remedy provided in the statute but can ignore the transfer and proceed directly on the property.

Note also that the Statute of Elizabeth requires "intent to delay, hinder or defraud." Since proof of a particular intent is a difficult task, courts soon developed "badges of fraud," i. e., circumstances indicative of intent to defraud. The first such case was Twyne's Case, 3 Coke 80b, 76 Eng. Rep. 809 (1601). There P was indebted to T for 400 pounds and to C for 200 pounds. C sued P and, while the action was pending, P secretly conveyed to T by deed of gift all of his chattels (worth 300 pounds) in satisfaction of T's claim. P, however, remained in possession of some of his property—some sheep—and treated them as his own. C obtained a judgment against P, but when the sheriff sought to levy on the sheep, friends of P prevented him from doing so, asserting that the sheep belonged to T. Thereupon C sued T to set aside the conveyance from P to T as a fraudulent conveyance. The court held that the transfer was fraudulent, noting the following "badges of fraud": (1) the conveyance is general, i. e., of all P's (the debtor's) assets; (2) the debtor continues in possession and deals with the property as his own; (3) the conveyance is made while a suit against the debtor is pending; (4) the transaction is secret; and (5) T (the transferee) takes the property in trust for the debtor.

In virtually every American jurisdiction, the Statute of 13 Elizabeth has been either recognized as part of the inherited common law or expressly adopted or enacted in more or less similar terms. The concept of "badges of fraud" has also been generally adopted, although what constitutes a "badge of fraud" varies from jurisdiction to jurisdiction. Among the most commonly recognized "badges of fraud" are those mentioned in *Twyne's Case;* intra-family transfers; voluntary transfers, i. e., transfers of property without consideration; and transfers of all or a substantial amount of property immediately prior to anticipated litigation. Not only do states differ as to what facts give rise to a "badge of fraud", there is also no uniformity as to what weight is to be given to a particular "badge": whether it is conclusive of fraud, prima facie evidence of fraud, or merely admissible evidence of fraud.

Because of the variations in state fraudulent conveyance statutes and the judicial decisions thereunder and the confusion caused thereby, the National Conference of Commissioners on Uniform State Laws in 1919 proposed the Uniform Fraudulent Conveyances Act (UFCA) which has now been adopted in twenty-three states. Sections 4 through 8 of the UFCA describe various forms of fraudulent conveyances. Of these four provisions, sections 4 and 7 are the ones most commonly used. Accordingly, this discussion of what is a fraudulent conveyance focuses on sections 4 and 7.

Section 4 labels fraudulent every conveyance made (1) without "fair consideration" (2) by a person who is or will thereby be rendered "insolvent." "Fair consideration" is defined in section 3 of the UFCA; it differs markedly from the common contracts concept of consideration. A mere peppercorn is not sufficient, although an antecedent indebtedness may be. Section 3 has a comparative value standard, or rather, two comparative value standards: "fair equivalent" if the transfer is an absolute transfer such as an exchange of property or a gift; "not disproportionately small" if the transfer is a security transfer

—a mortgage or an Article 9 security interest. Section 3 also requires good faith. Tacoma Association of Credit Men v. Lester, 72 Wash.2d 453, 433 P.2d 901 (1967) undertook to define "good faith" in UFCA section 3; the court attributed to the good faith concept: "(1) An honest belief in the propriety of the activities in question; (2) no intent to take unconscionable advantage of others; and (3) no intent to, or knowledge of the fact that the activities in question will, hinder, delay, or defraud others." 72 Wash.2d at 458, 433 P.2d at 904.

"Insolvent," the other element of a section 4 fraudulent conveyance, is defined in Section 2 of the UFCA. The section compares the "present salable value" of the debtor's assets and the "probable liability" on his existing debts. Neither of these phrases has an established accounting or business definition, and no reported case considers at length the meaning of these phrases. Most reported cases simply state that the transferor was or was not insolvent at the time of the transfer. Where the transfer is to a member of the transferor's family or for an inadequate consideration, some courts have presumed insolvency or shifted the burden of proof and required the transferee to show solvency of the transferor. These cases seem inconsistent with the language of section 4.

The language of section 7 differs markedly from the language of section 4. In section 7, the operative language is "made * * * or incurred with *actual* intent, as distinguished from intent presumed in law, to hinder, delay or defraud." Section 7 then focuses on intent—not the adequacy of the consideration or the financial condition of the transferor. How do you prove *actual* intent to defraud? Section 7 seems to present the same problem as was presented by the Statute of Elizabeth—the problem of proof of intent. "Badges of fraud" was the Statute of Elizabeth answer; the language of section 7— "actual intent as distinguished from intent presumed in law"—would seem to preclude the same answer for the UFCA. Notwithstanding this statutory language, cases under section 7 of the UFCA have considered the same factors as considered by Statute of Elizabeth cases and have even used the same "badges of fraud" terminology. In light of these section 7 cases, the cases presuming insolvency under section 4, and the element of good faith brought into section 4 by the definition of fair consideration, it would seem that there is a considerable overlap between sections 4 and 7.* While not all section 4 fraudulent conveyances are section 7 fraudulent conveyances and vice versa, most section 4 fraudulent convey-

---

* One case seems to suggest that the primary difference between proceeding under sections 4 and 7 of the UFCA is burden of proof—"substantial evidence" under section 4 and "clear and satisfactory" proof under section 7. Sparkman & McLean Co. v. Derber, 4 Wash.App. 341, 481 P.2d 585 (1971).

ances would also seem to be section 7 fraudulent conveyances. As is pointed out below, there is a possible practical difference between a determination of a section 4 fraudulent conveyance and a section 7 fraudulent conveyance.

It should be noted that neither section 4 nor section 7 of the UFCA, nor any other part of the UFCA, nor the Statute of Elizabeth condemns a debtor's giving preference to some of his creditors by paying them while leaving others unpaid. Common law, unlike the Bankruptcy Code, [see section 457 of the Bankruptcy Code discussed infra at page 175] does not condemn a preference. A debtor, though insolvent, may in good faith prefer one or more of his creditors, even to the extent of exhausing his assets without the preference being a fraudulent conveyance.

While neither the Statute of Elizabeth nor the UFCA expressly so provides, it is well settled under both types of statutes that a transfer of exempt property cannot be a fraudulent conveyance. The rationale is that since exempt property is not available to the creditor, the creditor has no grievance if the debtor should transfer exempt property.

b. WHAT IS THE PRACTICAL SIGNIFICANCE OF DETERMINING THAT A TRANSFER IS A FRAUDULENT CONVEYANCE?

The determination that a transfer is a fraudulent conveyance materially affects the rights and remedies of the creditor of the transferor, the transferee, and creditors of the transferee. Under section 9 of the UFCA (and in most Statute of Elizabeth jurisdictions) a creditor as to whom a conveyance is fraudulent has a choice of remedies: the creditor can either bring an action (usually a creditor's bill) to set the conveyance aside or ignore the transfer and levy on and sell the property fraudulently conveyed. Most practice books recommend setting the fraudulent conveyance aside. The validity of the conveyance is thus determined in advance of the sale of the property and so the sale is likely to be at a higher price. Also, this minimizes possible liability to the transferee in the event that the transfer was not fraudulent. Yet another factor in determining which remedy to use is the statute of limitations. Both the limitation period and the date that the statute begins to run may vary with the remedy used.

Under the Statute of Elizabeth, these remedies were available only to judgment creditors. The rule is now otherwise in most Statute of Elizabeth jurisdictions: a number of these states have adopted rules of practice modeled on the federal rules [Federal Rule of Civil Procedure 18b permits the joinder of a claim for money and a claim to have a fraudulent conveyance set aside]; others have eliminated the judgment requirement through case law or statutory modification. The UFCA does not distinguish between a judgment creditor and general creditors: rather the UFCA dividing line is whether a creditor's claim has matured. [Claims *ex contractu* can be mature notwithstanding the absence of any judgment.] If a creditor's claim has not matured, the option of ignoring the transfer and levying on the property is not available. See UFCA section 10.

Note that these statutory remedies are available to creditors as to whom the conveyance is fraudulent. As section 7 of the UFCA uses the phrase "both present and future creditors," the above described statutory remedies are available to all creditors of the transferor where the transfer is a section 7 fraudulent conveyance. Section 4, however, speaks only of "creditors." Thus, where the transfer is a section 4 fraudulent conveyance, these statutory remedies are available only to "present creditors"—creditors of the transferor who had extended credit prior to the making of the fraudulent conveyance.

To illustrate, on January 10, X lends D $1,000. On February 2, D transfers property to Y. On March 3, Z extends credit to D. The remedies of the UFCA will be available to X if the February 2nd transfer was a fraudulent conveyance under section 4 or 7. The remedies of the UFCA will be available to Z only if the February 2nd transfer was a fraudulent conveyance under section 7.

These statutory remedies are further restricted by statutory protection of certain transferees.

"Purchasers for fair consideration without knowledge" are completely protected. See UFCA section 9(1). Purchasers for "less than fair consideration" and "without fraudulent intent" are protected to the extent of consideration furnished. See UFCA section 9(2). And, if the transferee has conveyed the property to a bona fide purchaser for value, creditors of the transferor will not be able to reach the property. [Bona fide purchasers are similarly protected under the Statute of Elizabeth.] The creditors can, however, recover traceable proceeds of the second conveyance from the transferee or, in the absence of such proceeds, hold a fraudulent transferee personally liable for the value of the property.

For example, D fraudulently conveys her motorcycle to T. T then sells the motorcycle to X, a bona fide purchaser, for $2,000. The creditors of D have no rights to the motorcycle. They can, however, invoke the law of fraudulent conveyances to recover the $2,000 from T.

Creditors of one who makes a fraudulent conveyance also have common law remedies. Generally, a creditor who has a lien on property fraudulently conveyed can recover damages in tort against persons who prevent execution of the lien. General creditors, however, for the most part have not been allowed to bring an action in tort based upon a fraudulent conveyance. The reason given most frequently for denying general creditors a tort recovery for fraudulent conveyances is that the damages cannot be accurately measured. The most difficult measurement of damages problem would occur when the debtor has multiple creditors. If the sum of the debts is greater than the value of the property fraudulently conveyed, it will be difficult to determine to what extent each creditor has been damaged. Obviously if there had been no fraudulent conveyance, all of the creditors could not have satisfied their judgments from the property. On the other hand, there is no way of knowing which creditor might have acted first and thus satisfied his entire judgment from the transferred property.

Fraudulent conveyance cases do not always involve only the transferee and the creditors of the transferor. The effect of a fraudulent conveyance on the transferor or the creditors of the transferee also presents problems. A fraudulent conveyance does not eliminate the transferor's personal liability to his creditors. In fact, it increases such liability in jurisdictions that recognize tort liability for a fraudulent conveyance— the additional damages being the incidental costs of tracking down the property and attempting to set aside the fraudulent conveyance.

The affirmative rights of one who makes a fraudulent transfer are virtually nil. Generally the transferor cannot recover property fraudulently conveyed even where the transferee has promised to reconvey. Various rationales have been offered for this rule: *pari delicto,* unclean hands, the policy of discouraging fraudulent conveyances. Once the agreement to reconvey has been executed, however, a majority of jurisdictions reach a different result: an executed reconveyance will be enforced against either the transferee or non-lien creditors of the transferee. Here, the expressed rationale is that since the transferee agreed to reconvey, he was under a moral obligation to do so. It is said that moral obligation supplies consideration for the reconveyance and makes it enforceable. [What about *"pari delicto*, unclean hands, the policy of discouraging fraudulent conveyances"?]

Very few cases have considered the relative rights of the creditors of the transferor and the creditors of the transferee to property that has been fraudulently conveyed. To illustrate, A loans R $100. At the time of the loan, R owns a 1952 Hudson; while A does not take a security interest in the Hudson, she to some extent relies on R's ownership of the car in making the loan. R fraudulently conveys the car to E. E borrows $100 from B. B also relies on his debtor's ownership of the car without taking a security interest in the car. Now both R and E are in default. Both A and B are looking to the Hudson to satisfy their claims. Who has priority? Under the language of the UFCA it would seem that A should have priority; section 9 authorizes a creditor of one who transfers his property in fraud of creditors to pursue the statutory remedies against any person except a bona fide *purchaser*; B is not a bona fide purchaser—B is not even a purchaser. Notwithstanding this statutory analysis, the prevailing view in both UFCA and Statute of Elizabeth jurisdictions seems to be that the first creditor to obtain a lien on the property prevails, the reasoning being that the equities are equal. So, if B is the first to obtain an execution lien on the Hudson, B has priority.

The doctrine of fraudulent conveyances is also of considerable practical significance in bankruptcy. Under section 727(a)(2), the debtor's fraudulent conveyance can be used to deprive him of a discharge in a liquidation bankruptcy. Sections 544 and 548 empower the bankruptcy trustee to void pre-bankruptcy fraudulent conveyances of the bankrupt. These bankruptcy concepts and sections of the Bankruptcy Reform Act of 1978 are discussed at length later in the nutshell.

IV. CREDITORS WITH SPECIAL RIGHTS

A. CONSENSUAL LIENS

The preceding chapter focused on rights available to all creditors—rights afforded by the judicial process. Some creditors have rights in addition to those already discussed. Agreement of the parties is one source of such rights. The debtor and the creditor may agree that the creditor is to have a lien on certain real or personal property of the debtor.

Obtaining a consensual lien does not destroy or limit the creditor's rights. A lien creditor may proceed against the debtor personally, may utilize the various creditors' remedies discussed in the preceding chapter. Additionally, such a creditor has special rights in the property subject to its lien. The special rights include a right of foreclosure—the right to proceed against the security and apply it to the payment of the debt—and the right of priority—the right to take the security free from the claims of general creditors and later secured creditors.

1. SECURITY INTERESTS

a. TERMINOLOGY AND ORGANIZATION OF ARTICLE 9

Today in every state except Louisiana consensual liens are governed by Article 9 of the Uniform Commercial Code. Although the legislature of every state except Louisiana has adopted Article 9 of the Uniform Commercial Code, each state has adopted a different Article 9. Legislators in every state have made their own "improvements." Moreover, there are now two "official versions" of Article 9: the 1962 Official Text and the 1972 Official Text. Textual discussion in this book will be keyed to the 1972 Official Text.

Article 9 of the Code has a language all its own that can best be explained by illustration. Assume that D wants to borrow $5,500 from S to buy a new pick-up truck. S is only willing to make the loan if the truck will be security; D agrees. In "Code talk," D is the debtor; S is the secured party; the pick-up truck is the collateral; S's interest in the truck is a security interest; the agreement creating the security interest is a security agreement. See sections 1–201; 9–105. Since S is loaning D the $5,500 to acquire the collateral, S's security interest is a purchase money security interest. See section 9–107. [Similarly, if D had financed the car with the seller, and the seller had obtained a security interest in the car, the security interest would be a purchase money security interest.]

The creation of a security interest requires more than a security agreement. It is also necessary that the secured party give value and that the debtor acquire rights in the collateral. When these three requirements are satisfied, the security interest is said to have "attached."

To achieve maximum possible priority, it is necessary for the secured party to "perfect" its security interest. Depending on the kind of collateral involved, a security interest may be perfected when it attaches (e. g., a purchase money interest in consumer goods other than motor vehicles or fixtures, section 9–302(1)(d)), or it may require a transfer of possession from the debtor to the secured party (e. g., stock certificates, section 9–304(1)) or filing (the usual case, section 9–302). Where filing is required, the document filed is called a "financing statement." It need contain only the names, addresses, and signatures of the parties and a description of the types of items of collateral covered, section 9–402.

Article 9 of the Code is divided into five parts: Part 1 is mostly definitions; Part 2 controls disputes between the debtor and the secured party; Part 3 controls disputes between the secured party and third parties; Part 4 contains the mechanics of filing; and Part 5 governs the rights of the secured party on default. Parts 1 through 4 are ordinarily covered in detail in courses in commercial law. Accordingly, only Part 5 will be discussed at any length.

b. SECTION 9–301

There is, however, one section in Part 3 of Article 9 that merits consideration in a debtor-creditor law primer. Section 9–301 provides that an unperfected security interest is "subordinate" to a judicial lien on the same property.* In other words, section 9–301 contemplates a situation where a judicial lien arises in the gap between the creation and perfection of a security interest: if D gave S a security interest in her truck on October 7, and S perfected this security interest on October 21, any creditor who obtained an attachment or execution lien on the truck between October 7 and October 21 would have priority over S.

Section 9–301 is also important for what it does not say. It does not govern priority as between a secured creditor and a creditor with a statutory lien (see section 9–310) or between two secured creditors (see section 9–312). It does not expressly state that a creditor with an unperfected security interest has priority over general creditors although that is certainly implied. Moreover, section 9–301 is silent as to the relative priority when the judicial lien arises before the security interest attaches. In such cases, it would seem that the first in time rule should ap-

---

* The 1962 Official Text of section 9–301 requires that the judicial lienor be without knowledge of the security at the time the judicial lien arose.

ply regardless of whether the security interest is perfected immediately.

c. PART 5 OF ARTICLE 9

The application of Part 5 of the Uniform Commercial Code is conditioned on default by the debtor. The term "default" is not specifically defined in the Code. The circumstances which constitute default are a matter of agreement between the parties. Because the secured party usually has superior bargaining power, the security agreement will usually define default as broadly as possible. Common events of default include any impairment of the collateral such as failure to insure, impairment of the personal obligation such as bankruptcy of the debtor and any feeling of insecurity that the prospect for payment is uncertain (section 1–208). In the absence of any definition of "default" in the security agreement, default occurs only on a failure to pay.

When the debtor is in default, Part 5 of Article 9 gives the secured party the following cumulative remedies:

(1) Foreclose its security interest under the state's non-Code foreclosure law—9–501(1)

(2) Use real estate mortgage procedure when both realty and personalty are involved —9–501(4)

(3) Apply any special remedies provided in the security agreement—9–501(1), 9–501(2)

(4) Take judgment and levy execution on any non-exempt property of the debtor—9–501(1), 9–501(5)

(5) Collect accounts and instruments that are collateral—9–501(2), 9–502

(6) Foreclose its security interest under Code procedure—9–503, 9–504, 9–505, 9–506, 9–507.

While the first five alternatives seem fairly self-explanatory, discussion of the sixth and the Code concepts of repossession, redemption, retention and resale is necessary.

Section 9–503 of the Code authorizes a secured party to take possession of the collateral upon default of the debtor and to do so without judicial process if this can be done "without breach of the peace." "Breach of the peace" is another phrase that is not defined in the Code. Most cases in which there has been a finding of breach of peace under section 9–503 involve either unauthorized entry into the debtor's house or repossession after protests by the debtor or one acting on his behalf. Recent cases are divided as to whether repossession through trickery violates section 9–503's "breach of the peace" standard.

Recent cases are, however, uniform in upholding the constitutionality of section 9–503. While self-help repossession deprives the debtor of property without prior notice and hearing, *Sniadach* and the other due process decisions are inapplicable. Self-help repossession does not involve "state action."

If self-help repossession cannot be accomplished without a "breach of the peace," the secured party can "proceed by action," section 9–503. This "action" is variously referred to as replevin, claim and delivery, and sequestration. Regardless of the label, the remedy is essentially the same—the sheriff seizes the collateral pursuant to a court order. And, regardless of the label, there are constitutional requirements of notice and hearing. The state is issuing the writ; the state is seizing the property. State action! Due process requirements of notice and hearing must be satisfied. See pages 37–41 supra. Almost every state has amended its replevin, claim and delivery, or sequestration procedures to provide for some kind of probable cause hearing before the writ is issued by the court and the collateral is seized by the sheriff.

In theory, the debtor has a right to redeem repossessed collateral. Section 9–506 provides that a debtor may redeem by "tendering fulfillment of *all obligations* secured by the collateral as well as the expenses reasonably incurred by the secured party in retaking, holding and preparing the collateral for disposition * * *." Most security agreements contain language accelerating the entire balance due on default. Thus, a debtor who was unable to pay a single installment will have to come up with the entire balance plus expenses in order to redeem, Comment to 9–506.

Additionally, this "right of redemption" is terminated by the occurrence of any one of the following events:

(1) debtor's signing a written waiver after default, or

(2) secured party's disposing of the collateral, or entering into a contract for the sale of the collateral

(3) secured party's retaining the collateral pursuant to section 9–505, discussed below. In short, a debtor seldom redeems repossessed property.

In the event that the repossession is not followed by redemption, the secured party may either retain the collateral or resell it. There are two significant limitations on the retention alternative.

First, section 9–505 provides that retention of repossessed collateral results in complete satisfaction of the debtor's obligation. If, for example, D owes S $5,000 and S repossesses D's car and elects to retain it, D's entire $5,000 debt is extinguished, regardless of the value of D's car. Accordingly, S is likely to elect the retention alternative only if the collateral is worth as much as or more than the debt owed. The second limitation on retention makes it unlikely that S will be permitted to retain collateral worth more than the debt owed: Retention requires debtor acquiescence.* If the collateral is worth more than the amount of the secured debt, the debtor will generally insist that the secured party resell the collateral. Any surplus from a resale goes to the debtor, section 9–504(2).

Section 9–504 governs the disposition of the collateral by the secured party. Reasonable notice of the sale must be given to the debtor (and, except in the case of consumer goods, to other secured creditors from whom the repossessing secured party has received written notice) unless the collateral is perishable, or threatens to decline rapidly in value or is of a type "customarily sold on a recognized market." The sale may be either public or private; the secured party may bid-in only if the sale is public or if the collateral is of a type "customarily sold on a recognized market or is of a type which is the subject of widely distributed price quotations."

Additionally, section 9–504(3) requires that every aspect of sale of a repossessed item "including the method, manner, time, place and terms must be commercially reasonable." "Commercially reasonable" is nowhere defined in the Code.

---

* If the collateral is consumer goods and the debtor has paid 60% of the debt, the debtor must expressly consent to the retention. Otherwise, section 9–505 gives the debtor the opportunity to object to the retention.

Notwithstanding the statement in section 9–507(2) that low resale price is not itself sufficient to establish that the sale was not commercially reasonable, both the courts and the commentators seem to regard the price as a major consideration.

If the proceeds of the sale is not sufficient to satisfy the indebtedness, the debtor is liable for any deficiency, absent any agreement to the contrary. In seeking recovery of a deficiency, the creditor has all of the rights of a general creditor. In the unlikely event that the section 9–504 sale yields a sum greater than that owed by the debtor to the secured creditor, the secured party must account to the debtor for any surplus.

The debtor may recover under section 9–507 for any losses caused by the secured party's failure to comply with the provisions of Part 5. Particularly, in consumer credit transactions it is difficult to prove damages resulting from noncompliance with Part 5. Accordingly, if the collateral is consumer goods, the debtor is assured a minimum recovery regardless of the lack of any provable damages: "the credit service charge plus ten per cent of the principal amount of the debt or the time price differential plus ten per cent of the cash price," section 9–507(1).

Noncompliance with the requirements of Part 5 of Article 9 may also affect the secured party's right to a deficiency judgment. The Uniform Commercial Code nowhere mentions denial of the section 9–504(2) right to recovery of any deficiency as a remedy for noncompliance with the requirements of Part 5 of Article 9. Nevertheless, a number of courts have held that the noncomplying secured party loses its right to a deficiency judgment. More courts hold that the right to a deficiency judgment is *not* lost by a violation of the requirements of Part 5. However, a growing number of the courts that permit recovery of a deficiency judgment limit the deficiency judgment to the difference between the debt and the value of the collateral, with a rebuttable presumption that the value of the collateral equals the amount of the debt.

2. MORTGAGES

There is no single uniform law governing real property security, and the rights of a mortgagee on default of the mortgagor vary considerably from state to state. There are, however, a number of similarities between Article 9 of the Uniform Commercial Code and the law of mortgages in most jurisdictions.

The mortgagor's equitable redemption rights virtually mirror the debtor's rights under section 9–506. The redeeming party must pay the entire debt; the right to redeem is terminated by the sale of the property or by strict foreclosure. In about one half of the states, however, statutes augment the mortgagor's redemption rights. These statutes extend the period of redemption beyond foreclosure; the additional period varies from several months to several years. This statutory redemption differs from equitable redemption with regard to the sum payable to effect redemption: the basic factor is the sale price (plus interest at specified rate and other costs), not the debt secured by the mortgage.

In only a few states does the mortgagee have both the options that are available to a secured party under Article 9 of the Uniform Commercial Code: retention or resale. Retention of the mortgaged property, i. e., strict foreclosure, is available in certain circumstances in nineteen states, but is commonly used in only three states. In other states, foreclosure results in a sale of the property.

There are two types of foreclosure sales generally used in the United States: judicial sale and sale pursuant to a power of sale. Judicial sale is more commonly used. The mechanics of such a sale are mostly a matter of local law. The legislation ordinarily provides for notice of a hearing, a hearing, judicial determination of default, notice of sale, sale, confirmation of sale, possible redemption (statutory) and entry of a judgment for any deficiency.

Until court confirmation, the judicial sale is not enforceable by the buyer. There are legal rules limiting the court's discretion in confirming the sale. Absent a statutory provision to the contrary, mere inadequacy of price without more does not justify a refusal to confirm—the inadequacy must be so gross as to shock the conscience. Nevertheless, in cases involving confirmation of the sale, as in cases involving section 9–504(3)'s "commercially reasonable" standard, adequacy of the price seems the primary concern. Moreover, in a number of states, there are "statutory provisions to the contrary." For example, in several states an appraisal in advance of the sale is required, and the sale is not confirmed unless the sales price is at least a certain percentage of the appraisal.

Because of the delays and expenses incident to foreclosure by judicial sale, mortgagees included provisions in the mortgage permitting sale without any judicial proceeding in case of default. This approach to foreclosure has only limited recognition in the United States. Several states legislatively exclude this extrajudicial procedure, and in only eighteen states is foreclosure under a power of sale the prevailing practice. The conduct of the sale under a power of sale is determined by the provisions of the instrument creating it and by any statutory regulations governing its exercise. In the majority of jurisdictions using this type of procedure, the sale must be public, and preceded by notice (usually advertisement) specifying the amount of debt due, description of the property, date and location of sale and such other matters as either the mortgage or the applicable statute may provide. The critical attitude of the courts toward powers of sales makes them quick to grant relief against even slight irregularities. This willingness to overturn sales results in uncertainty of title and is probably the chief reason for the power of sale's failure to gain greater acceptance.

B. LIENS BY OPERATION OF LAW

1. COMMON LAW LIENS

Some creditors are given additional rights by operation of law. Common law grants to certain creditors a possessory lien on property of their debtors. A common law possessory lien is the right to retain the property of another for some particular claim or charge upon the property so detained.

Common law from very early times gave the innkeeper a lien on the goods of the guest brought by him into the inn. Similarly, a common carrier has a lien for freight charges on all goods delivered by it. And an artisan who, at the request of the owner, performs services on a chattel has a common law possessory lien on such chattels.

A common law possessory lien is either specific or general. The former attaches to specific property as security for some demand which the creditor has with respect to that property. A general lien is one that the holder thereof is entitled to enforce as security for all the obligations which exists in his favor against the owner of the property. Specific liens have been favored by the courts. General liens exist only when (1) contracted for, (2) conferred by statute or (3) so common and well-established that the parties to the transaction must be taken to have made their contracts in relation to such custom and usage. The burden of establishing the general lien is on the party claiming it, and courts have been reluctant to find the burden sustained. In certain callings, however, such as those of attorney, banker, factor and innkeeper, the general lien is well-established.

A common law possessory lien is merely a device to coerce the debtor into payment of his debts by the retention of his property from him until he pays. In general, there is no remedy for enforcing the lien; the lienor has no right to sell the subject matter of the lien to satisfy his claim unless such right is expressly conferred by statute or agreement of the parties.

Although possession is essential to the creation of liens under common law and the lien is in essence a right to retain the goods until certain debts are paid, a change of possession does not necessarily destroy the lien. When the lienholder has parted with possession, it is a question for the jury whether he has so far voluntarily parted with possession as to warrant the conclusion that he has waived the lien. For example, if the owner of the property obtains possession thereof without the knowledge or consent of the lienor, the latter is not divested of his lien. A lienor who has voluntarily and unconditionally surrendered possession of the property cannot thereafter assert a lien on the property. Even if such a lienor subsequently regains possession of the property his lien is not restored. To illustrate, C makes D a dress and unconditionally delivers the dress to D before D pays the $35 charge. Subsequently, D returns the dress to C to have the hem lowered. C only has a lien on the dress for the hemming work.

2. EQUITABLE LIENS

Equitable liens do not depend on the possession of the debtor's property by a creditor. Rather, the basis for an equitable lien is one of two equitable maxims.

First, as equity looks upon as done that which is agreed or intended to be done, an agreement that evidences an intention to create a consensual lien but fails to do so, creates an equitable lien. For example, a mortgage which, through some informality or defect in terms or mode of execution, is not valid as a mortgage, will nevertheless generally create an equitable lien on the property described. Similarly, an agreement to give a mortgage creates an equitable lien.

Second, equity regards as done that which ought to be done and so creates equitable liens to avoid unjust enrichment. To illustrate, B enters into a contract to buy Greenacre from S for $10,000. B makes a partial payment of $2,000. S is unable to comply with the covenants of the contract as to the title she is to convey. Under these facts, B would have an equitable lien on Greenacre to secure the repayment of the $2,000, notwithstanding the absence of any agreement to this effect. A buyer under an executory contract for the sale of land has an equitable lien on the land for purchase money advanced, where the contract fails due to the fault of the seller.

Equitable liens also differ from common law liens in terms of rights available to the lienor. A holder of an equitable lien can enforce his lien by having the subject property sold to satisfy his claim.

C. STATE STATUTORY LIENS

Other sources of additional rights for certain creditors are state and federal statutes. Legislation has enlarged many of the liens recognized at common law and many of those asserted in equity. And, statutes have in many instances gone beyond the liens previously recognized in law or equity and created a number of additional liens. It is not feasible within the scope of this nutshell to do more than indicate this source of liens and mention some of the more common statutory liens: employees' liens on the employer's personalty to secure payment of back wages; landlord's lien on tenant's property (codification of a common law possessory lien) ; materialmen's and mechanics' liens on land and the improvements thereon to secure the compensation of persons who, under contract with the owner or his agent, contributed labor or materials to the improvement of said land; and tax liens.

D. FEDERAL CLAIMS

The largest creditors are, of course, the various governmental entities. For example, at the close of fiscal 1970 the Internal Revenue Service had some 788,000 delinquent accounts involving $1,812,265,000 of taxes in arrears. A governmental creditor may be either a general creditor or a lien creditor. When its claim is secured, the government has all the rights of a secured creditor; when its claim is not secured, it has all the rights of a general creditor.

Additionally, a number of states statutorily prefer governmental claims against delinquent debtors to those of private creditors. The federal government's claims are given preference over claims of other creditors primarily by two statutory provisions: the federal priority provision, 31 U.S.C.A. § 191, more commonly referred to by its Revised Statute designation, R.S. 3466; and the Federal Tax Lien Act, Internal Revenue Code of 1954, sections 6321–23.

1. FEDERAL PRIORITY PROVISION

Section 3466 applies to every kind of debt owing to the federal government: tax and non-tax. The statute, as recently amended, provides:

> "Whenever any person indebted to the United States is insolvent, or whenever the estate of any deceased debtor, in the hands of the executors or administrators, is insufficient to pay all the debts due from the deceased, the debts due to the United States shall be first satisfied; and the priority established shall extend as well to cases in which a debtor, not having sufficient property to pay all his debts, makes a voluntary assignment thereof, or in which the estate and effects of an absconding, concealed, or absent debtor are attached by process of law, as to cases in which an act of bankruptcy is committed. The priority established under this section does not apply, however, in a case under Title 11 of the United States Code."

On its face, section 3466 confers absolute priority on the United States whenever a person indebted to the United States becomes insolvent. No exceptions are expressly made for administrative expenses—the costs incurred in collecting, liquidating and distributing the debtor's property. No exceptions are expressly made for earlier liens on the debtor's property.

The scope of the statute has been judicially limited in several significant respects. There are a substantial number of cases recognizing that administrative expenses are to be paid prior to federal claims. More important, there are cases holding that creditors who have obtained specific and perfected liens before the government's priority attached take before the federal government. There is, however, considerable confusion as to when a lien is sufficiently specific and perfected, or, to use section 3466 terminology, when the lien is "choate."

The United States Supreme Court in Illinois ex rel. Gordon v. Campbell, 329 U.S. 362 (1946), said that "the lien must be definite * * * in at least three respects * * * : (1) the identity of the lienor; * * * (2) the amount of the lien * * * and (3) the property to which it attaches." The lien there involved was a state statutory lien for unemployment contributions. The Court found the lien "not sufficiently specific or perfected" for federal purposes. The statutory language—"all the personal property * * * used * * * in business"—was too vague and comprehensive. Thus, it would seem that judgment liens and any statutory liens reaching all property of the debtor would similarly fall unless some specific property is seized by the lienor before the federal priority arises.

United States v. Gilbert Associates, Inc., 345 U.S. 361 (1953), added yet another factor to be considered in determining whether a lien is choate for purposes of section 3466. Without considering the three elements set out in *Campbell*, the Court found the lien "general" and "unperfected" as the debtor "had not been divested by the Town [the lienor] of either title or possession." Thus, at least a statutory lien on personalty cannot prevail in insolvency even if it satisfies the *Campbell* tests as to certainty of the lienor, amount and property, unless in addition either title or possession has passed to the lienor before the federal priority attaches. It is less than completely clear that a statutory lien can prevail even then. In the sixteen years since *Campbell* the *Supreme Court* has never found a lien to be choate for purposes of section 3466; moreover, the Court has on several occasions expressly reserved the question of whether even the most specific and perfected of liens could defeat the federal priority.*

Lower courts have consistently held that certain liens take prior to the federal government in insolvency proceedings: possessory liens; liens of creditors who have levied on the property; mortgages. A mortgage or security interest that contains an after-acquired property clause is incho-

---

* There were six Supreme Court decisions in the first half of the 19th century that permitted consensual liens to take prior to the government. These cases came long before the "choateness" doctrine, and the Court intimated in *Campbell* that the old "mortgage cases" may require re-examination.

ate—the property subject to lien is not identified with sufficient specificity. Similarly a mortgage or security interest with a future advances clause falls as the amount of the lien is not sufficiently specific.

United States v. Oklahoma, 261 U.S. 253 (1923), further judicially limited the federal government's priority under section 3466 through an artificial construction of the word "insolvency." The Court there first indicated that the statute contemplated insolvency in the bankruptcy sense of having debts in excess of assets, rather than in the equity sense of inability to pay debts as they mature. Additionally, *United States v. Oklahoma* held that except in the case of decedent's estate something more than insolvency in the bankruptcy sense is required. The insolvency must be manifested in one of the three forms mentioned in the second clause of section 3466; by assignment; by having effects attached after absconding, concealing or absenting oneself; or by committing an act of bankruptcy. [It would be more logical to say that these three forms were included in the statute as illustrations rather than limitations on the scope of the statute. *United States v. Oklahoma*, however, has been consistently followed.]

The commission of an "act of bankruptcy" by an insolvent is one of the events that triggers section 3466. Section 3 of the Bankruptcy Act of 1898 lists six acts of bankruptcy; the Bankruptcy

Reform Act of 1978 does not use the concept of "act of bankruptcy."

Section 3466 did not apply in bankruptcy proceedings under the Bankruptcy Act of 1898, cf. section 64a(5). And, it will not apply in bankruptcy proceedings under the Bankruptcy Reform Act of 1978. Section 322 of the Bankruptcy Reform Act of 1978 amends section 3466 by adding to the end of it: "The priority established under this section does not, however, apply in a case under Title 11 (Bankruptcy) of the United States Code."

Section 507 establishes which claims are entitled to priority treatment in a proceeding under the Bankruptcy Reform Act of 1978. Section 507 is considered infra at pages 272–276. The only governmental claims afforded a priority under section 507 are certain tax claims and unpaid custom duties, and these claims are given only a sixth priority. Thus, creditors with inchoate liens that are valid in bankruptcy and creditors with claims that would be given a priority in bankruptcy may receive more from a bankruptcy proceeding where 3466 is inapplicable than from a state insolvency proceeding where 3466 controls.

Consider the following illustration. Lawyer D has non-exempt property worth $3,000. She owes the following debts:

> $2,200 to the federal government for law school loans

> $340 to her secretary for salary
>
> $660 to a creditor who has a judgment lien on real property owned by D that is worth more than $600
>
> $800 to general creditors.

In short, D's debts exceed her assets; she is unable to pay her debts. D makes an assignment for the benefit of creditors. (Assignment for the benefit of creditors is covered infra at pages 119–127). The assignment coupled with her insolvency triggers section 3466. Assuming administrative expenses of $300, the distribution under section 3466 would be as follows:

> $300 for administrative expenses
>
> $2,200 for federal government
>
> $500 to the creditor with the judgment lien.

[The judgment lien is inchoate and thus subordinate to the federal claim because it is not sufficiently definite as to the property subject to the lien. In most jurisdictions, the docketing of a judgment creates a general lien on all real property owned by the debtor—the lien is not restricted to any specific property.]

A general assignment for the benefit of creditors is a basis for a creditor-initiated bankruptcy proceeding. See section 303 considered infra at page 148. Thus, creditors of the requisite number with required amounts of claims may transfer administration of D's assets to the bankruptcy court. Assuming higher administrative expenses in bankruptcy—$500—the bankruptcy distribution would be as follows:

$660 to the creditor with the judgment lien [Liens not invalidated by some specific provision of the Bankruptcy Act are enforceable against the property to which they attach or the proceeds of the sale of such property. Valid liens must be statisfied in full before any payments are made to general creditors—even general creditors with a section 507 priority.]

$500 to administrative expenses [section 507(a)(1).]

$340 to secretary [section 507(a)(3).]

$1,100 to the federal government and $400 to the private creditors [After liens and priorities are satisfied, the remainder is distributed pro rata. Here, there was $1,500 available to satisfy the $3,000 ($2,200 + $800) of unsecured, non-priority claims held by the government and by private creditors. Accordingly, each received 50 cents on the dollar.]

2. FEDERAL TAX LIEN

a. CREATION OF A FEDERAL TAX LIEN

The United States has a lien on "all property and rights to property" of a taxpayer who neglects or refuses to pay a tax for which s/he is liable, Internal Revenue Code, section 6321. In this context, "all" truly does mean all. The federal tax lien reaches not only all property owned by the taxpayer at the time that the lien arises but also property subsequently acquired by the taxpayer. Moreover, the federal tax lien attaches to that part of the taxpayer's property that would otherwise be exempt by state law from the reach of creditors.

The creation of the federal tax lien is conditioned on the following three events: assessment, demand and failure to pay. Although no lien exists until the taxpayer "neglects or refuses to pay the same after demand," the tax lien dates from the "time the assessment is made," sections 6321, 6322. When a person files a return acknowledging liability in excess of remittances, assessment involves nothing more than the notation of the acknowledged tax liability on a list in the office of the district director of Internal Revenue, section 6203. Assessment in the instance of an acknowledged liability will occur almost immediately after the return is received. Demand follows "as soon as practicable, and within 60 days," section 6303(a).

Where tax liability is understated on the return, considerably more time will elapse between the filing of the return and assessment. First, of course, the deficiency must be discovered through an audit of the return. Then, section 6213(a) prohibits assessment of a deficiency until ninety days after mailing to the taxpayer of the formal notification of the deficiency found by the Internal Revenue Service, as provided in section 6212. Once this notice of deficiency, commonly called the "statutory notice" or the "ninety-day letter," is sent, the taxpayer may file a petition in the Tax Court, and if s/he does so, assessment is further barred until the decision of the Tax Court has become final.

There are essentially only two ways the government can avoid the prohibition of section 6213(a) and make an assessment before completion of an audit and issuance of the statutory notice: the "jeopardy assessment" (section 6861(a)) and the immediate assessment permitted for bankruptcy and receivership proceedings (section 6871(a)). The latter assessment cannot be made until after bankruptcy. The former requires a finding by the district director personally, reviewed by the regional counsel of the Internal Revenue Service, that assessment or collection of a deficiency will be jeopardized if an immediate assessment is not made.

The actual assessment of a deficiency is the same as the assessment of a liability disclosed on a return—recordation on a list in the district director's office. Thus, in all instances a valid federal tax lien results without the federal government's filing notice thereof in any public recordation system. An unfiled federal tax lien is valid as against the taxpayer and most third parties. There are, however, certain third persons identified in section 6323(a) affected only by prior filed federal tax liens. Section 6323(a) is considered infra at page 110.

The mechanics of filing a federal tax lien are set out in section 6323(f). It provides for filing of notice of a tax lien (1) in a public index at the district IRS office for the district where the property is located, (2) in the case of real property, in one office designated for such filing by the state in which the realty is located, and, (3) in the case of personal property, whether tangible or intangible, in one office designated for such filing by the state within which the personalty is situated and the taxpayer resides.

Section 6322 provides that the tax lien continues until the amount assessed or a judgment against the taxpayer arising from the liability is satisfied or becomes unenforceable by the running of the statute of limitations provided for in section 6502(a), which period is 6 years from the date of assessment of the tax or such extension of time as may be expressly agreed upon by the government and the taxpayer. There are certain circumstances which may suspend or toll the statute. See, e. g., section 6503(b).

By reason of tolling of the statute of limitations, a lien may run beyond the initial 6-year period. To achieve this result, the government must refile its notice of lien within the one-year period ending 6 years and 30 days after the date of the assessment. Further extensions are possible and require similar refiling during each successive 6-year interval affected.

b. EFFECT OF FEDERAL TAX LIEN ON THIRD PARTY INTERESTS

A person who is not paying his federal taxes is probably not paying his non-governmental creditors and probably lacks sufficient assets to pay all claims against him. Which claims have priority? Because of the federal tax lien, IRS has priority over all creditors except:

(1) creditors who obtain choate liens before the federal tax lien *arises*, or

(2) creditors protected by the Federal Tax Lien Act of 1966.

United States v. Security Trust & Sav. Bank, 340 U.S. 47 (1950), was the first case to apply the "choate lien doctrine" to a priority problem under the Federal Tax Lien Act. *Security Trust* involved the relative priority of a federal tax lien and an attachment lien. Since an attachment lien is subject to contingencies that might terminate its enforceability, the lien was deemed inchoate and therefore ineffective against the subsequently arising federal tax lien.

Security Trust relied on section 3466 choateness cases as precedent. Subsequent federal tax lien cases have followed this practice. Nevertheless, the federal tax lien standard of "choateness" seems less stringent than that of the federal priority provisions. As noted previously, the Supreme Court has yet to find a competing lien choate in a case arising under section 3466. There are several Supreme Court federal tax lien cases in which the competing lien was held to be choate. In United States v. Crest Finance Co., 368 U.S. 347 (1961), the Supreme Court accepted the government's contention that the competing lien was choate. The lien there involved was an assignment of accounts; the accounts were earned and due prior to the time that the federal tax lien attached.

In both United States v. City of New Britain, 347 U.S. 81 (1954) and United States v. Vermont, 377 U.S. 351, 370 (1964), prior statutory liens on personal property were held choate. The liens involved in these cases are difficult to distinguish from the lien held *inchoate* in United States v. Gilbert Associates, Inc., supra. In neither *New Britain* nor *Vermont* was the taxpayer divested of title or possession. The Court in *Vermont* distinguished *Gilbert* saying "different standards apply where the United States' claim is based on a tax lien arising under §§ 6321 and 6322." 377 U.S. at 358. The exact nature of these "different standards" is less than clear. There is considerable dicta that the competing lien still must meet the "three identities test": lienor, amount of lien, and property subject to the lien.

As noted above, the IRS tax lien is inferior not only to prior choate liens but also to interests protected by the Federal Tax Lien Act.

Section 6323(a) of the Federal Tax Lien Act recognizes and protects certain "purchasers, holders of security interests, mechanics lienors, and judgment lien creditors" whose interests arise before notice of the tax lien is filed. For example, the rights of one who purchases from the taxpayer in the interim between the date of assessment and the date of filing would not be affected by the federal tax lien.

Section 6323(h) should be consulted for a definition of the interests protected by 6323(a). "Purchaser" is defined so as to include a lessee. "Security interest" includes consensual liens on both personalty and realty. The "security interest" is deemed to exist only after the collateral exists, the lien creditor has made disbursements, *and* the security interest is valid under local law against a judgment lien. The last element was obviously intended to limit section 6323(a)'s protection of "security interests" to *perfected* security interests and *recorded* real property mortgages.*

---

* Unfortunately, Congress used the term "judgment lien" and not "judicial lien." Under the law of almost all states, a judgment lien does not attach to personal property, and therefore, even an unperfected UCC security interest would be superior to a judgment lien. Cf. UCC 9–201. Such a result would be inconsistent with prior law, and there is no indication that in revising the Act, Congress intended

The following hypotheticals illustrate the application of section 6323(a):

> (1) January 10, federal tax lien arises
>
> February 2, S makes a secured loan to the taxpayer and perfects its security interest
>
> March 3, IRS files its federal tax lien in accordance with section 6323(f).

S's security interest would have priority.

> (2) April 4, federal tax lien arises
>
> May 5, X makes a secured loan to the taxpayer but neglects to file a financing statement or otherwise perfect its lien
>
> June 6, IRS files its federal tax lien in accordance with section 6323(f).

IRS would have priority. X did not obtain a security interest AS DEFINED IN THE FEDERAL TAX LIEN ACT prior to federal tax lien filing.

Article 9 security interests are often "floating liens." Security agreements commonly contain after-acquired property clauses "This debt is secured by all of the debtor's inventory, now owned

to accord priority to unperfected security interests over tax liens. Instead, it is more likely that Congress did not understand what a judicial lien was and that the courts will have to interpret judgment lien to include some other types of judicial liens which would be superior to unperfected security interests under 9–301. Unfortunately, however, at least one court failed to get the message. Major Electrical Supplies, Inc. v. J. W. Pettit Co., 427 F.Supp. 752 (M.D.Fla.1977).

or hereafter acquired"—or future advances clauses—"This collateral secures all of the debtor's debts to the secured party, whenever incurred."

Section 6323(c) governs the extent to which the priority enjoyed by a secured party extends to property acquired by the taxpayer after the federal tax lien filing. Section 6323(c) imposes the following limitations:

1. The secured party must have obtained and perfected its security interest prior to the filing of the federal tax lien.

2. The collateral must be commercial financing security, i. e., accounts, chattel paper, or inventory—not equipment.

3. The property must have been acquired within 45 days of the federal tax lien filing.

Assume for example that:

January 10, S lends D $100,000 and obtains and perfects a security interest in all of D's present or future inventory

February 2, federal tax lien arises

March 3, federal tax lien is filed

April 4, D acquires additional inventory.

S's priority extends to the April 4 inventory. S's $100,000 claim must be satisfied in full before IRS has any rights in any of D's inventory.**

** Consider the following variations of the above hypothetical:
  (1) January 10, S lends D $100,000 and obtains and perfects a security interest in all of D's present or future inventory;

Section 6323(c) and (d) both extend the secured party's priority to future advances in certain situations.

1. The secured party must have obtained and perfected its security interest prior to the filing of the federal tax lien.

2. The extension of credit must have occurred within 45 days of the federal tax lien filing *or* before the creditor obtained knowledge of the federal tax lien filing, whichever first occurs.†

3. Section 6323(c) is limited to "commercial financing security" *but* section 6323(d) is *not*.

Assume for example that:

> January 10, S lends D $100,000 and obtains and perfects a security interest in D's *equipment*

February 2, federal tax lien arises;
March 3, federal tax lien is filed;
May 5, D acquires additional inventory.
S has priority as to the original inventory; IRS has priority as to the inventory acquired on May 5. It was not acquired within 45 days of the federal tax lien filing.
(2) January 10, S lends D $100,000 and obtains and perfects a security interest in all of D's present or future equipment;
February 2, federal tax lien arises;
March 3, federal tax lien is filed;
April 4, D acquires additional equipment.
S has priority as to the original equipment; IRS has priority as to the equipment acquired on April 4. Equipment is not "commercial financing security."

† There is no time limitation on future advances made pursuant to an "obligatory disbursement agreement" as defined in section 6323(c)(4).

February 2, federal tax lien arises

March 3, federal tax lien is filed

April 4, S lends D an additional $40,000.
S's priority would extend to the April 4 loan unless S on April 4 knew of the federal tax lien filing. In other words, S must be paid $140,000 be-
fore IRS has rights to D's equipment.

Section 6323(b) defines certain limited interests that take priority over a federal tax lien
even though they arise after the tax lien has been
filed. Most of these "super-priorities" are either
casual and common transactions of limited
amounts for which an individual cannot be ex-
pected to check for filed tax liens or transactions
which tend to increase the value of the taxpayer's
property.

In light of these judicial and statutory limitations on the priority of the federal tax lien and
the applicability of section 3466 to federal tax
claims, the federal government may fare better
asserting a federal priority than a federal tax
lien. It should be remembered, however, that the
federal priority provision will not always be applicable. Its use is limited to situations in which
the debtor is insolvent and one of the three
events specified in the second clause of section
3466 has occurred.

3. CIRCUITY OF PRIORITY PROBLEMS

Both section 3466 and the federal tax lien, by imposing a second priority system on the state priority system, cause circuity of priority (circular priority) problems. Circuity of priority can be best explained by illustration. Assume that D owns property worth $700 and owes A $600, owes B $400 and owes the federal government $500. Both A and B have liens on D's property. A obtained her lien first and under the common law rule of "first in time, first in right" has priority over B under state law. As noted in the previous sections, both the federal priority provision and the Federal Tax Lien Act distinguish between choate and inchoate liens for priority purposes. Thus, if B's lien is choate but A's is not, and either section 3466 or the Federal Tax Lien Act is applicable, the federal claim would be superior to A's claim, but junior to B's.

In summary, A "beats" B under state law; B "beats" U.S. under federal law. U.S. beats A under federal law. It is like the children's game of paper, scissors, and rock.

How should the $700 be distributed? If B is paid before A, state law is ignored. If A is paid before B, it would seem that federal law is being ignored since under federal law B, but not A, is to be paid before the U.S.

The Supreme Court in United States v. City of New Britain, 347 U.S. 81 (1954), adopted a two-step analysis to resolve this dilemma. The federal law of priorities was first applied. An amount equal to the interests that take prior to the federal claim under federal law was set aside to be paid out first. State law was then used to divide the amount so set aside. In the example given in the preceding paragraph only B's lien is prior to the federal government so $400, the amount of B's claim, would be set aside. As A has first priority under state law, the $400 would be paid to A; the remaining $300 would be paid to the federal government. If the value of D's property had been $1000, A would receive the first $400, the government would then receive $500 and the remaining $100 would be paid to A. This seems to be a logical way of resolving the circuity problem, consistent with both federal and state law. The concern of the federal law is what amount is paid prior to the federal claim, not who is paid prior.

4. OTHER FEDERAL CLAIMS

Most federal claims are governed by neither the federal priority provision nor the Federal Tax Lien Act. Assume, for example, that the SBA guarantees a secured loan to O.K. Supermarkets. The inventory that secures the SBA guaranteed loan is also collateral for an earlier in time loan by Kimbell Foods. If O.K. is unable to pay both debts in full, whose lien has priority: SBA or Kimbell Foods?

Obviously, the Federal Tax Lien Act does not apply. And the federal priority provision does not apply since O.K. is not "insolvent" as defined under section 3466. What law controls a federal claim in a non-tax, "non-insolvent" creditor conflict?

The Supreme Court in United States v. Kimbell Foods, Inc., 99 S.Ct. 1448 (1979), recently held that:

1. Federal law determines the priority of liens stemming from federal lending programs;

2. Whether federal law incorporates state priority rules or fashions a separate federal rule such as the choateness rule is a matter of judicial policy;

3. A federal rule such as the choateness doctrine is not necessary to protect the governmental interests underlying SBA and FHA programs;

4. Accordingly, state priority rules and not the federal choateness rule control.

The holding in *Kimbell* is expressly limited to federal claims arising from SBA and FHA loans. The Court carefully leaves open the possibility that in some credit transactions protection of governmental interests may require some special federal rule such as the choateness doctrine. Nevertheless, it would seem that state priority rules and not the choateness doctrine will control most priority contests involving non-tax, federal claims if the debtor is not "insolvent" for purposes of section 3466.

V. DEBTOR'S STATE LAW REMEDIES, A/K/A COLLECTIVE CREDITOR ACTION

The remedies previously considered are all similar in that (1) all are creditor-initiated and (2) all benefit the specific creditor that invokes the remedy. The next pages will consider a couple of state debtor-creditor remedies—compositions/extensions and assignments for the benefit of creditors—that are at least in theory debtor-initiated. The qualifying words "in theory" are used because people just don't wake up in the morning, and, for the lack of anything else interesting to, do make an assignment for the benefit of creditors or enter into a composition and extension agreement. While these two remedies are debtor-initiated, they are creditor induced.

A. ASSIGNMENTS FOR THE BENEFIT OF CREDITORS

An assignment for the benefit of creditors is a voluntary transfer of assets by the debtor to another person in trust to liquidate the assets and distribute the proceeds to the creditors of the debtor/transferor. The assignee takes legal title to the property transferred.* To illustrate, D

* In the absence of a recording statute specifically applicable to assignments for the benefit of creditors, general statutes providing for the recording of transfers of real

makes an assignment for the benefit of creditors to A. C, D's creditor, will not be able to attach or execute on the property transferred. Legal title to the property is now in A. A is not indebted to C.

Basically an assignee acquires only the title of the debtor-assignor. The title of the assignee is subject to liens, claims and encumbrances which are valid as against the debtor. Section 9–301 of the Uniform Commercial Code sets out the major exception to this rule. Under Section 9–301(1) of the 1972 Official Text of the UCC, an unperfected security interest is subordinate to the rights of a lien creditor.** Section 9–301(3) grants the status of "lien creditor" to the assignee. Accordingly, a security interest that is unperfected at the date of the assignment can be invalidated by the assignee. To illustrate, on January 10, M extends credit to D Inc. and takes a mortgage on D Inc's building. On February 2, S, another of D Inc.'s creditors, obtains a security

property will apply to an assignment which includes real property. A general assignment for the benefit of creditors of merchandise, however, is specifically excepted from compliance with the bulk sales law. See section 6–103(2)

** Under the 1962 Official Text of section 9–301, an unperfected security interest is subordinate to a lien creditor only if the lien creditor was without knowledge of the unperfected security interest. Section 9–301(3) grants the assignee the status of a lien creditor without knowledge unless *all* of the creditors represented by the assignee had knowledge of the unperfected security interest at the time the assignment for the benefit of creditors was made. The assignee's own personal knowledge is irrelevant.

interest on D Inc.'s inventory. On March 3, D Inc. makes an assignment for the benefit of creditors. The assignment will not affect M's rights under its mortgage. If, however, S's security interest is unperfected on March 3rd, it will be invalid.

In the absence of special statutes, assignments for the benefit of creditors are regulated according to trust law. The assignee is accountable to creditors as a trustee is accountable to his beneficiaries. The assignee may be removed and may be personally surcharged for any breach of fiduciary duties.

The assignee's duties and responsibilities are those of any trustee. S/he derives power and authority from the assignment, and, absent any statutory provision, s/he must be guided by the terms of the assignment. Under the common law, the primary duty of the assignee is to liquidate the assets and distribute the proceeds to creditors as expeditiously as possible. Even where an express power of sale is not contained in the instrument of assignment, the assignee has the power and the obligation to sell the debtor's property to convert it to cash to be distributed to creditors.

Consent of creditors is not a condition precedent to the making of an assignment for the benefit of creditors. The right to make an assignment is regarded as an incident of ownership.

The primary common law limitation on use of an assignment for the benefit of creditors is the law of fraudulent conveyances. As an assignment for the benefit of creditors places the debtor's property out of the reach of his creditors—legal title passes to the assignee so that creditors of the assignor can no longer levy on the property—it would seem that creditors would be able to void an assignment for the benefit of creditors under a fraudulent conveyance statute. However, common law early took the position that creditors could not attack an assignment as a fraudulent conveyance if it was truly for their benefit.

An assignment for the benefit of creditors which reserves to the assignor any interest, benefit, or advantage out of the property conveyed to the injury of creditors is a fraudulent conveyance. For example, an assignment is invalidated by the reservation to the assignor of control of the assigned property such as the power to revoke the assignment or to declare the uses and trusts to which the property shall be subject. Similarly, provisions in the assignment which require the assignee to delay liquidation render the assignment invalid as a fraudulent conveyance.

Some jurisdictions consider a partial assignment for the benefit of creditors, i. e., an assignment of less than all of the debtor's property, a fraudulent conveyance. The rationale for this position is that creditors are "hindered" and "delayed" if they are referred to the assignee for satisfaction and then have to come back to the debtor. Some states regard any assignment for the benefit of creditors by a solvent debtor as a fraudulent conveyance: since an immediate sale of the property of a solvent debtor would, theoretically at least, provide funds for the payment of all debts in full, the only result of an assignment by a solvent debtor is to hinder and delay creditors.

A common law assignment for the benefit of the creditors does not discharge the debtor from any deficiencies arising or resulting from the fact that the assigned property is liquidated for less than the amount required to pay creditors in full. [If creditors voluntarily discharge or release the assignor under such circumstances that a composition agreement can be found, the release or discharge will be effective; composition agreements are considered infra at page 127.] This lack of discharge is obviously a major disadvantage of assignments to the debtor and a major reason that assignments for the benefit of creditors are used primarily by corporate debtors.

As the common law permits preferences, a common law assignment for the benefit of creditors which provides for preferential payments to designated creditors is not a fraudulent conveyance. Most courts, however, have held that debtors can not use preferences to obtain discharges from creditors; assignments that condition preferential treatment on release of the unpaid portion of any claim are generally voided as fraudulent conveyances. To appreciate the reason for this rule, it is necessary to remember that the assignment places the debtor's property beyond the reach of his creditors. If the debtor could prefer creditors willing to grant a discharge, the creditor would virtually have to accept the debtor's terms. Should the creditor refuse, it would probably receive little if anything from the assignee and would have no rights against the property of the debtor.

Today, assignments for the benefit of creditors are regulated by statute in most states. Some of these state statutes are mandatory; others merely directory. A state statute that is mandatory in its terms must be complied with in order that the assignment be valid. On the other hand, where the state statute is merely directory, the debtor may make a common law assignment or a statutory assignment. If the former is chosen, common law rules apply; if the latter is used, the statute must be complied with.

The state statutes customarily require recording of the assignment, filing schedules of assets and liabilities, giving notice to the creditors and bonding of the assignee, and subject the assignor to court supervision. Virtually all state statutes prohibit the granting of a preference—all creditors except those with liens or statutorily created priorities are to be treated equally. Some statutes, however, expressly provide for the very relief sought by a preferential assignment at common law, i. e., a discharge. Such provisions are, at best, of questionable validity. Article 1, section 8, clause 4 of the Constitution empowers Congress to establish "uniform laws on the subject of Bankruptcies throughout the United States." The exercise by Congress of this power suspends the power of states to enact bankruptcy laws. States may regulate the debtor-creditor relationship, but this regulation may not be a bankruptcy law. In determining whether a state statute is invalid as a bankruptcy law, the Supreme Court has seemed to place primary importance on the presence or absence of discharge provisions. See, e. g., Johnson v. Star, 287 U.S. 527 (1933); International Shoe Co. v. Pinkus, 278 U.S. 261 (1929).

A number of state assignment statutes authorize the assignee to set aside prior fraudulent conveyances, and some empower the assignee to void pre-assignment preferences by the assignor-debtor. Even in these states, however, a bankruptcy trustee has an additional bundle of important rights which are unavilable to an assignee —rights granted by sections 544–549 of the Bankruptcy Code. [These sections are discussed infra in pages 175–226.]

When the debtor has made substantial preferences or fraudulent conveyances or allowed liens, voidable in bankruptcy to attach to his property, creditors may decide that an assignment for the benefit of creditors does not adequately protect their rights. If so, the creditors may be able to force the debtor into bankruptcy. A general assignment for the benefit of creditors is a basis for ordering relief against the debtor in a creditor-commenced bankruptcy. See Bankruptcy Code section 303(h)(2). This means that if creditors of the requisite number with the required amount of claims wish to transfer the administration of the assignor's assets to the bankruptcy court, within the 120 days stipulated by section 303(h)(2) of the Code, it is their privilege to do so. [Section 303(h)(2) requires that the debtor transfer all or substantially all of his property to the assignee. Remember, however, that in at least some states, anything less than a general assignment is a fraudulent conveyance.] Section 543 empowers the bankruptcy court to require an assignee whose administration is superseded by bankruptcy to turn over the debtor's estate to the bankruptcy trustee, and to make an accounting.

An assignment for the benefit of creditors has certain advantages over bankruptcy to creditors. Its flexibility and informality save time and expense, and frequently result in better liquidation prices. Generally, the costs of administration of an assignment will be lower than those of bankruptcy proceedings. Thus, in the absence of fraudulent conveyances, preferences or liens voidable in bankruptcy, the dividends to creditors from an efficiently administered assignment will probably be larger than those received from the administration of the same property in bankruptcy.

B. COMPOSITION AND EXTENSION

A composition is a contract between a debtor and two or more creditors in which the creditors agree to take a specified partial payment in full satisfaction of their claims.* An extension is a contract between the debtor and two or more creditors in which the creditors agree to extend the time for the payment of their claims against the debtor. An agreement can be both a composition and an extension: an agreement to take less over a longer period of time.

The same rules of law govern compositions and extensions. Both are governed more by principles of contract law than by state debtor-creditor rules. Compositions and extensions encompass all of the essential elements of a simple contract, and the absence of any of these elements ren-

---

* A number of early cases make mention of "bankruptcy composition." From 1874 to 1938, the Bankruptcy Act provided for a composition in bankruptcy with the added feature that an agreement accepted by the requisite number of creditors was binding on all creditors. The Chandler Act of 1938 repealed these composition provisions and replaced them with Chapter XI (Arrangements), Chapter XII (Real Property Arrangements by Person Other Than Corporations) and Chapter XIII (Wage Earners' Plans). The Bankruptcy Reform Act of 1978 replaced these provisions with Chapters 11 and 13. These federal debtor rehabilitation provisions, similar in nature to a composition, are considered infra at pages 279–315.

ders the agreement invalid. Thus, there must be consideration.

The doctrine of Foakes v. Beer, 9 App.Cas. 605 (1884), that part payment in money of a liquidated debt constitutes no consideration for a release of the unpaid balance would seem to invalidate composition agreements. Courts, however, have been able to find consideration in the agreement of creditors each with the other to scale down his claim and accept a lesser sum. Thus, a composition agreement requires the participation of at least two creditors.

While more than one creditor must participate in a composition agreement, there is no requirement that all creditors agree. Creditors who do not agree to the composition are not affected by it. For example, D is indebted to W, X, Y, and Z. D proposes to pay each creditor 10% of its claim each month for the next six months, in full satisfaction of all liability. W, X, and Y agree to this composition/extension. Z does not. As a non-assenting creditor, Z is unaffected by the agreement between W, X, and Y. Z will not receive the monthly payments as provided in the agreement, but Z will be free to attempt to collect the full amount of its claim from D through extrajudicial or judicial means. If W, X and Y are aware that Z is not taking part in the composition/extension, Z's collection of 100% of its claim from D will not affect the composition/extension agreement.

Similarly, all is well where the other creditors know that one or more of the creditors are being paid more or are being benefited in a way different from the rest. As noted previously, the common law does not condemn preferences; but the law is zealous in seeing that no creditor receives any secret consideration. Accordingly, where a creditor is given a secret preference, the other creditors have the right to void the agreement. The creditor with the preference can neither enforce nor void the agreement, and the debtor has a right to recover preferential payments from him. This last "rule" is almost always explained by the presumption of duress: the debtor is presumed to be vulnerable to creditor pressure because of the creditor's *de facto* power to refuse to enter into the composition and therefore to force the debtor to file a bankruptcy petition.

There are a number of reasons that a debtor might prefer a composition to bankruptcy. By making a composition with his creditors, the debtor avoids the stigma that attaches to bankruptcy while he achieves the same result—discharge from all or a substantial portion of his debts. The composition discharge is even broader in scope than that of bankruptcy. A composition releases a surety while a discharge in bankruptcy does not. See Bankruptcy Code section 524(E). A debt discharged by a composition is not revived by a new promise to pay it unless that new promise is supported by new consideration; a promise to pay a debt discharged in bankruptcy need not be supported by consideration in order to be enforceable. Cf. section 524(c). Further a composition does not bar future bankruptcy—a Chapter 7 bankruptcy discharge bars further Chapter 7 bankruptcy relief for six years. See section 727(a)(8). The main disadvantage of a composition is that it is voluntary. Creditors unwilling to accept its terms are not required to do so. Non-assenting creditors are not affected by the composition.

The following chart compares assignments for the benefit of creditors and compositions:

ASSIGNMENT FOR THE BENEFIT OF CREDITORS	COMPOSITION
1. Common law; statutory	1. Contractual
2. Affects all general creditors	2. Only affects creditors who enter into the composition
3. Only debts voluntarily released by creditors discharged	3. Discharges all creditors who enter into composition
4. In most jurisdictions, all nonexempt property is delivered to a third person for sale with distribution of proceeds to creditors	4. Debtor retains property except as provided in the agreement
5. Basically liquidation device	5. Basically debtor rehabilitation device
6. General assignment for benefit of creditors basis for involuntary bankruptcy under section 303(h)(2)	6. *Not* a basis for an involuntary bankruptcy proceeding

[C514]

VI. BANKRUPTCY: AN OVERVIEW

The remainder of the nutshell will focus on bankruptcy. Initially, a couple of basic differences between bankruptcy and state debtor-creditor law should be noted. State law puts a premium on prompt action by creditors. The first creditor to attach the debtor's property, the first creditor to execute on the property, etc. is the one most likely to be paid. Bankruptcy, on the other hand, emphasizes equality of treatment, rather than a race of diligence. While bankruptcy law does not require equal treatment for all creditors, all creditors within a single class are treated the same. After the initiation of bankruptcy proceedings, a creditor can not improve its position *vis-a-vis* other creditors by seizing the assets of the debtor. Similarly, the debtor's ability to make preferential transfers to creditors before bankruptcy is considerably limited.

Second, the prospects for debtor relief are much greater in bankruptcy. While no debtor is guaranteed a discharge, most debtors do receive a discharge. "One of the primary purposes of the bankruptcy act is to 'relieve the honest debtor from the weight of oppressive indebtedness and permit him to start afresh. * * *'" Local Loan Co. v. Hunt, 292 U.S. 234, 244 (1934).

A. BANKRUPTCY LAW

The law of bankruptcy is federal law, consisting primarily of (1) the Bankruptcy Reform Act of 1978 (BRA), (2) the Bankruptcy Act of 1898 as amended and (3) bankruptcy rules. With few exceptions, the substantive provisions of BRA apply to bankruptcy proceedings initiated on or after October 1, 1979. BRA has four titles:

I. Title I of BRA contains the substantive law of Bankruptcy. It is Title 11 of the United States Code. It is divided into the following Chapters:

Chapter 1. General Provisions, Definitions and Rules of Construction.

Chapter 3. Case Administration.

Chapter 5. Creditors, the Debtor, and the Estate.

Chapter 7. Liquidation.

Chapter 9. Adjustment of the Debts of a Municipality.

Chapter 11. Reorganization.

Chapter 13. Adjustment of the Debts of an Individual With Regular Income.

Chapter 15. United States Trustees.

The provisions in Chapter 1, 3, and 5 apply to Chapter 7, 11, and 13 cases unless otherwise specified.

II. Title II establishes a new bankruptcy court and sets out the jurisdiction of this court. It amends Title 28 of the United States Code.

III. Title III contains amendments to a number of federal nonbankruptcy statutes that affect bankruptcy proceedings.

IV. Title IV provides for the transition from the Bankruptcy Act of 1898 to BRA.

This book will focus on BRA. Nevertheless, the Bankruptcy Act of 1898, as amended, will also be considered. All bankruptcy proceedings commenced prior to October 1, 1979, will continue to be governed by this law. Additionally, the provisions of the Bankruptcy Act of 1898 and the cases construing it will be helpful in understanding the new bankruptcy statute.

It is also necessary to deal with the Bankruptcy Rules. From 1973 to 1976, the United States Supreme Court pursuant to the authority of 28 U.S.C.A. § 2075 promulgated bankruptcy rules. These rules superseded a considerable part of the Bankruptcy Act of 1898. All statutory provisions in conflict with the rules were repealed.

No rules have yet been prescribed for use with BRA. The Supreme Court still has the rule-making power. The rule-making authority is, however, limited. The new rules may not supersede provisions of BRA. Until new rules are adopted, the existing bankruptcy rules apply to bankruptcy proceedings commenced on or after October 1,

1979, to the extent such rules are not inconsistent with the provisions of BRA.

B. FORMS OF BANKRUPTCY RELIEF

There are two basic types of bankruptcy proceedings: (1) liquidation and (2) rehabilitation.

Chapter 7 of BRA is entitled "Liquidation." The provisions in Chapters 1, 3 and 5 of BRA also apply in liquidation cases unless otherwise specified.

In a liquidation proceeding, the trustee collects the non-exempt property of the debtor, converts that property to cash, and distributes the cash to the creditors. The debtor gives up all of the non-exempt property s/he owns at the time of the filing of the bankruptcy petition in the hope of obtaining a discharge. A discharge releases the debtor from any further liability for his or her pre-bankruptcy debts. Assume, for example, that B owes C $2,000. B files a bankruptcy petition. C only receives $300 from the liquidation of B's assets. If B receives a bankruptcy discharge, C will be precluded from pursuing B for the remaining $1,700.

As the preceding paragraph implies, every liquidation proceeding under the bankruptcy laws does not result in a discharge. Section 727(a), considered infra at pages 233–237, lists a number of grounds for withholding a discharge. And, even if the debtor is able to obtain a discharge, s/he will not necessarily be freed from all creditors' claims. Section 523, considered infra at pages 237–245, sets out exceptions to discharge.

The vast majority of bankruptcy cases are liquidation cases. Chapters VIII–X deal with liquidation proceedings under BRA. The term "bankruptcy" is often used to describe liquidation proceedings under the bankruptcy laws. References to "bankruptcy" in this nutshell should generally be regarded as references to liquidation proceedings.*

Chapters 11 and 13 deal with debtor rehabilitation, not liquidation, of the debtor's assets. Again, the provisions of Chapters 1, 3, and 5 apply unless otherwise specified.

In a rehabilitation proceeding under the bankruptcy laws, creditors usually look to future earnings of the debtor, not the property of the debtor at the time of the initiation of the bankruptcy proceeding, to satisfy their claims. The debtor retains its assets and makes payments to creditors, usually from post-petition earnings, pursuant to a court-approved plan.

Chapter 11, like Chapter 7, is available to all forms of debtors—individuals, partnerships and

---

* Liquidation proceedings under the Bankruptcy Act of 1898 are commonly referred to as "straight bankruptcy" cases. Rehabilitation proceedings under the Bankruptcy Act of 1898 are commonly referred to as "chapter proceedings." It is likely that these phrases will also be used to describe cases brought under BRA.

corporations. Chapter 11 is considered infra at pages 279–302. Chapter 13 can be used only by individuals with a "regular income" (as defined in section 101(24)) who have unsecured debts of less than $100,000 and secured debts of less than $350,000. Chapter 13 is considered infra at pages 303–315.

C. BANKRUPTCY COURTS

The Bankruptcy Act of 1898 provides for bankruptcy referees. Originally, the judicial role of bankruptcy referees was relatively minor. The referee was primarily an administrator and supervisor of bankruptcy cases, not a judge. Amendments to the Bankruptcy Act of 1898 made the bankruptcy referee more of a judicial officer. In 1973, the Bankruptcy Rules changed the title of the office from "bankruptcy referee" to "bankruptcy judge."

Under the Bankruptcy Act of 1898, bankruptcy judges are appointed by federal district judges for six-year terms. Appeals from bankruptcy judges' decisions and orders lie to the district court and from there to the court of appeals. The practice and standard on appeal from a bankruptcy judge to a district judge are essentially the same as the practice and standards governing the appeal from any trial court to an appellate tribunal.

BRA establishes bankruptcy courts in every federal judicial district as adjuncts of the United

States District Court. Beginning on April 1, 1984, bankruptcy judges will be appointed by the President for 14-year terms. Incumbent bankruptcy judges whose terms expire prior to March 31, 1984, will be continued in office until that date unless found unqualified by the Chief Judge of the Circuit, after consultation with a merit-screening committee.

Appeals from decisions of this new bankruptcy court will be taken to the district court of the district within which the bankruptcy court is located subject to two exceptions. First, BRA permits appeal directly to the court of appeals if all parties to the appeal so agree. Second, BRA permits a judicial circuit to create an appellate panel of bankruptcy judges to hear appeals from the bankruptcy court.

D. BANKRUPTCY JURISDICTION

Under the Bankruptcy Act of 1898, bankruptcy courts had limited jurisdiction. This jurisdiction, commonly referred to as "summary jurisdiction," * extended to (1) *all* matters concerned with

---

* The phrase "summary jurisdiction" is somewhat misleading. First, it incorrectly implies that under the Bankruptcy Act of 1898, bankruptcy courts have a second, "non-summary" form of jurisdiction. Summary jurisdiction is the only form of jurisdiction that a bankruptcy judge possesses under the Bankruptcy Act of 1898. Bankruptcy courts have only summary jurisdiction; other courts have plenary jurisdiction. Second, the words "summary jurisdiction" suggest that in resolving the controversy the bankruptcy judge always conducts summary pro-

the administration of the bankrupt estate and (2) *some* ** disputes between bankruptcy trustee and third parties involving rights to money or property in which the bankrupt estate claimed an interest. There has been considerable litigation over whether a dispute is within the bankruptcy court's summary jurisdiction.

BRA should eliminate such litigation in bankruptcy proceedings filed on or after October 1, 1979.† 28 U.S.C.A. § 1471 gives the bankruptcy court jurisdiction over all cases arising under Title 11 (bankruptcy) and "all civil proceedings arising in or related to cases under Title 11." This jurisdiction has been described by both Senator DeConcini and Congressman Butler as "pervasive," Congressional Record, October 6, 1978, p. S.1424, S.1432.

---

ceedings—that there are fewer procedural safegurds in bankruptcy court than in federal or state court. This impression is also invalid.

** The summary jurisdiction of the bankruptcy court over such matters depends on (1) the property in question being in the actual possession of the bankrupt at the time of the initiation of the bankruptcy proceeding, (2) the property in question being in the "constructive" possession of the bankrupt at the time of the initiation of the bankruptcy proceeding, (3) actual or implied consent, or (4) specific statutory grant of jurisdiction.

† A case filed before October 1, 1979 "shall be conducted and determined * * * as if this Act (BRA) had not been enacted," section 403. Accordingly, the principles of summary jurisdiction will continue to apply to cases pending on October 1, 1979. Cases filed on or after October 1, 1979, will be subject to the new jurisdictional provisions, section 405(B).

The bankruptcy court may abstain from exercising its jurisdiction when a particular proceeding could be better handled by another court, 28 U.S.C.A. § 1471(d). The decision whether to abstain may not be appealed.

Litigation in other courts "related to cases under Title 11" is generally stayed by the filing of the bankruptcy petition, section 362.†† Either party to a civil action in a non-bankruptcy forum may remove it to the bankruptcy court if the bankruptcy court would have had original jurisdiction over the proceeding under 28 U.S.C.A. § 1478. The bankruptcy court has a power to remand a removal action; the decision whether to remand may not be appealed.

While BRA expands a bankruptcy judge's judicial powers, it limits his administrative responsibilities. The Commission on the Bankruptcy Laws of the United States concluded that the bankruptcy judges' involvement in administering bankrupt estates impairs their ability to handle their judicial responsibilities. "After a referee has read the debtor's petition, schedules, and statement of affairs, and has examined him and others at the first meeting of creditors, it is obviously difficult to resolve questions arising in a proceeding to determine whether the debtor ought to be discharged or even whether a particular debt

†† The automatic stay is considered at pages 150–160 infra.

is dischargeable, without being influenced by information and impressions gained during his previous contact with the debtor and the papers in the case. When the referee has appointed, or approved the appointment of, a trustee to take charge of the property of the estate, has supervised and perhaps instructed the trustee in the performance of his duties, and has approved the trustee's choice of counsel and the initiation of an action, the referee may not appear to the trustee's adversary as one fitting the model of judicial objectivity." Report of the Commission on the Bankruptcy Laws of the United States, 93d Cong. 1st Sess., 1973, p. 93.

Under BRA, the bankruptcy judge does not preside at the first meeting of creditors; indeed, s/he is not permitted to attend the meeting. Thus, the bankruptcy judge will not be influenced by information revealed at that meeting at which the Federal Rules of Evidence do not apply.

Removal of the bankruptcy judge from administrative duties is accomplished to an even greater extent in eighteen judicial districts that will participate in a five-year experimental program using United States trustees. In these "pilot districts", the United States trustee, rather than the bankruptcy court, will supervise the administration of bankruptcy cases. If it is necessary to appoint a trustee, the United States trustee, rather than the bankruptcy judge, will appoint the trustee. In no-asset cases where no private trustee is willing to serve, the United States trustee will serve as trustee.

E. TRUSTEES/UNITED STATES TRUSTEES

An underlying premise of the Bankruptcy Act of 1898 was that the property of the bankrupt was essentially a trust for the benefit of the bankrupt's creditors. Consequently, the creditors themselves should control the collection, liquidation and distribution of the bankrupt's property through their elected representative, the trustee in bankruptcy.

The trustee is a private citizen, not an employee of the government. S/he is an active and not a passive trustee. The trustee is given a number of very important rights and duties by the Bankruptcy Act of 1898 and the Bankruptcy Rules. In essence, the duties of the trustee are to collect the bankrupt's property; invalidate certain pre-bankruptcy and post-bankruptcy transfers of such property; set apart to the bankrupt his exempt property; reduce the assets of the bankrupt estate to cash; determine which creditors have valid claims and the amounts thereof; distribute the funds of the estate to these creditors; and, in appropriate cases, object to the bankrupt's discharge.

The Bankruptcy Act of 1898 thus relies heavily on a system of private trustees, supervised by the bankruptcy judges. It is contemplated that the trustee will be elected by the creditors. If, however, creditors do not elect a trustee, the bankruptcy judge may appoint a trustee.

BRA also relies on a system of private trustees. And, the rights and duties of a bankruptcy trustee in a Chapter 7 liquidation proceeding are very similar to the rights and duties of a bankruptcy trustee in a straight bankruptcy case under the 1898 Act.

BRA does change the method of selecting the trustee. Promptly, after the "order for relief", the bankruptcy judge must appoint an interim trustee, section 701. This interim trustee will be a private citizen, not a government employee. In selecting an interim trustee, the bankruptcy judge is limited to private citizens who are members of a "panel" of private trustees established and maintained by the Director of the Administrative Office of the United States Courts. This interim trustee will serve at least until the first meeting of creditors.

At the first meeting of creditors, the creditors may elect a new trustee to replace the interim trustee if creditors holding at least 20% in amount of certain, unsecured claims vote in the election, section 702(c). This percentage requirement is designed to insure that trustees are elected only in cases in which there is significant creditor interest and to discourage election of trustees by attorneys for creditors who hope to be attorneys for the trustee, as was often the practice under the Bankruptcy Act of 1898. If the creditor interest in the case is sufficient to permit election of a trustee, the creditors are not required to select a trustee who is a member of the panel of private trustees.

If the creditors do not elect a trustee, the interim trustee becomes the trustee and serves in that capacity for the duration of the case.

The United States trustee does not replace private trustees. The United States trustee merely performs some of the appointing and supervisory duties of the bankruptcy judge. Private trustees will serve in the eighteen judicial districts participating in the pilot program using the United States trustee. However, in these "pilot districts", the United States trustee, not the bankruptcy judge, will appoint interim trustees and supervise the activities of trustees.

VII. COMMENCEMENT OF A BANKRUPTCY PROCEEDING

A bankruptcy proceeding begins with the filing of a petition with the bankruptcy court, section 301. Generally, the debtor files the petition. Such debtor-initiated proceedings are often referred to as "voluntary." Creditors have a limited right to initiate "involuntary" bankruptcy proceedings against the debtor under Chapters 7 and 11.

A. VOLUNTARY CASES

Section 301 deals with the commencement of voluntary cases. It provides that a bankruptcy petition may be filed by "any entity that may be a debtor under such chapter." Section 109 sets out who is eligible to be a debtor under each chapter.

Section 109 contains two limitations on the availability of Chapter 7 (liquidation) relief to a debtor:

1. The debtor must be a "person." "Person" is defined in section 101(30) as including partnerships and corporations. A sole proprietorship would not be a "person."

2. The debtor may not be a railroad, insurance company or banking institution. Railroads are eligible for bankruptcy relief only under Sub-

chapter IV of Chapter 11; insurance companies and banking institutions are excluded from relief under the Bankruptcy Act of 1978 because their liquidations are governed by other state and federal regulatory laws.

With two exceptions, any person who is eligible to file a petition under Chapter 7 is also eligible to file a petition under Chapter 11. The first exception is railroads. As noted above, railroads are eligible for Chapter 11, but not Chapter 7. The second exception is stockbrokers and commodity brokers; they are eligible for Chapter 7, but not Chapter 11.

There are three significant limitations on the availability of Chapter 13:

1. The debtor must be an individual. A Chapter 13 petition may not be filed by a corporation or a partnership.

2. The individual must have "income sufficiently stable and regular to enable such individual to make payments under (Chapter 13 plan)," section 101(24), 109(e). This includes wage earners, some self-employed individuals, and individuals on welfare, pensions, or investment income.

3. The debtor must have unsecured debts totalling less than $100,000 and secured debts of less than $350,000.

Please note that insolvency is not a condition precedent to any form of voluntary bankruptcy action. A debtor may file a petition under Chapter 7, 11 or 13 even though s/he is solvent.

A husband and a wife may file a single petition for voluntary relief under any chapter that is available to *each* spouse. If a husband and a wife jointly file under Chapter 13, their aggregate debts are subject to the $100,000/$350,000 limits.

A debtor who files a bankruptcy petition must pay a filing fee—$60 for Chapters 7 or 13, $200 for Chapter 11, 28 U.S.C.A. § 1930(a). The court may dismiss the bankruptcy case for non-payment of fees, sections 707, 1113, 1307. No provision is made for *in forma pauperis* bankruptcy.

A voluntary bankruptcy case is commenced when an eligible debtor files a petition. No formal adjudication is necessary; the filing operates as an "order for relief," section 301.

B. INVOLUNTARY CASES

Section 303 deals with bankruptcy petitions filed by creditors. It contains a number of significant limitations on involuntary petitions:

1. Creditors may file involuntary petitions under Chapters 7 or 11 but *not* Chapter 13.

2. Certain debtors are protected from involuntary petitions. Debtors excluded from voluntary bankruptcy—railroads, insurance companies, banking institutions—are also excluded from in-

voluntary bankruptcy. Additionally, farmers and charitable corporations may not be subjected to involuntary petitions. (Legislative history shows that farmers are excluded because of the cyclical nature of agriculture.)

3. The petition must be filed by the requisite number of creditors. Generally, three creditors with unsecured claims totalling at least $5,000 must join in the petition. If, however, the debtor has less than twelve unsecured creditors *, a single creditor with an unsecured claim of $5,000 is sufficient.

An involuntary petition does not operate as an adjudication, as an order for relief. The debtor has the right to file an answer. If the debtor does not timely answer the petition, "the court shall order relief," section 303(h). If the debtor does timely answer the petition, the court "shall order relief against the debtor" only if one of the two grounds for involuntary relief are established.

The first basis for involuntary relief is that the debtor is *generally* not paying debts as they come due. This is sometimes referred to as "equitable insolvency."

---

* In determining whether the debtor has 12 creditors, certain creditors are ignored: employees of the debtor; "insiders" such as relatives of individual debtors, directors of corporate debtors, or partners of debtor partnerships; and creditors who have received a voidable transfer, 303(b)(2).

The alternative basis for involuntary relief is that within 120 days before the petition was filed, a general receiver, assignee or custodian took possession of substantially all of the debtor's property or was appointed to take charge of substantially all of the debtor's property. The appointment of a receiver in a mortgage foreclosure action to take possession of Greenacre, less than substantially all of the debtor's property, would not be a basis for involuntary relief.

Usually there will be an interval of at least several weeks between the filing of an involuntary petition and the order of relief against the debtor. During this period, the debtor may continue to buy, use, or sell property and to operate its business, section 303(f).** The bankruptcy court may appoint an interim trustee to take possession of the debtor's property or operate the debtor's business "if necessary to preserve the property of the estate or to prevent loss to the estate," section 303(g). If an interim trustee is appointed, the debtor may regain possession by posting a bond.

Notwithstanding the protection of section 303(f), the filing of an involuntary petition adversely affects the debtor's financial reputation and business operations. Section 303(i) attempts

** Sections 502(f) and 507(a)(2) protect third parties who deal with a debtor after an involuntary petition has been filed. These provisions are considered infra at pages 269, 273–274.

to protect debtors from ill-founded petitions by setting out the following remedies in cases in which an involuntary petition is dismissed after litigation:

1. The court *may* grant judgment for the debtor against the petitioning creditors for costs and a reasonable attorney's fee.

2. If an interim trustee took possession of the debtor's property, the court *may* grant judgment for "any damages proximately caused by the taking."

3. If the petition was filed in "bad faith," the court *may* award "any damages proximately caused by such filing," such as loss of business, and also punitive damages.

C. DISMISSAL

The bankruptcy court may dismiss or suspend a voluntary bankruptcy proceeding even though it was filed by an eligible debtor. And, the bankruptcy court may dismiss or suspend an involuntary bankruptcy proceeding even though all of the requirements are satisfied. Section 305 *empowers* the bankruptcy court to dismiss or suspend a case if there is a foreign bankruptcy proceeding pending concerning the debtor or if "the interests of creditors and the debtor would be better served by such dismissal or suspension." *

* The bankruptcy court may also dismiss a bankruptcy case for failure to pay filing fees.

To illustrate, D, Inc., is generally not paying its debts as they come due. D, Inc. is trying to negotiate a workout with its creditors. Three of D, Inc.'s creditors are dissatisfied with the terms proposed in the workout and file an involuntary Chapter 11 petition against D, Inc. The bankruptcy court may decide to dismiss this petition if D, Inc. is making progress in negotiating a workout with its creditors.

A section 305 dismissal must be preceded by "notice and a hearing." The decision to dismiss (or not to dismiss) is not appeable. If an involuntary petition is dismissed under section 305, the petitioning creditors are *not* liable for costs, attorneys' fees or damages under section 303(i).

D. STAY

A debtor who files a bankruptcy petition needs immediate protection from the collection efforts of his or her creditors. A bankruptcy trustee needs time to collect the "property of the estate" (section 541, considered *infra* at pages 161–164) and make pro rata distributions to creditors. Accordingly, the filing of a bankruptcy petition automatically "stays", i. e., restrains, creditors from taking further action to collect their claims or enforce their liens.

1. SCOPE OF THE STAY

The scope of the stay is extremely broad. It bars virtually all debt collection efforts. Section

362(a) defines the scope of the automatic stay by listing the acts and actions that are stayed by the commencement of the case. Use of dunning letters or other informal collection methods is stayed, section 362(a)(6). Obtaining, perfecting or enforcing a lien is stayed, section 362(a)(5). Section 362(a)(7) stays post-petition setoffs. Commencing or continuing a collection action is stayed, section 362(a)(1). Enforcing a pre-petition judgment against "property of the estate" or the debtor is stayed, section 362(a)(2).

Section 362(b) sets out eight exceptions to the automatic stay. Section 362(b)(1) excepts criminal prosecutions. Section 362(b)(2) provides a limited exception from the stay for alimony and child support. Such claims may be collected from property acquired after the filing of the petition and other property that is not "property of the estate."

Section 362(b)(3) permits post-petition perfection of purchase money security interest within the ten-day "grace period" of UCC section 9–301(2). To illustrate, on March 3, S sells D equipment on credit and retains a security interest in the equipment. The equipment is delivered to D on March 6. On March 9, D files a bankruptcy petition. Notwithstanding the automatic stay, S may file its financing statement until March 16.

Governmental enforcement of its police or regulatory powers is not affected by the automatic stay, section 362(b)(4). For example, a state environmental agency suit to stop clean air violations would not be stayed by section 362.

Section 362 is not the only statutory basis for restraining creditors' collection efforts. For example, section 105 grants a bankruptcy court the power to issue orders necessary or appropriate to carry out the provisions of Title 11, and 28 U.S. C.A. § 243(a) gives a bankruptcy court all the powers of a court of law, equity, and admiralty. An injunction or stay issued under one of these provisions will not be automatic; rather, it will be granted or issued pursuant to the usual rules for injunctions. Accordingly, a bankruptcy trustee may request the bankruptcy court to stay a state agency environmental suit or any of the other actions listed in section 362(b). The actions listed in section 362(b) are merely excepted from the *automatic* stay.

2. DURATION OF THE STAY

Section 362(c)(1) provides that an automatic stay automatically terminates as to particular property when that property ceases to be "property of the estate" (section 541, considered infra at page 161, describes "property of the estate"). If, for example, the bankruptcy trustee sells part of the property of the estate, Redacre, and the sale is not free and clear of liens, a creditor with a lien on Redacre may foreclose its lien.

An automatic stay also terminates automatically when the bankruptcy proceeding is closed or dismissed or the debtor receives or is denied a discharge, section 362(c)(2). Accordingly, the automatic stay in a Chapter 7 case has a very limited life. The automatic stay in a Chapter 11 or 13 case, however, will probably not automatically terminate for years.

A bankruptcy court may order the earlier end of automatic stay. It may terminate the automatic stay on request of a "party in interest." Sections 362(d)–(g) governs requests for relief from the bankruptcy stay. These provisions are considered below.

3. RELIEF FROM THE STAY

On request of a "party in interest",* the bankruptcy court may terminate, annul, modify, or condition a bankruptcy stay. The grounds for such relief are set out in section 362(d).

The general statutory ground for relief from the bankruptcy stay is "for cause," section 362(d)(1). The automatic stay rules promulgated under the Bankruptcy Act of 1898 used the same standard and so cases decided under Rules 401, 601, 11–44, and 13–401 should be helpful in

---

* The phrase "party in interest" is not statutorily defined. Section 1109 suggests that for purposes of Chapter 11 "party in interest" includes "the debtor, the trustee, a creditors' committee, an equity security holders' committee, a creditor, an equity security holder, or any indenture trustee."

determining what is "cause" for relief from the stay.**

There are two additional, more specific statutory grounds for relief from the bankruptcy stay that apply primarily to secured creditors. First, under section 362(d)(2), a secured party or a mortgagee may obtain relief from the stay if it can establish both that:

> (1) the debtor does not have any equity in the encumbered property, and

> (2) the encumbered property is not necessary to an effective reorganization.

Note that in a Chapter 11 or 13 proceeding, proof only that the amount of the secured claim exceeds the value of the collateral will not be sufficient. If, for example, Cocky Locky Motel Corp., CLMC, files a Chapter 11 petition, First Dacron Bank, FDB, with a mortgage on the motel will not be entitled to relief from the stay merely by establishing CLMC's lack of equity.

FDB, or any other creditor with a lien on a debtor's property, may also obtain relief from the bankruptcy stay by showing that its interest in the debtor's property is not adequately protected, section 362(d)(1). Assume, for example, that Helen Wheels Chrysler Co. sells Warren Pease a

---

** For a comprehensive and comprehensible study of the automatic stay rules under the Bankruptcy Act of 1898, see Kennedy, The Automatic Stay in Bankruptcy, 11 U. Mich.J.L.Ref. 177 (1978).

new Chrysler on credit. Helen Wheels Chrysler obtains and perfects a security interest in the automobile. Pease files a Chapter 13 petition still owing Helen Wheels Chrysler Co. $5,000 for his car. Section 362(a)(5) prevents Helen Wheels Chrysler Co. from repossessing and reselling the car. The value of the car and of Helen Wheels' lien on the car declines each month. Under section 362(d)(1) Helen Wheels is entitled to relief from the stay unless it is adequately protected.

"Adequate protection" is a very important concept in the Bankruptcy Reform Act of 1978. "Adequate protection" is the critical issue in most controversies under section 362(d) (relief from the stay), section 363 (use, sale or lease of property) and section 364 (obtaining credit).

Section 361 governs "adequate protection." It does not define "adequate protection"; rather, section 361 specifies three non-exclusive methods of providing adequate protection.† The first method of adequate protection specified is periodic cash payments to the lien creditor equal to the decrease in value †† of the creditor's interest in

---

† The phrase "adequate protection" appears in the "cram down" provisions in the Bankruptcy Act of 1898. Cases under sections 216(7) and 461(11) of the Bankruptcy Act of 1898 should be helpful in deciding what is "adequate protection."

†† How and when "value" is to be determined is not specified in the new Bankruptcy Act. Legislative history indicates that the time and method of valuation will vary according to the circumstances of the case.

the collateral. Thus, a bankruptcy court may condition the stay on lien foreclosure by Helen Wheels Chrysler Co. on monthly cash payments equal to the depreciation on the car.

Section 361(2) indicates that adequate protection may take the form of an additional lien or substitute lien on other property. Assume, for example, that P Potato Processing Co., files a Chapter 11 petition. C Bank has a perfected security in P's potato processing equipment. P needs to use the encumbered equipment to continue operation of its business, to accomplish a successful Chapter 11 reorganization. Such use will, however, decrease the value of the equipment and C's lien in the equipment. Under section 361(2) adequate protection may take the form of a lien on other property owned by P; the new collateral does not necessarily have to be the potato processing equipment.

Section 361(3) grants the debtor in possession or trustee considerable flexibility in providing adequate protection. Section 361(3) recognizes such other protection, other than providing an administrative expense claim, that will result in the secured party's realizing the "indubitable equivalent" * of the value of its interest in the

---

* The term "indubitable equivalent" is not statutorily defined. Congressional reports indicate that the phrase was taken from In re Murel Holding Corp., 75 F.2d 941 (2d Cir.1935). While *Murel* uses the words "indubitable equivalent", it provides little insight as to their meaning. In *Murel,* the secured creditor was protected by a lien on oth-

collateral. An example of such other protection is a guarantee by a solvent third party to cover any losses suffered by the secured party as a result of the stay.

While § 361 specifies three methods of "adequate protection," it does not require the bankruptcy court to provide adequate protection. The bankruptcy trustee or the debtor in possession proposes a method of adequately protecting the interest of a lien creditor. If the affected lien creditor objects, the court will determine whether the protection proposed is adequate. If the method of adequate protection approved by the court proves to be inadequate, the lien creditor is granted an administrative expense priority for its losses, section 507(b).**

To illustrate, Chaste Manhattan Bank, C, has a perfected security interest in the inventory of Burt Rentals, Inc., B. B files a Chapter 11 petition. At the time of the petition, B owes C $100,000, and the encumbered inventory has a "value" of $60,000. C requests relief from the automatic stay. B offers a personal guarantee of

er property of the debtor. This form of adequate protection is specifically recognized by section 361(2).

** A debtor in possession or bankruptcy trustee may not propose an administrative expense priority as "adequate protection," section 361(3). If, however, the form of adequate protection proposed by the debtor in possession or bankruptcy trustee and approved by the bankruptcy proves to be "inadequate", section 507(b) awards the lien creditor an administrative expense priority for its losses.

payment by Debbie Rentals to protect C. The court finds that this is "adequate protection" and denies C request for relief. The bankruptcy court proves to be wrong. When B's Chapter 11 fails, Debbie Rentals is insolvent. The value of the inventory securing C's $100,000 claim is now worth only $40,000. Under § 507(b), C will have a $20,000 ($60,000 − $40,000) administrative expense priority claim.†

The party requesting relief from the stay (e. g., the secured creditor) has the burden of establishing the debtor's lack of equity in the encumbered property. The party opposing the relief from the stay (e. g., the bankruptcy trustee) has the burden of proof on all other issues.

Section 362(f) permits ex parte relief from the stay in cases in which "irreparable damage" might occur to the stayed party before there is an opportunity for notice and hearing. Otherwise, relief from the stay must be preceeded by "notice and hearing." ††

Section 362(e) provides for expeditious handling of hearings on requests for relief from stay.

† C will also have a $40,000 secured claim and a $40,000 unsecured claim, section 506.

†† "Notice and hearing" is described in section 102 as "such notice as is appropriate in the particular circumstances and such *opportunity* for a hearing as is appropriate in the particular circumstances." Thus, in some cases, "notice and hearing" may take the form of a telephone call from the bankruptcy judge to the secured creditor's attorney.

If, within 30 days of the request for relief, the bankruptcy court does not make at least a preliminary determination that the bankruptcy trustee or debtor will prevail, the stay is automatically terminated as to the requesting party. The final hearing must then be commenced within 30 days after such a preliminary hearing.* There is no time limit within which the final hearing must be concluded.

The hearings under § 362(e) will deal only with the grounds for relief from the stay. According to the Senate Judiciary Committee Report that accompanied S.B. 2266:

> " * * * At hearings on relief from the stay, the only issue will be the lack of adequate protection, the debtor's equity in the property, and the necessity of the property to an effective reorganization of the debtor, or the existence of other cause for relief from the stay. This hearing will not be the appropriate time at which to bring in other issues, such as counterclaims against the creditor, which, although relevant to the question of the amount of the debt, concern largely collateral or unrelated issues. * * * However, this would not preclude the party seeking continuance of the stay from presenting evidence on the existence of

---

* In a number of cases the final hearing will be consolidated with the preliminary hearing.

claims which the court may consider in exercising its discretion. What is precluded is a determination of such collateral claims on the merits at the hearing." Senate Committee on the Judiciary Report No. 95–989, p. 55.

VIII. CHAPTER 7 AND THE DEBTOR

In determining whether to file a Chapter 7 petition, a debtor has two primary concerns:

(1) What will bankruptcy cost?

(2) How will I benefit from bankruptcy?

Costs of bankruptcy to the debtor include not only the attorney's fee (usually around $600 in a simple, liquidation bankruptcy case) and the filing fee of $60 but also loss of property. As the next 3 pages indicate, in a Chapter 7 proceeding virtually all of the debtor's non-exempt property as of the date of the filing of the bankruptcy petition becomes "property of the estate" to be liquidated and distributed to creditors.

The primary benefits of bankruptcy to a debtor are (1) the temporary relief from creditor action provided by the automatic stay and (2) the permanent relief from creditor action provided by the bankruptcy discharge. The automatic stay is considered supra at pages 150–160. Bankruptcy discharge is considered infra at pages 232–248.

A. PROPERTY OF THE ESTATE

1. SECTION 541

The filing of a bankruptcy petition creates an estate, section 541. In a Chapter 7 case, the "property of the estate" is distributed to the creditors of the debtor, section 726.

With two minor exceptions *, the property of the estate includes all of the property of the debtor as of the time of the filing of the petition. The seven numbered paragraphs of section 541(a) specify what property becomes property of the estate. Paragraph one is by far the most comprehensive and significant. Section 541(a)(1) provides that property of the estate includes "all legal or equitable interests of the debtor in property as of the commencement of the case."

This is a very broad statement. Property of the estate thus includes both real property and personal property, both tangible property and intangible property, both property in the debtor's possession and property of the debtor possessed by another. Third parties holding property of the estate are statutorily required to return such property to the bankruptcy trustee, sections 542, 543.

Note that section 541(a)(1) limits property of the estate to the debtor's property as of the filing of the petition. Generally, the bankruptcy petition "fixes a line of cleavage." Property ac-

---

* Section 541(b) excludes from the property of the estate any power such as a power of appointment that the debtor may exercise solely for the benefit of another. Section 541(c)(2) excludes from the property of the estate spendthrift trusts recognized under applicable state law.

quired prior to the petition becomes property of the estate and passes to the bankruptcy trustee for distribution to creditors; property acquired after the petition remains the debtor's. For example, if Ben Walton files a Chapter 7 petition on October 2, the money he earns for playing the piano at the Dew Drop Inn after October 2 is *not* "property of the estate."

There are four significant exceptions to the rule that property acquired after the filing of a bankruptcy petition remains the bankrupt's property.

1. Property of the estate includes property that the debtor acquires or becomes entitled to within 180 days after the filing of the petition by:

    a. bequest, devise or inheritance

    b. property settlement or a divorce decree

    c. as beneficiary of the life insurance policy, section 541(a)(5).

2. Property of the estate also includes the earnings from property of the estate, section 541(a)(6). If, for example the Ropers file a Chapter 7 petition, the apartments that they own would be property of the estate, and post-petition rents from the apartments would be property of the estate.

3. Property of the estate includes property received from a conversion of property of the es-

tate. Assume that James Rockford files a Chapter 11 petition and that the next day his mobile home is destroyed by a tidal wave. Any insurance proceeds would be property of the estate.

4. Property of the estate includes property acquired by a debtor after s/he files a Chapter 13 petition and before the Chapter 13 proceeding is converted to a Chapter 7 case, section 1306. For example, D files a Chapter 13 petition on January 10. On December 12, he converts from Chapter 13 to Chapter 7, section 1307(a). Property acquired by D from January 10 until December 12 is "property of the estate."

2. EXEMPT PROPERTY

a. WHAT PROPERTY IS EXEMPT IN BANKRUPTCY?

Under non-bankruptcy law, Jim Rockford's mobile home would probably be exempt property.* Under the Bankruptcy Reform Act of 1978, all property of the debtor becomes property of the estate but an individual debtor is permitted to exempt certain property from "property of the estate," section 522(*l*).

Under section 522, an individual debtor may assert the exemptions to which s/he is entitled under the laws of the state of his domicile and un-

---

* Non-bankruptcy exemption law is considered supra at pages 16–20.

der federal laws other than Title 11.** Alternatively, the individual debtor may claim the exemptions set out in section 522(d) unless the state of the debtor's domicile has provided by legislation that this alternative exemption is not available to its residents.

Section 522(d) creates four kinds of exemptions:

1. *Specified property not limited as to amount.* For example, health aids, section 522(d)(9) and social security benefits, section 522(d)(10)

2. *Specified property to "the extent reasonably necessary for the support of the debtor."* For example, alimony, section 522(d)(10)(D), and life insurance proceeds, section 522(d)(11)(C).

3. *Specified property to a limited value.* For example, $7,500 for a homestead, section 522(d)(1); $200 for each item of household furnishings, section 522(d)(3). The dollar limitations in section 522(d) refer to the value of the debtor's interest, not the value of the property. To illustrate, assume that Ward Cleaver files a Chapter 7 petition. If the Cleaver's $40,000 house is subject to a $35,000 mortgage, the house

---

** Some of the items that may be exempted under Federal laws other than Title 11 include:
  Social security payments, 42 USCA 407
  Civil service retirement benefits, 5 USCA 729, 2265
  Veterans benefits, 45 USCA 352(E).
For most debtors, the state exemptions are far more significant.

is exempt. The exemption for household furnishings in section 522(d)(3) is limited only as to the value of the debtor's interest in a particular item; there is no limitation as to the number of items. If for example, Tom Bradford filed a bankruptcy petition he could assert this $200 exemption for each of the beds in the Bradford's house.

4. Any property with a value no greater than the total of $400 and the unused portion of the homestead exemption, section 522(d)(4). Assume that Lucy Ricardo files a bankruptcy petition. Since she and Ricky live in a rented apartment, she would have a general exemption of $7,900, section 522(d)(4) [$400 from (d)(4) + the unused $7,500 from (d)(1)].

An individual debtor may *not* select some exemptions from state law and some exemptions from section 522(d). S/he must elect *either* the state exemptions or section 522(d). The Bankruptcy Reform Act does not indicate when the election is to be made. [This will probably be dealt with by the rules.] In a joint case, each spouse is entitled to claim an exemption. It would seem that one spouse could claim the state exemption and the other spouse could claim section 522(d) exemptions.

Whether an individual elects to claim under state exemption law or section 522(d), waivers of exemptions made before or after bankruptcy are not enforceable, section 522(e).

b. WHAT IS THE SIGNIFICANCE IN BANKRUPTCY OF EXEMPT PROPERTY?

Generally, an individual debtor is able to retain his or her exempt property. Exempt property is not distributed to creditors in the bankruptcy proceeding and is protected from the claims of most creditors after the bankruptcy proceeding. After bankruptcy, there are only four groups of creditors who have recourse to property set aside as exempt in a bankruptcy proceeding:

1. creditors with tax claims excepted from discharge by section 523(a)(1);

2. creditors with domestic claims excepted from discharge by section 523(a)(5);

3. creditors whose claims arise after the filing of the bankruptcy petition; *

4. creditors with liens on exempt property that are neither avoided nor extinguished through redemption.

As #4 suggests, some liens on exempt property that are valid outside of bankruptcy are invalidated as a result of bankruptcy. The general invalidation provisions, discussed infra at pages 175, 226, are applicable to liens on exempt property. More importantly, section 522(f) empowers

---

* If the debtor chooses the set of exemptions set out in section 522(d), post-petition creditors will be able to reach items not exempted under relevant state law.

the debtor to avoid judicial liens on any exempt property and security interests that are both non-purchase money, and nonpossessory on certain household goods, tools of the trade, and health aids.

To illustrate, assume that the list of property that an individual claims as exempt includes a stereo system and an automobile. If a creditor has an attachment or execution lien on the stereo, the debtor may avoid the lien, section 522(f)(1). If a creditor has a security interest in the stereo, the security interest may be avoided unless it is either possessory or purchase money, section 522(f)(2). If a creditor has an attachment lien or execution lien on the automobile, the debtor may avoid the lien. If, on the other hand, a creditor has a security interest in the automobile,** it is valid.

As the preceding paragraph illustrates, section 522(f) avoids any judicial lien on any exempt property. It avoids only those consensual liens that:

    (1) are non-possessory, *and*

    (2) are non-purchase money, *and*

** It can perhaps be argued that, for some debtors, an automobile is "implements * * * or tools of the trade" for purposes of section 522(f)(2)(B). There are cases holding that the phrase "tools of the trade" in state exemption statutes includes an automobile used by the debtor in his work. Note, however, that section 522(d) makes separate provisions for motor vehicles, section 522(d)(2), and tools of the trade, section 522(d)(6).

(3) encumber exempt personal property of a type mentioned in section 522(f)(2).

Possessory security interests in exempt personal property, purchase money security interests in exempt personal property, and any security interests on exempt personal property not covered by section 522(f) may be extinguished through "redemption." Section 722 † authorizes an individual debtor to discharge a lien on exempt personal property by paying the lienor the value of the property encumbered.†† To illustrate, assume that Susan Vance, V, owes the Bank of the Potomac, BP, $3,000. BP has a security interest in V's Subaru. If V files a bankruptcy petition and the value of the Subaru is only $1,200, V can discharge BP's lien by paying BP $1,200.

A waiver of exemptions is unenforceable in bankruptcy, section 522(e).

Section 522(e) and section 522(f) apply in every personal bankruptcy. Even if the debtor elects to claim exemptions under state law in-

---

† Section 722 does not apply to liens on tools of the trade. It is limited to liens on "tangible personal property intended for personal, family or household use." In theory, section 722 applies to all liens "securing a dischargeable consumer debt" on such property. As a practical matter, however, a debtor will not invoke section 722 to redeem property from liens which can be avoided under section 522(f).

†† It is unclear whether the payment under section 722 must be a cash payment. Section 524(c)(4)(B)(II) seems to contemplate redemption by means of a promissory note. stead of section 522(d), section 522(e) nullifies

any waiver of exemptions and section 522(f) invalidates certain liens on certain exempt property.

3. LEASES AND EXECUTORY CONTRACTS, SECTION 365

The effect of the filing of a bankruptcy petition on a debtor's leases and executory contracts * is governed by section 365. Under section 365, a bankruptcy trustee may either:

1. assume and retain leases and executory contracts

2. assume and assign leases and executory contracts

3. reject leases and executory contracts.

According to section 365(a), the trustee's assumption or rejection of a lease or executory contract is "subject to court approval." Perhaps, the Rules will specify whether notice and a hearing is required. In a Chapter 7 case, a lease or executory contract is deemed rejected by operation of law unless it is assumed by the trustee within 60 days after the order for relief.**

---

* The term "executory contract" is not statutorily defined. According to legislative history, "it generally includes contracts on which performance remains due to some extent on both sides."

** There is no similar time limit for Chapters 11 and 13 cases. In a rehabilitation proceeding, a lease or executory contract may be assumed or rejected as a part of the plan or prior to the formulation of the plan. The court may, upon request of the other party to the lease or contract, set a time by which the trustee or debtor in possession must act.

Why would a bankruptcy trustee decide to assume and retain a lease or executory contract? If, for example, Cunningham Hardware Store, Inc., files a Chapter 11 petition, the trustee (or debtor in possession) needs hardware and needs a store to continue operating the business. Accordingly, the trustee will probably decide to assume and retain the store lease.

In a Chapter 7 case, the bankruptcy trustee will rarely decide to assume *and retain* a lease or executory contract. If Cunningham Hardware Store, Inc., decides to liquidate and files a Chapter 7 petition, there is no reason for the bankruptcy to *assume and retain* the store lease.

There may, however, be reasons to *assume and assign* a lease or executory contract in a Chapter 7 (or Chapter 11 or Chapter 13) case. Consider the following illustration:

Cunningham Hardware Store, Inc., C, leases a store in Northwest Plaza for 10 years at a rental of $1,000 a month. Three years later, C files a Chapter 7 petition. Because of an increase in rents and the lack of available space in Northwest Plaza, Kinky Friedman's Kosher Fried Chicken Corp., K, offers to pay C's bankruptcy trustee $5,000 for an assignment of its lease. Under these facts, the bankruptcy trustee would want to assume and assign the lease.

There are a number of limitations on the trustee's power to assume and retain or assume and assign leases and executory contracts.

Common law limitations on assignment of rights and delegation of duties *will* be recognized in bankruptcy, section 365(c). If, for example, Chico Escuela files a bankruptcy petition, the bankruptcy trustee can *not* assume and assign Escuela's contract to play baseball for the New York Mets.

Contract provisions limiting assumption and assignment of leases and executory contracts will *not* be recognized in bankruptcy, section 365(e), 365(f)(1). Even if Cunningham's lease contains a "bankruptcy clause," i. e., a clause that makes the filing of a bankruptcy petition an event of default and authorizes the lessor to terminate the lease, or an "ipso facto clause," i. e., a clause that makes the filing of a bankruptcy petition an event of default and automatically terminates the lease, the bankruptcy trustee will be able to assume and assign the Northwest Plaza lease.

If there has been an event of default other than a default by reason of the filing of a bankruptcy petition, the trustee may not assume the lease or executory contract unless s/he first either cures the default or provides "adequate assurance" * that the default will be promptly cured and provides "adequate assurance of future perform-

* "Adequate assurance" is not statutorily defined. Section 365(b)(3) indicates what "adequate assurance" contemplates in one specific situation: lease of real property in a shopping center. Note also that section 2–609 of the Uniform Commercial Code uses the phrase "adequate assurance of performance."

ance", section 365(b)(2). For example, a Chapter 11 debtor that is behind in its rent payments will probably have to pay the back rent and/or post a substantial security deposit in order to assume a lease.

After the trustee assumes a lease or executory contract, the other party to the contract looks to the property of the estate and not the debtor for payment for the post-petition obligations under the lease or contract. Assumption creates a first priority administrative expense for performance of the debtor's obligation. [Administrative expenses are considered infra at pages 272–273.] The trustee's assignment of assumed contracts or leases, however, "relieves the trustee or the estate from any liability for any breach of such contract or lease occurring after such assignment," section 365(k).

After the assumption and assignment of a lease or executory contract, the other party to the lease or contract may look only to the assignee for the payment of the debtor's post-assignment obligations under the lease or contract. To protect the non-bankrupt party, section 365(f)(2) requires that the assignee provide "adequate assurance of future performance" as a condition precedent to any assignment.

Section 365 contemplates that some leases and executory contracts will be rejected rather than assumed and retained or assumed and assigned. Rejection by the trustee does not give rise to any rights against the debtor personally. Rather, the non-bankrupt party to a lease or executory contract rejected by the trustee has a general, non-priority claim against the property of the estate, sections 365(g) and 502. Such claims are considered infra at pages 259–278.

Section 365(h) deals with the rejection of a lease by the bankruptcy trustee for a debtor/lessor. A trustee for a debtor who owns rental real estate may not use section 365 to evict tenants. Even if the trustee decides to reject the debtor/lessor's leases, the tenant has the right to remain in possession. The trustee for the debtor/lessor may, however, terminate some of the services required in the lease such as maintenance.** The lessee may then offset any damages caused by such termination against its rent obligations.

Section 365(h) provides similar protection for a buyer of real property under an installment sales contract who is in possession. Even if the seller/debtor's bankruptcy trustee rejects the contract of sale, a buyer in possession may elect to remain in possession and continue making payments under the contract.

** It is unclear whether the trustee is free to terminate all services. Legislative history indicates that section 365(h) is designed to prevent the lessee from being deprived of his estate. Can the lessor terminate elevator service to the tenants in a 47 floor office building?

4. AVOIDANCE OF PRE–BANKRUPTCY TRANSFERS

Some transfers that are valid outside of bankruptcy can be invalidated by a bankruptcy trustee. The Bankruptcy Reform Act of 1978 empowers the bankruptcy trustee to invalidate certain pre-bankruptcy transfers. These invalidation provisions reach both absolute transfers such as payments of money, gifts, and sales, and security transfers such as creation of mortgages and security interests. When the bankruptcy trustee invalidates a pre-bankruptcy absolute transfer, the property becomes property of the estate, sections 550, 541(a)(3). When the bankruptcy trustee invalidates a security transfer, the encumbered property becomes property of the estate free from encumbrances.

The various invalidation provisions reflect certain basic bankruptcy policies. The provisions and underlying policies are considered below.

a. PREFERENCES

Common law * does *not* condemn a preference. Under common law, a debtor—even an insolvent

---

* Some state statutes void certain transfers because of their preferential character. The trustee may take advantage of such statutes by virtue of his powers under section 544(b): if the state anti-preference provision protects any actual creditor of the debtor, it protects the bankruptcy trustee. Section 544(b) is considered infra at pages 199, 208.

debtor—may treat certain creditors more favorably than other similar creditors. Although D owes X, Y, and Z $1,000 each, D may pay X's claim in full before paying any part of Y's claim or Z's claim.

Bankruptcy law *does* condemn *certain* preferences. A House report that accompanied a draft of the Code explained the rationale for such a bankruptcy policy as follows:

> "The purpose of the preference section is two-fold. First, by permitting the trustee to avoid pre-bankruptcy transfers that occur within a short period before bankruptcy, creditors are discouraged from racing to the courthouse to dismember the debtor during his slide into bankruptcy. The protection thus afforded the debtor often enables him to work his way out of a difficult financial situation through cooperation with all of his creditors. Second, and more important, the preference provisions facilitate the prime bankruptcy policy of equality of distribution among creditors of the debtor. Any creditor that received a greater payment than others of his class is required to disgorge so that all may share equally." House Report 95–595 at 117–78.

(1) ELEMENTS OF A PREFERENCE

Section 547(b) sets out the five elements of a preference; the bankruptcy trustee may void any transfer of property of the debtor if s/he can establish:

(1) the transfer was "to or for the benefit of a creditor"; and

(2) the transfer was made for or on account of an "antecedent debt", i. e., a debt owed prior to the time of the transfer; and

(3) the debtor was insolvent at the time of the transfer; and

(4) the transfer was made within 90 days before the date of the filing of the bankruptcy petition, *or,* was made between 90 days and 1 year before the date of the filing of the petition to an "insider" who had reasonable cause to believe that the debtor was insolvent at the time of the transfer; and

(5) the transfer has the effect of increasing the amount that the transferee would receive in a Chapter 7 proceeding.

The first three requirements of section 547(b) will usually be easy to apply. To illustrate, a true gift is not a preference—not to or for the benefit of a creditor. A pledge of stock to secure a new loan is not a preferential transfer—not for or account of antecedent debt. The third requirement—insolvency of the debtor at the time of transfer—is made easy by section 547(f)'s creation of a rebuttable presumption of insolvency for the 90-days immediately preceding the filing of the bankruptcy petition.

In determining whether the transfer was made within 90 days of the filing of the petition, look to Federal Rule of Civil Procedure 6(a) which provides that the day on which the transfer occurred is not included.* In determining whether the transfer was made to an "insider" so that the relevant time period is 1 year, not merely 90 days, look to BRA section 101(25)'s definition of insider.

Remember that the presumption of insolvency is limited to the 90-days immediately preceding the bankruptcy petition. Accordingly, in order to invalidate a transfer that occurred more than 90 days before the filing of the bankruptcy petition the trustee must establish that (i) the transferee was an "insider"; (ii) the debtor was insolvent at the time of the transfer; and (iii) the transferee had reasonable cause to believe that the debtor was insolvent.

The fifth element, which essentially tests whether the transfer improved the creditor's position, will be satisfied unless the creditor was fully secured before the transfer or the property of the estate is sufficiently large to permit 100% payment to all general claims. Assume, for ex-

---

* If under state law, a transfer is not fully effective against third parties until public notice of the transfer has been given and such public notice is not timely given, then section 547(e) deems the transfer to have occurred at the time public notice was given. The use of section 547 to invalidate transfers not recorded in a timely fashion is considered infra at pages 214, 219.

ample, that D makes a $1,000 payment to C, a creditor with a $10,000 general claim, on January 10. On February 20, D files a bankruptcy petition. The property of the estate is sufficient to pay each general creditor 50% of its claim. A general creditor with a $10,000 claim will thus receive $5,000. S, however, will receive a total of $5,500 from D and D's bankruptcy unless the January 10th transfer is avoided. ($1,000 + 50% × (10,000 − 9,000)). Accordingly, the bankruptcy trustee may avoid the January 10th transfer under section 547(b) to "facilitate the prime bankruptcy policy of equality of distribution among creditors."

The following hypotheticals illustrate the application of the five elements of section 547(b).

(1) On January 10, C lends D $10,000 and obtains and records a mortgage on Redacre. Redacre has a fair market value at all times of $20,000. On March 3, D repays C $3,000 of the $10,000. On April 4, D files a bankruptcy petition.

D's bankruptcy trustee may *not* avoid the March 3 transfer under section 547(b). Element # 5 is not satisfied. Even if the transfer had not been made, C would recover $10,000. [Payment to a fully secured creditor is not a preference.]

(2) On February 2, D borrows $2,000 from S and gives S a security interest in equipment which S perfects. At all relevant times, the

equipment has a fair market value of $1,300. On April 4, D repays S $400 of the $2,000 loan. On May 5, D files a bankruptcy petition. The property of the estate is sufficient to pay each general creditor 10% of its claim.

The trustee may avoid the April 4 payment and recover the $400 for the estate. All of the elements of section 547(b), including element # 5, are satisfied. The transfer would enable S to receive $560 ($400 + 10% × 1,600.) If the transfer had not been made, D would receive only $200. [Payment to a partially secured creditor is a preference.]

(3) On March 3, D borrows $300,000 from S. On April 4, S demands security for the loan and D gives S a mortgage on Redacre. Redacre has a fair market value of $400,000. On May 5, D files a bankruptcy petition. The property of the estate is sufficient to pay each general creditor 20% of its claim.

The trustee may avoid the April 4 mortgage so that Redacre is property of the estate free and clear of S's lien. Again all of the elements of section 547(b) are satisfied. The transfer would enable S to receive $300,000. If the transfer had not been made, S would receive only $60,000. [Section 547(b) invalidates liens to secure past debts.]

(4) On April 4, D borrows $40,000 from S and gives S a security interest on equipment. The

equipment has a fair market value of $50,000. On June 6, D files a bankruptcy petition.

The trustee may not avoid the April 4 security interest. The April 4 transfer was for present consideration, not "for or on account of an antecedent debt." Element # 2 is not satisfied. [Section 547 does not invalidate liens to secure new debts.]

(2) EXCEPTIONS (SECTION 547(c))

Section 547(b) sets out the elements of a voidable preference. Section 547(c) excepts certain pre-petition transfers from the operation of section 547(b). If a transfer comes within one of section 547(c)'s exceptions, the bankruptcy trustee will not be able to invalidate the transfer even though s/he is able to satisfy the five requirements of section 547(b).

The first exception is for a transfer that was intended to be for new value and is in fact a "substantially contemporaneous exchange," section 547(c)(1). For example, on September 3, D lends J $1,600 in what both parties intend to be a secured loan. On September 11, J executes a mortgage giving D a lien on Redacre. On September 15, J's creditors file an involuntary bankruptcy petition.

The bankruptcy trustee may *not* avoid D's mortgage. Even though the September 11 "transfer" satisfies the five elements of section 547(b), it is protected by section 547(c)(1).

Remember that section 547(c)(1) requires that the transfer both be a "substantially contemporaneous exchange" and be intended by the parties to be a transfer for new value. If C makes an unsecured loan in the morning and then learns that the debtor is in financial difficulty and so demands and obtains a security interest in the afternoon, the bankruptcy trustee may avoid the security interest under section 547(b).

Section 547(c)(2) protects payments of debts within 45 days after the debt arose if:

> (1) the debt was incurred in the ordinary course of business (or ordinary course of financial affairs);

> (2) payment was made in the ordinary course of business (or ordinary course of financial affairs);

> (3) payment was made "according to ordinary business terms." To illustrate, D receives a water bill for January water use on February 2 and pays the debt on February 20. On March 3, D files a bankruptcy petition.

D's bankruptcy trustee may *not* recover the February 20th payment. Even though it satisfies the five tests of section 547(b), it is excepted from the operation of section 547 by section 547(c)(2).

The third exception protects "enabling loans." Section 547(c)(3) requires that:

> (1) the creditor gives the debtor "new value" to acquire certain real or personal property;

> (2) the debtor signs a security agreement giving the creditor a security interest in the property;

> (3) the debtor in fact uses the "new value" supplied by the creditor to acquire the property;

> (4) the creditor perfects its security interest within ten days after the security interest attaches.

For example, on April 4, F borrows $14,000 from S to buy a new tractor and signs a security agreement that describes the tractor. S files a financing statement. On April 20, F uses S's $14,000 to buy a new tractor. On May 5, F files a bankruptcy petition.

F's bankruptcy trustee may *not* avoid S's security interest. While all of the elements of section 547(b) are satisfied,* all of the elements of section 547(c)(3) are also satisfied.

---

* The creation of a lien is a transfer of property of the debtor. It was, of course, "to or for the benefit of a creditor." And, it was "for or on account of an antecedent debt." "For purposes of this section, a transfer is not made until the debtor has acquired rights in the property transferred," section 547(e)(3). The other elements of section 547(b) are discussed supra on pages 176–181.

Section 547(c)(4) protects a creditor who has received a preference and then extends further unsecured credit to the debtor, by creating an offset. For example, on June 6, C lends D $60,000. On July 7, D repays $20,000 of the loan. On August 8, C lends D an additional $8,000. On September 9, D files a bankruptcy petition.

D's bankruptcy trustee may recover $12,000 from C ($20,000 − $8,000). The July 7th payment of $20,000 was a preference. The trustee's recovery is, however, reduced by the amount of the August 8th unsecured advance, section 547(c)(4).

(3) UCC Floating Liens (Section 547(c)(5))

Section 547(c)(5) creates a limited exception from preference attack for certain Article 9 floating liens. As noted on page 111, Article 9 provides a mechanism for establishing a "floating lien." Such liens are most commonly used in financing accounts or inventory which normally "turn-over" in the ordinary course of the debtor's business. For example, on January 10 Port Phillips Credit Co. lends Calderwood Department Store $100,000 and takes a security interest in the store's inventory. Obviously, Port Phillips wants Calderwood to sell its inventory so that it can repay the loan. It is equally obvious that as inventory is sold, the collateral securing Port Phillips' loan decreases unless Port Phillips' lien "floats" to cover the proceeds from the sale of the inventory and to cover the new inventory Calderwood acquires. Accordingly, the security agreement Calderwood signs on January 10 will probably contain an after-acquired property clause—will probably give Port Phillips a security interest in inventory now owned *or hereafter acquired.*

Under Section 547(e)(3), "For purposes of this section, a transfer is not made until the debtor has acquired rights in the property transferred." Thus, if Calderwood Department Store acquires new inventory on March 3d and files a bankruptcy petition on April 4th, it would *seem* that Calderwood Department Store's bankruptcy trustee can invalidate Port Phillips Credit Co. security interest in the March 3d inventory because there was:

    1. a transfer of property of the debtor to a creditor

    2. for an antecedent debt

[The debt was incurred on January 10th; section 547(e)(3) dates the transfer of the security interest in the March 3d inventory as of March 3d.]

    3. presumption of insolvency

[Remember section 547(f).]

    4. transfer made within 90 days of the bankruptcy petition

    5. transfer increased bankruptcy distribution to Port Phillips Credit Co. (unless

[*185*]

Port Phillips Credit Co. was already fully secured.)

Section 547(c)(5), however, may protect Port Phillips Credit Co. A creditor with a security interest in inventory or accounts receivable is subject to a preference attack only to the extent that it improves its position during the 90-day period before bankruptcy. The test is a two-point test and requires determination of the secured creditor's position 90 days before the petition and on the date of the petition. If new value was first given after 90 days before the case, the date on which it was first given substitutes for the 90-day point.

There are seven steps involved in applying section 547(c)(5)'s "two-step" test:

1. Determine the amount of debt on the date of the bankruptcy petition;

2. Determine the value of the debtor's accounts and/or inventory encumbered by the secured creditor's lien on the date of the petition;

3. Subtract # 2 from # 1;

4. Determine the amount of debt 90 days before the petition;

5. Determine the value of the debtor's accounts and/or inventory encumbered by the secured creditor's lien 90 days before the petition;

6. Subtract # 5 from # 4;

[*186*]

7. Subtract the answer in # 3 from the answer in # 6. That is the amount of preference.

The following hypotheticals illustrate the application of section 547(c)(5).

(1) D files a bankruptcy petition on April 11. At the time of the filing of the petition, D owes S $100,000. S has a valid in bankruptcy floating lien on D's inventory of furniture. On April 11, D's inventory has a value of $80,000. On January 11, 90 days before the bankruptcy petition, D owed S $125,000, and D's furniture had a value of only $70,000. [D increased its furniture inventory in March when S threatened to "call in the loan."] D's bankruptcy trustee may reduce S's secured claim to $45,000.* [80,000 − ((125,000 − 70,000) − (100,000 − 80,000))].

(2) D files a bankruptcy petition on April 22. At the time of the filing of the petition, D owes S $200,000. S has a valid in bankruptcy security interest in D's inventory of oriental rugs. On April 22, D's inventory of rugs has a value of

---

* Ninety days before the petition, "the amount by which the debt secured by such security interest exceeded the value of all security interest for such debt" was by $55,000. ($125,000 − $70,000). On the date of the petition, this amount was only $20,000. ($100,000 − $80,000) S's security interest is effective "except to the extent that (the debtor's acquisition of new inventory) * * * caused a reduction * * * of any amount by which the debt secured by such security interest exceeded the value of all security interest * * *." Accordingly, S's $80,000 security interest must be reduced by $35,000. ($55,000 − $20,000). Accordingly, section 547(c)(5) limits S to a $45,000 secured claim.

$200,000. On January 22, 90 days before the bankruptcy petition was filed, D owed S $200,000, and the rugs had a fair market value of $150,000. D did not acquire any additional rugs after January 11; the value of D's rugs increased because of market considerations. The trustee has no section 547 rights against S. There is no transfer to invalidate. S's improvement in position was not "to the prejudice of other creditors holding an unsecured claim."

(3) D Manufacturing Co., D, files a bankruptcy petition on April 4. At the time of the filing of the bankruptcy, D owes C Credit Corp., C, $40,000. C has a valid in bankruptcy security interest in all of D's equipment. The D–C security agreement has an after-acquired property clause. On the date of the filing of the petition, D's equipment has a fair market value of $31,000. On January 4, 90 days before the filing of the bankruptcy petition, D owed C $40,000 and D's equipment had a fair market value of $32,000. On February 2, D sold a piece of equipment for $6,000. (D used the $6,000 to pay taxes,) On March 3, D bought other equipment for $5,000. The trustee can limit S's security interest to the equipment owned on January 4. The March 3d "transfer" is a preference under section 547(b).** The March 3d "transfer" of a security inter-

---

**Remember, that March 3 is the date that the transfer is deemed made for purposes of section 547, section 547(e)(3).

est in equipment is not protected by section 547(c)(5) because section 547(c)(5) only applies to security interests in inventory or accounts.

b. SETOFFS (SECTION 553)

At times, a party is both a creditor and a debtor of another party. Assume, for example, that Stephen Weed, W, has a checking account at Kane Citizens Bank, B, with a $1,000 balance. W borrows $4,000 from B to buy a new car. B is in the position of a creditor of W's on the car loan; B, however, is in the position of a debtor of W's on the checking account. B is thus both W's creditor and W's debtor.

In attempting to collect the $4,000 loan from W, B may assert its right of setoff. Professor Skilton defines "setoff" as follows: "Setoff is a time honored right of one who is indebted to another to reduce or balance off such indebtedness by charging against the debt sums which his creditor in that transaction may owe him in some other transaction. It may be viewed as a form of self-help, and not merely * * * a defense to be pleaded in case he is sued by his creditor * * *. One might have supposed that this time honored right originated with a common law rule based on common sense. But historically, it owes much to statutes, although equitable setoff supplemented statutory setoff. Today, however setoff may exist without a statutory base." Skilton, The Secured Party's Rights in a Debtor's

[*189*]

Bank Account Under Article 9 of the Uniform Commercial Code, 1977 So.Ill.L.J. 120, 186.

The use of setoff is not limited to banks. Bank setoff is, however, the most common setoff transaction. Accordingly, this book will deal with setoff primarily in a banking context.

To illustrate, if Kane Citizens Bank, B, asserts its right of setoff against Stephen Weed, W, it will reduce W's checking account balance from $1,000 to 0 and reduce the amount owed by W on the $4,000 loan to $3,000.

What if Stephen Weed files a bankruptcy petition one day after the setoff? Can the bankruptcy trustee recover the $1,000 from Kane Citizens Bank? If one day before the filing of a bankruptcy petition, W withdraws $1,000 from his savings account and uses that $1,000 to reduce his indebtedness to B, the trustee can recover the $1,000 under section 547. Is there any reason to treat B's setoff differently?

Section 547 does not apply to setoffs. Section 553 is the only provision of the Bankruptcy Reform Act of 1978 that limits pre-petition setoffs. It contains a number of limitations on setoffs:

(1) "Mutual Debt"

The debts must be between the same parties in the same right or capacity. For example, a claim against a "bankrupt" * as an administratrix can-

---

*The Bankruptcy Reform Act of 1978 uses the term "debtor", not the term "bankrupt". Nevertheless, in dis-

not be set off against a debt owed to the "bank-rupt" as an individual.

(2) "Arose before the commencement of the case"

Both the debt owed to the "bankrupt" and the claim against the "bankrupt" must have preceded the filing of the bankruptcy petition.

(3) "Disallowed", section 553(a)(1)

Certain claims against a "bankrupt" are disallowed. See section 502 considered infra at pages 264, 270. A claim that is disallowed under section 502 may not be used as the basis for a setoff. To illustrate, A owes B $4,000. B files a bankruptcy petition. The debt from A to B is property of the estate. The trustee attempts to collect the $4,000 from A. A only pays the trustee $3,000. A alleges that it set off a $1,000 claim it had against B. If that $1,000 claim would be barred by the statute of limitations in a state collection action, it would be disallowed under section 502(a)(1) and the setoff would be disallowed under 553(a)(1).

(4) "Acquired" Claims, section 553(a)(2)

Section 553(a)(2) prevents a debtor of an insolvent from obtaining claims against the insol-

cussing setoffs in which each party is the debtor of the other, it seems less confusing to use the term "bankrupt" to identify the party that filed a voluntary bankruptcy petition (or the party whose creditors filed an involuntary bankruptcy petition).

vent to use to offset against the debtor's own obligations in an ensuing bankruptcy. Assume for example, that A owes B $4,000; B owes C $1,000. B is insolvent. Because B is insolvent, C's $1,000 claim is of little value to C. C would be willing ˎto sell its claim against B to A for less than $1,000. A would be willing to buy C's claim for less than $1,000 if it could then assert that claim as a setoff to reduce its debt to B from $4,000 to $3,000. Under section 553(a)(2) claims against the "bankrupt" acquired from a third party may *not* be set off against a debt owed to the "bankrupt" if:

> a. the claim was acquired within 90 days before the bankruptcy petition or after the bankruptcy petition, *and*

> b. the "bankrupt" was insolvent when the claim was acquired. [Section 553(c) creates a rebuttable presumption of insolvency.]

(5) Build-ups, section 553(a)(3)

Section 553(a)(3) precludes a setoff by a bank ** if:

> a. money was deposited by the "bankrupt" within 90 days of the bankruptcy petition, and

> b. the "bankrupt" was insolvent at the time of the setoff (Remember section 553(c)'s presumption of insolvency.), and

** Again, section 553(a)(3) is not limited to bank setoffs.

    c. the purpose of the deposit was to create or increase the right of setoff.

For example, X Bank makes a loan to D Corp. Payment of the loan is guaranteed by P, the president of D Corp. D Corp. suffers financial reverses. X Bank pressures D Corp. and P to increase the balance of the corporation's general bank account. D Corp. moves $100,000 from other banks to its X Bank account before filing its bankruptcy petition. Section 553(a)(3) would preclude X Bank from taking the $100,000 by way of setoff.

(6) Improvement in position, section 553(b)

Section 553(b) is similar to section 547(c)(5), considered supra at pages 186–189. Both are designed to prevent an improvement in position within 90 days of bankruptcy. Application of section 553(b) requires the following simple computations:

1. Determine amount of claim against the debtor 90 days before the date of the filing of the petition; † 2. Determine the "mutual debt" owing to the "bankrupt" by the holder of such claim 90 days before the filing of the petition; † 3. Subtract #2 from #1 to determine the "insufficiency." † 4. Determine the amount of

---

† If there is no "insufficiency" (as defined in section 553(b)(2)) 90 days before the petition, examine the 89th day, then the 88th day, etc. until a day is found that has an "insufficiency." Computations 1–3 will then focus on that day.

the debt on the date that the right of setoff was asserted; 5. Determine the amount of the setoff; 6. Subtract # 5 from # 4 to determine the insufficiency; 7. Subtract the answer in # 6 from the answer in # 3, to what part, if any, of the amount setoff the trustee may recover.

The following problems illustrate the application of section 553(b):

1. D files a Chapter 13 petition.

90 days before the petition, D owes B Bank $100,000 and has $40,000 on deposit.

10 days before the petition, B exercises its right of setoff. At that time, D owes B Bank $70,000 and the account has $60,000 balance.

The trustee may recover $50,000 from B Bank.††

2. D files a Chapter 7 petition.

90 days before the petition, D owes $200,-000 to B Bank and has $200,000 on deposit at B Bank.

††There was a $60,000 ($100,000 – $40,000) "insufficiency" 90 days before the bankruptcy petition was filed. At the time of the setoff, the "insufficiency" was only $10,000 ($70,000 – $60,000). There was a $50,000 improvement in position ($60,000 – $10,000). The bankruptcy trustee may recover $50,000 of the amount of offset under section 553(b).

88 days before the petition D withdraws $80,000 from the account; 5 days before the petition, B exercises its right of setoff. At that time, D owes B $70,000 and has $60,000 on deposit in B Bank.

The trustee may recover $60,000 from B Bank.*

In summary, a bankruptcy trustee will apply the above six tests to any setoff that has occurred prior to the filing of the bankruptcy petition.

The filing of a bankruptcy petition automatically stays any further setoffs. Section 553 subjects the right of setoff to limitations provided in sections 362 and 363. Section 362(a)(7) stays setoffs. Thus, in order, to exercise a right of setoff after the filing of the bankruptcy petition it is necessary to obtain relief from the stay. Section 362(d), considered supra at pages 153–158, governs relief from the stay.

In assessing the practical significance of the limitations on post-petition setoffs imposed by

----

* On the first date within the 90 day period that there was an "insufficiency," it was an insufficiency of $80,000. At the time of the setoff, the "insufficiency" was only $10,000 ($70,000 − $60,000). There was an improvement in position of $70,000 ($80,000 − $10,000). Nevertheless, the trustee may recover only $60,000 under section 553(b). "The amount so offset" establishes the ceiling for recovery under section 553(b).

section 362, it is important to remember section 363. Consider the following illustration:

On Thursday, X Inc. files a Chapter 11 petition. X Inc. owes B Bank $700,000 and has an account at B Bank with a $300,000 balance. Each Friday, X Inc. issues paychecks to its employees in an amount in excess of $200,000. What can B Bank do? B Bank may under 362(f) seek ex parte relief from the stay on setoffs. Alternatively, B Bank may invoke section 363(c)(2) to refuse X Inc.'s use of the "cash collateral" without notice and hearing on the issue of "adequate protection."

If a stay is terminated or modified to permit a post-petition setoff, the setoff will be limited by section 553(a)—requirements 1–5, discussed on pages 189–196. Section 553(b) applies only to pre-petition setoffs.

c. FRAUDULENT CONVEYANCES

(1) SECTION 548

The Bankruptcy Code, like non-bankruptcy law, invalidates fraudulent conveyances. Indeed, the Bankruptcy Code fraudulent conveyance provisions are very much like the non-bankruptcy fraudulent conveyance statutes considered supra at pages 67–79.

Section 548 is based on the Uniform Fraudulent Conveyances Act. Section 548(a)(1) corresponds to section 7 of the UFCA; it empowers the trustee to invalidate transfers made with actual intent to hinder, delay or defraud creditors. Section 548(b) is similar to the partnership provisions of section 8(a) of the UFCA.* And section 548(a)(2) resembles UFCA section 4-7; it provides for avoidance of transfers where the debtor received less than a "reasonably equivalent value" *and* (i) was insolvent or became insolvent as a result of the transaction, *or* (ii) was engaged in business or was about to engage in a business transaction for which his remaining property was unreasonably small capital; *or* (iii) intended to incur or believed that he would incur debts beyond his ability to pay.

Section 548 differs from the UFCA in several significant respects:

1. Section 548 applies to transfers of both non-exempt and exempt property. The UFCA is limited to transfers of non-exempt property.

2. The test in section 548(a)(2) is "reasonably equivalent value." The test in sections 4-7 of the UFCA is "fair consideration." The "fair consideration" standard requires an inquiry into both the amount of consideration and the parties' good faith. Section 548's use of "reasonably equivalent value" eliminates a good faith require-

---

* Under section 548(b), the trustee of a bankrupt partnership may avoid a transfer of partnership property to a general partner if the partnership was or thereby became insolvent. The consideration given the partnership by the partner is irrelevant since a general partner is individually liable for the payment of the partnership's debts. Transfers by a partnership to a nonpartner are governed by section 548(a).

ment from value determination. However, the "good faith" of the *transferee* remains significant under section 548. Section 548(c) protects a transferee who takes "for value and in good faith." Accordingly, the practical significance of the use of "reasonably equivalent value" instead of "fair consideration" is the elimination of any inquiry into the good faith of the *transferor* in determining whether a trustee can recover property under section 548(a)(2).**

3. Section 548 eliminates the requirement of actual unpaid creditors as to whom the transfer was fraudulent. Under the UFCA a transfer by an insolvent not for fair consideration may be set aside only by creditors who were creditors at the time of the transfer. Under section 548(a)(2), such a transfer may be avoided even though all who were creditors at the time of the transfer have been paid.

(4). The UFCA does not have its own statute of limitations. States generally have a three to six year limitations period for actions to invalidate fraudulent conveyances. Under section 548, the bankruptcy trustee may only reach transfers made † within one year of the filing of the bank-

---

** The transferor's good faith (or lack of good faith) is, of course, a very important factor in determining whether the trustee may invalidate a transfer under section 548(a)(1): "made such transfer * * * with actual intent to hinder, delay or defraud."

† For purposes of section 548, a transfer will be *deemed* made when it becomes so far perfected that a bona fide

ruptcy petition.†† To illustrate, assume that in June of 1979, Mrs. Lupner gave her daughter Lisa a new piano as a graduation present. Mrs. Lupner was insolvent at the time of the gift. On August 1, 1980, Mrs. Lupner files a bankruptcy petition. By the date of bankruptcy, Mrs. Lupner has repaid all of her June, 1979 creditors except Todd DilaMuca whom she owed $10. Mrs. Lupner's bankruptcy trustee will not be able to recover the piano under section 548. The transfer was a fraudulent conveyance (a transfer for less than "reasonably equivalent value" while insolvent) but it was made more than a year prior to the bankruptcy petition.

(2) SECTION 544(b)

Section 548 is not the only provision in the Bankruptcy Code that invalidates fraudulent conveyances. The trustee may also use section 544(b) to invalidate fraudulent conveyances.

purchaser from the debtor could not acquire an interest in the property transferred superior to the interest of the transferor, section 548(d). The problems of determining the date that a transfer will be *deemed* made are considered at pages 219, 221 infra.

†† The one-year period of section 548 is not a true statute of limitations. It does not require that the trustee's action to invalidate the transfer be commenced within one year of the time the transfer was made. If the transfer was made within one year of the date of the filing of the bankruptcy petition, the bankruptcy trustee has up until the closing or dismissal of the case or two years after his or her appointment, whichever first occurs, to commence the invalidation action, section 546.

Section 544(b) does not specifically provide for the invalidation of fraudulent conveyances. Rather it empowers the bankruptcy trustee to avoid any pre-bankruptcy transfer that is "voidable under applicable law by a creditor holding an unsecured claim that is allowable." *

Section 544(b) incorporates state fraudulent conveyance law into the Bankruptcy Code. If, outside of bankruptcy, the transfer would be governed by a Statute of Elizabeth fraudulent conveyance statute, section 544(b) is a Statute of Elizabeth statute; if the state statute is the UFCA, then section 544(b) is UFCA. Section 544(b) reflects not only the state substantive law of fraudulent conveyances but also the state limitations period ** for fraudulent conveyances.

In the Lupner problem, the June gift of a piano would be a fraudulent conveyance under nonbankruptcy law, Statute of Elizabeth or Uniform

---

* Section 502 governs allowance of claims. Section 502 is considered infra at page 264.

** The state limitations period determines which transfers may be challenged, not when the challenge must be made. Section 546 again gives the trustee time after his or her appointment to commence the action. To illustrate, D makes a fraudulent conveyance in January of 1979. State law imposes a five-year limitation period on fraudulent conveyance actions. If D files a bankruptcy petition in December of 1983 that satisfies or tolls the state law limitations period, and D's bankruptcy trustee will have the additional section 546 period to commence a fraudulent conveyance action.

Fraudulent Conveyance Act, as to Todd Dila-Muca. Todd DilaMuca was a creditor holding an unsecured claim that is allowable. Accordingly, Mrs. Lupner's bankruptcy may use section 544(b) to recover the piano.

While the existence of the trustee's section 544(b)'s avoiding powers depend upon the existence of an avoiding power held by an actual creditor, the extent of the trustee's section 544(b) avoidance powers is greater than the power of the actual creditor. In the Lupner problem, under state fraudulent conveyance law, if Lisa Lupner paid Todd DilaMuca $10, she could keep the piano. Under section 544(b), Lisa is not so fortunate. Legislative history clearly indicates that section 544(b) retains the rule of Moore v. Bay, 284 U.S. 4 (1931).

Under the rule of *Moore v. Bay,* the trustee is not limited in his recovery by the amount of the claim of the actual creditor. A transfer which is voidable by a single, actual creditor, may be avoided entirely by the trustee, regardless of the size of the actual creditor's claim. Thus Lisa may *not* keep the piano by simply paying the bankruptcy trustee $10.

(3) COMPARISON OF SECTIONS 548 AND 544(b)

The Lupner hypothetical points up the similarities and differences of sections 548 and 544(b).

These provisions are also compared by the following chart:

548		544b	
1.	Essentially UFCA	1.	UFCA or Statute of Elizabeth whichever is the state law
2.	Reaches transfers made within one year of bankruptcy petition [limitations period is measured from the time the transfer is *deemed* made. See page 219 infra]	2.	Reaches all transfers made with state limitations period [limitations period is measured from the time the transfer was actually made]
3.	Elements of fraudulent conveyance tested as of time that transfer was *deemed* made. See page 219 infra	3.	Elements of fraudulent conveyance tested as of time that the fraudulent conveyance was actually made
4.	Transferee that takes for value and in good faith protected	4.	Transferee that takes for value and in good faith protected
5.	No requirement of actual creditor as to whom conveyance is fraudulent	5.	Voidable only if transfer is fraudulent as to an actual creditor with an unsecured, allowable claim
6.	Complete invalidation	6.	Complete invalidation

[C515]

d. TRANSFERS NOT TIMELY RECORDED OR PERFECTED

A bankruptcy trustee may avoid certain pre-petition transfers that are not timely recorded or perfected. A failure to record or a delay in recording can adversely affect other creditors. If creditor X does not record its lien on D's property, creditor Y might not know that D's property is encumbered. Relying on the mistaken belief that D holds his property free from liens, Y might extend credit, refrain from obtaining a lien, or forebear from instituting collection proceedings.

State law requires recordation or other public notice of a number of transfers. Real estate recording statutes require the recording of deeds and real property mortgages. Article 6 of the Uniform Commercial Code requires that creditors be notified in advance of any bulk transfer. Section 2–326 of the Code calls for public notice of sales on consignment. And, Article 9 of the Uniform Commercial Code calls for public notice, i. e., perfection, of security interests.

The Bankruptcy Act does not have its own public notice requirements. It does *not* simply invalidate all transfers not recorded within 10 days. Rather, the Bankruptcy Act makes use of the notoriety requirements of state law in the following invalidation provisions: sections 544, 547 and 545.

(1) SECTION 544(b)

Section 544(b) empowers the bankruptcy trustee to invalidate any transfer that under non-bankruptcy law is voidable as to any actual creditor of the debtor with an unsecured, allowable * claim. In applying section 544(b), it is thus necessary to determine:

(1) whether non-bankruptcy law public notice requirements have been timely satisfied;

(2) which persons are protected by the non-bankruptcy requirement of public notice;

(3) if any actual creditor of the debtor with an unsecured allowable claim comes within the class of persons protected by such state law.

The following hypotheticals illustrate the application of section 544(b):

1. On January 10, D makes a bulk transfer to X. X fails to give notice to C, one of D's creditors. Under section 6–104, such failure to notify renders the transfer "ineffective" against C. On March 3, D files a bankruptcy petition. On that date, C is still one of D's unsecured creditors. The bankruptcy trustee will be able to invalidate the January 10 transfer to X.

The applicable public notoriety requirement, section 6–104, was not timely satisfied. Section 6–104 protects all creditors of the transferor

---

* Most creditors' claims are allowable. Section 502, particularly section 502(b), indicates the extent to which claims are disallowed. Section 502 is considered infra at pages 264–270.

whose claims arose before the bulk transfer. C is such a creditor. C is an actual creditor of the debtor/transferor with an unsecured, allowable claim. Since the transfer is ineffective as to C, the bankruptcy trustee can invalidate the transfer.**

\# 2. On January 10, D borrows $10,000 from M and gives M a mortgage on Redacre. On February 2, C lends D $10,000. On March 3, M records its mortgage. On July 7, D files a bankruptcy petition. On the date of the perfection, D still owes $10,000 to M and $10,000 to C. D's bankruptcy trustee will not be able to invalidate M's mortgage.

The public notoriety requirements were not timely satisfied. M delayed in recording its mortgages. Most real property recording statutes only protect purchasers, and/or lien creditors. C is not within the class of persons protected by the applicable recording statute. Section 544(b) empowers the trustee to invalidate transfers that are invalid as to actual creditors such as C. Since C can not invalidate the transfer, the bankruptcy trustee can not invalidate the transfer *under section 544(b)*.

** Remember that under section 544(b), the bankruptcy trustee is not limited by the amount of the actual creditor's claim. A transaction which is voidable (or ineffective) as to a single actual creditor can be completely avoided by the trustee, regardless of the size of that creditor's claim. See page 201 supra.

\# 3.   On January 10, D borrows $10,000 from S and gives S a security interest in equipment. On February 2, C lends D $10,000.   On March 3, S perfects its security interest.   On July 7, D files a bankruptcy petition.   On the date of the petition, D still owes $10,000 to S and $10,000 to C.   D's bankruptcy trustee will *not* be able to invalidate S's security interest.

The public notoriety requirements of the UCC were not timely satisfied.   S delayed in perfecting its security interest.   Article 9's perfection requirements, however, protect only certain gap secured creditors and buyers.   C is not within the class of persons protected by the applicable recording statute.   Section 544(b) empowers the bankruptcy trustee to avoid transfers that are invalid as to actual creditors.   Since no actual creditor can ~~not~~ invalidate the transfer, the bankruptcy trustee can not invalidate the transfer.

\# 4.   On January 10, D borrows $10,000 from S and gives S a security interest in equipment. On February 2, L obtains an execution lien on the same equipment.   On March 2, S perfects its security interest.   On July 7, D files a bankruptcy petition.   On the date of the petition, D is still indebted to S and L.   The bankruptcy trustee will not be able to invalidate S's security interest.

Again, the public notoriety requirements of the UCC were not timely satisfied.   Article 9's perfection requirements do protect a lien creditor such as L, section 9–301. L is a holder of a secured claim. Section 544(b) only gives the bankruptcy trustee the invalidation powers of any actual holders of *un*secured claims.* While L has the power to invalidate S's security interest, the bankruptcy trustee does not have L's invalidation powers.

As problems $\#2$, $\#3$ and $\#4$ illustrate, the use of section 544(b) to invalidate pre-petition

---

* Under section 544(b), the bankruptcy trustee may assert the rights of an actual lien creditor whose lien has been invalidated. Section 551 provides for preservation of invalidated liens.

Preservation of an invalidated lien benefits only the bankruptcy estate—not the lien creditor. Where an invalidated lien is preserved, the trustee is able to assert the status of that lien creditor in attacking other liens on the property. If there are no other creditors with liens on the same property, or if all such other liens are superior to the lien that the trustee avoids, nothing is gained by preserving the invalidated lien. Preservation of a lien is of practical significance only where there are other liens on the property, subordinate to the lien avoidable by the trustee, that the trustee may not attack in any other manner.

To illustrate, on February 2, S lends D $20,000 and takes a security interest in D's equipment. On March 3, X, another creditor of D, obtains an execution lien on the equipment. On March 13, S perfects its security interest. On March 23, D files a bankruptcy petition. X defeats S, section 9–301. The bankruptcy trustee, T, defeats X if D was insolvent on March 3, section 547, (considered supra at page 175). T may preserve X's lien under section 551. T may then assert the rights of X to invalidate S's security interest under section 544(b).

Note that in the hypothetical in the preceding paragraph, the trustee could also use section 547 to invalidate S's lien if D was insolvent on March 13, see page 175 supra. The rule that, under section 544(b), the trustee may assert the rights of an actual lien creditor whose lien has been invalidated is of very limited practical significance.

transfers that were not timely recorded is severely limited. Section 544(b) gives the trustee the invalidation powers of any actual unsecured creditors. Most recording statutes protect lien creditors or bona fide purchasers, but not unsecured creditors.

(2) SECTION 544(a)

Section 544(b) looks to the rights of actual creditors of the debtor; section 544(a) focuses on the rights of hypothetical lien creditors and bona fide purchasers of real property. Section 544(a) empowers the bankruptcy trustee to invalidate any transfer that under non-bankruptcy law is voidable as to a creditor who extended credit and obtained a lien on the date of the filing of the bankruptcy petition or is voidable as to a bona fide purchaser of real property whether or not such a creditor or purchaser actually exists. In applying section 544(a), it is thus necessary to determine whether:

(1) non-bankruptcy law public notice requirements have been timely satisfied;

(2) a creditor who extended credit and obtained a lien on the date that the bankruptcy petition was filed or a bona fide purchaser of real property on the date of the bankruptcy petition comes within the class of persons protected by such state law.

PROPERTY OF THE ESTATE

The following hypotheticals illustrate the application of section 544(a):

1. On January 10, D borrows $10,000 from M and gives M a mortgage of Redacre. On February 2, D files a bankruptcy petition. As of the date of the petition, M had not recorded its mortgage. D's bankruptcy trustee may invalidate M's mortgage under section 544(a).

The public notice requirements of the state real property recording statutes were not satisfied. Real property recording statutes typically protect bona fide purchasers. Since the mortgage was unrecorded on the date that the bankruptcy petition was filed, M's mortgage would be ineffective as against a bona fide purchaser of Redacre on the date that the petition was filed. Section 544(a) gives the bankruptcy trustee the same powers as a person who was a bona fide purchaser on the date that the bankruptcy petition was filed.

2. On January 10, D borrows $10,000 from S and gives S a security interest in equipment. On February 2, D files a bankruptcy petition. S fails to perfect its security interest prior to February 2. The bankruptcy trustee will be able to invalidate S's security interest under section 544(a).

The applicable public notice requirement was not satisfied. Article 9's perfection requirements protect creditors with judicial liens, section 9–

301. Since the security interest was unperfected on the date that the bankruptcy petition was filed, S's security interest would be subordinate * to the claim of a creditor who obtained a judicial lien on the date that the petition was filed, section 9–301. Section 544(a) gives S the same invalidation powers as a person who extended credit and obtained a judicial lien on the date that the bankruptcy petition was filed.

3. On January 10, D borrows $10,000 from S to buy equipment and gives S a purchase money security interest in the equipment. On January 18, D files a bankruptcy petition. On January 19, S perfects its security interest.** The bankruptcy trustee may not invalidate S's security interest.

Section 544(a) empowers the bankruptcy trustee to invalidate security interests that would be subordinate to the claims of a creditor who obtained a judicial lien on the date that the petition

---

* Even though the Uniform Commercial Code uses the term "subordinate" instead of "voidable", a security that would be "subordinate" to a creditor that obtained a judicial lien on the date of the filing of the bankruptcy petition is "voidable" by the bankruptcy trustee.

** The filing of a bankruptcy petition stays or stops most creditor collection efforts. Section 362(a), considered infra at pages 150–151, defines the scope of the stay, by listing the acts that are stayed by the commencement of the bankruptcy case. Section 362(a)(4) stays lien perfection. Section 362(b) lists exceptions to the automatic stay. Section 362(b)(3) excepts perfection of purchase money security interests from the scope of the stay.

was filed. By reason of section 9–301(2),† S's purchase money security interest would be effective as against a creditor who obtained a lien on January 18, the date that the bankruptcy petition was filed. Accordingly, S's purchase money security interest is effective against the bankruptcy trustee.

4. On January 10, Dudley Doright, D, borrows $10,000 from Snidely Whiplash, S and gives S a security interest in equipment. On December 29, S properly files his financing statement. On December 30, D files a bankruptcy petition. The bankruptcy trustee may not invalidate S's security interest UNDER SECTION 544(a).††

The public notice requirements of Article 9 were not timely satisfied; S delayed in perfecting its security interest for almost a year. Article 9's perfection requirements protect *"gap"* lien creditors and buyers. In this hypothetical, the

---

† Section 9–301(2) provides in part: "If the secured party files with respect to a purchase money security interest before or within ten days after the debtor receives possession of the collateral, he takes priority over the rights of * * * a lien creditor which arise between the time the security interest attaches and the time of filing." This "ten-day grace period" is also effective against a bankruptcy trustee, see section 546(b).

†† The bankruptcy trustee will probably be able to invalidate S's security interest under some other provision of the Bankruptcy Reform Act of 1978. If D was insolvent on December 29, the bankruptcy trustee may invalidate S's security interest under section 547. The applicability of section 547 to transfers not timely perfected or recorded is considered infra at page 214.

bankruptcy trustee has the right of a lien creditor, but not a gap lien creditor. Section 544(a) gives the bankruptcy trustee the invalidation powers of a creditor who obtained a judicial lien as of the date of the bankruptcy petition. On the date of the bankruptcy petition, December 30, S's security interest was perfected. A perfected security interest is effective against lien creditors, cf. sections 9–201, 9–301. Accordingly, S's security interest may not be invalidated under section 544(a).

The above hypotheticals suggest three general rules for the use of section 544(a) in invalidating transfers:

(1) If the transfer has been recorded or otherwise perfected prior to the date that the bankruptcy petition was filed, the trustee will not be able to invalidate the transfer under section 544(a).

(2) Except as noted in (3) below, if the transfer was not recorded or otherwise perfected by the date that the bankruptcy petition was filed, the bankruptcy trustee will be able to invalidate the transfer under section 544(a).

(3) The bankruptcy trustee will not be able to invalidate a purchase money security interest perfected within ten days after the delivery of the collateral to the debtor even if the debtor files a bankruptcy petition in the gap between the creation of the security interest and perfection.

(3) COMPARISON OF SECTION 544(a) AND 544(b)

COMPARISON OF SECTION 544(a) AND SECTION 544(b)

	544(a)	544(b)
I. STATUS (federal law) A. Necessity of protected actual creditor with allowable claim	NOT NECESSARY	NECESSARY
B. Effect of amount of actual creditor's claim	IRRELEVANT	IRRELEVANT
II. PRACTICAL SIGNIFICANCE OF STATUS (non-bankruptcy law) A. Real property transfers	1. Recording statute protects either creditors or purchasers 2. Transfers not recorded at time bankruptcy petition filed may be avoided	1. Recording statute must protect unsecured creditors 2. Transfers not timely recorded may be invalidated if an actual creditor with an unsecured allowable claim extended credit in the gap
B. Personal Property transfers governed by UCC	Article 9 security interests not perfected at the date of filing of the bankruptcy petition may be invalidated	Subject to the very limited exception noted on the bottom of p. 207. Section 544(b) may not be used to invalidate Article 9 security interests. Section 544(b) may be used to invalidate a bulk transfer if an actual creditor with unsecured, allowable claim failed to receive the notice required by Article 6

[C518]

(4) SECTION 547(e)

In the Dudley Doright/Snidely Whiplash hypothetical above, the bankruptcy trustee was not able to invalidate Snidely's security interest under section 544(a) notwithstanding Snidely's long delay in giving public notice of his lien. Should Doright's bankruptcy trustee be able to invalidate Snidely's lien?

As noted on page ——, there are a number of reasons for invalidating such "secret liens." Creditors of Doright may have been misled by Snidely's failure to record or a delay in recording. Unaware of this "secret", unrecorded lien, Nell Fenwick might extend credit to Doright she would not extend if aware of the lien. Unaware of a "secret", unrecorded lien, Mr. Peabody might delay in collecting a delinquent debt from Doright he would try to collect if aware of the lien. The Bankruptcy Code should invalidate transfers that are not timely recorded. And it does. In section 547.

Although it is easy to see the reason for invalidating liens that are not timely perfected, it is difficult to understand why section 547 should be the mechanism for invalidating such liens. The easy way to invalidate such secret liens would be to add a section to the Bankruptcy Code to the effect that any lien that can be recorded or otherwise perfected under state law must be recorded within 10 (30?) days after it is obtained in order

[*214*]

to be valid in bankruptcy. While that is the "easy way", it is not the way of the Bankruptcy Code. Basically, the Bankruptcy Code's method is to "deem" that for purposes of applying the requirements of section 547,* the date of transfers not timely recorded is the date of perfection,** not the actual date of transfer.

The Doright/Whiplash hypothetical illustrates the practical significance of the statutory delay

---

* The elements of section 547 are considered supra at pages 176, 180.

** Section 547 does not specify the means of perfection. Rather, section 547(e)(1) provides that for purposes of section 547, transfers shall be perfected when effective under non-bankruptcy law against certain specified third parties. In a transfer of real property other than fixtures, the third parties are bona fide purchasers, i. e., the date of perfection is the date that the transfer is effective against bona fide purchasers. Non-bankruptcy law generally requires that transfers of interests in real property other than fixtures be recorded in order to be effective against bona fide purchasers.

A transfer of personal property or fixtures is perfected for purposes of section 547 when it is effective against a creditor with a judicial lien. Absolute transfers of personal property are generally effective against subsequent lien creditors of the transferor without any recording. For example, A pays B $1,000. This transfer is effective against subsequent lien creditors of A without any recording. X delivers 200 widgets to Y. Again, the transfer is effective as against subsequent lien creditors of the transferor without recordation.

Security transfers of liens in personal property or fixtures are not effective against subsequent judicial lien creditors of the transferor without recordation or other perfection. For example, D gives S a security interest in equipment to secure a debt. Under UCC section 9–301(1)(b), S's security interest is not superior to the rights of a subsequent judicial lien creditor of D until S perfects.

of the effective date of the transfer until public notice of the transfer has been given. Remember, Doright borrowed $10,000 from Snidely on January 10 and gave Snidely a security interest in equipment which Snidely perfected on December 29. Doright filed a bankruptcy petition on December 30. At first, it might seem that section 547 is not applicable—that the security transfer from Doright to Snidely was not for an antecedent indebtedness and did not occur within 90 days of the bankruptcy petition. For purposes of section 547, however, the transfer will be *deemed* made on December 29, not January 10. [Under section 9–301, Snidely's security interest would not be effective as against subsequent judicial lien creditors until that date. Accordingly, by reason of section 547(e), the transfer will not be deemed made until that date.] Thus, the "December 29 transfer" would be within 90 days of the bankruptcy petition. Thus, the "December 29 transfer" would be for an antecedent indebtedness, i. e., the $10,000 loaned on January 10. Thus, the trustee would be able to invalidate S's security under section 547 if D was insolvent on December 29. [Remember section 547(f) creates a rebuttable presumption of insolvency.]

The above hypothetical illustrates that a delay in perfection can result in a security interest actually given for present consideration being deemed made for an antecedent indebtedness and thus a section 547 preference.

Section 547(e) does not require immediate perfection; it provides a ten-day "grace period" for perfection.

Section 547(e)(2) describes three situations. First, § 547(e)(2)(A) deals with transfers perfected within ten days. Such a transfer will be deemed made at the time of the transfer. A transfer deemed made at the time of the transfer is not vulnerable to attack by the bankruptcy trustee under section 547.

Second, section 547(e)(2)(B) deals with transfers not perfected within ten days. Such a transfer will be deemed made at the time of perfection. A transfer deemed made at a point in time later than the time of the transfer is vulnerable to attack by the bankruptcy trustee under section 547.

Third, section 547(e)(2)(C) deals with the effect of filing a bankruptcy petition during the ten-day "grace period." Under such facts, the transfer will be deemed made at the time of the transfer if it is perfected within ten days of the transfer or will be deemed made at the time of the filing of the bankruptcy petition if it is not perfected within ten days.

The operation of section 547(e) is illustrated in the following five hypotheticals:

1. On January 10, S lends D $10,000 and obtains a security interest in D's equipment. S perfects this security interest on January 19. For purposes of section 547, the security transfer will

be deemed to have occurred on January 10, section 547(e)(2)(A). S perfected within ten days after the transfer so the transfer is deemed made when it was actually made.

2. On January 10, S lends D $10,000 and obtains a security interest in D's equipment. S perfects its security interest on February 2. For purposes of section 547, the security transfer will be deemed to have occurred on February 2, section 547(e)(2)(B). S did not perfect within ten days so the transfer is deemed made when it was finally perfected.

3. On January 10, S lends D $10,000 and obtains a non-purchase money security interest in D's equipment. D files a bankruptcy petition on January 15. S perfects its security interest on January 19.* For purposes of section 547, the security transfer will be deemed to have occurred on January 10, section 547(e)(2)(A), section 547(e)(2)(C)(ii). [Same facts as # 1 except that D filed a bankruptcy petition before the security interest was perfected.]

4. On January 10, S lends D $10,000 and obtains a security interest in D's equipment. D files a bankruptcy petition on January 15. S perfects its security interest on February 2. For purposes of section 547, the security transfer will

---

* It would seem that S would have to request and obtain relief from the automatic stay of section 362 in order to file a financing statement after the bankruptcy petition was filed.

be deemed to have occurred on January 15, section 547(e)(2)(C). Transfers not perfected within ten days are deemed made at the date of the bankruptcy petition if the filing of the petition preceded perfection. [Same facts as # 2 except that D filed a bankruptcy petition before the security interest was filed.]

5. On January 20, M lends D $10,000 and obtains a mortgage on Redacre. The applicable state recording statute contains a twenty-day grace period. M records its mortgage on February 2. D files a bankruptcy petition on March 3. For purposes of section 547, the security transfer will be deemed to have occurred on February 2. Section 547(e) recognizes only a ten-day grace period. M failed to perfect within that ten-day period. Accordingly, the time of the transfer will be deemed to be the date of perfection.

(5) SECTION 548(d)

Section 548(d) is similar to section 547(e). Section 547(e) fixes the time when a transfer is deemed made for purposes of the preference invalidation provisions of section 547. Section 548(d) fixes the time when a transfer is deemed made for purposes of the fraudulent conveyance invalidation provisions of section 548: when the transfer is so far perfected that no subsequent bona fide purchaser of the property from the debtor can acquire rights in the property superior to those of the transferee.

The purpose of section 548(d) is to prevent a fraudulent conveyance from escaping invalidation by being kept secret for over a year. For example, on January 10, 1979, D an insolvent, gives Redacre to X. X does not record the deed until November 11, 1980. On December 12, 1980, D files a bankruptcy petition. Remember, section 548 has a one year limitations period.* The transfer of Redacre was actually made more than one year before the bankruptcy petition was filed. The transfer, however, was not effective against a subsequent bona fide purchaser until it was recorded on November 11. Accordingly, under section 548(d), the transfer is deemed made on November 11, 1980. Without section 548(d), the bankruptcy trustee could not invalidate the gift by an insolvent under section 548.

The transfer from D to X in the preceding paragraph was a "true" fraudulent conveyance: a transfer by an insolvent without "reasonably equivalent value." Section 548(d), however, also may enable the bankruptcy trustee to invalidate some transfers that are not "true" fraudulent conveyances—transfers in which there has been merely a delay in recordation or perfection. Consider the following illustration.

Wallace Cleaver, W, gives Redacre to his brother Theodore, T, in December of 1979. W is sol-

* This one year limitation period and the other requirements of section 548 are considered supra at pages 198, 199.

vent at that time. T, however, does not record the transfer until June of 1981. At that time, W is insolvent. In July of 1981, W files a bankruptcy petition. The bankruptcy trustee will be able to use section 548(a)(2) to invalidate the 1979 gift of Redacre.

Note that T's delay in recordation is crucial to the bankruptcy trustee's section 548 case. At the time that the gift is actually made, the donor, W, is solvent. There are no legal problems with people who are solvent making gifts. This happens every Chanukah and Christmas. Gifts are fraudulent conveyances when made by people who are insolvent.

While the donor, W, was solvent when the gift was actually made, he is insolvent when the gift is deemed made under section 548(d)—at the time the transfer is perfected against bona fide purchasers from the transferor. Section 548(d), like section 547(e), enables the trustee to test all aspects of the transaction as of the time of recordation rather than as of the time of the actual transfer. Since W was insolvent when the transfer is deemed made—at the time of recordation —the transfer was fraudulent as a transfer by an insolvent without reasonably equivalent value.

(6) SECTION 545(2)

Section 545(2) invalidates statutory liens that are not perfected or enforceable on the date of the petition against a hypothetical bona fide purchaser. Section 546(b) recognizes any applicable state law "grace period." If under state law, the statutory lien may still be perfected and that perfection relates back to a pre-bankruptcy petition date, then the bankruptcy trustee will not be able to invalidate the lien.

Section 545(2) is of very limited practical significance. First, most statutory liens satisfy section 545(2)'s bona fide purchaser test. Second, statutory liens are also subject to section 544(a) which can be used to invalidate any statutory lien on real property that is voidable by a hypothetical bona fide purchaser and any statutory lien on personal property that is voidable by a hypothetical lien creditor.

e. LANDLORDS' LIENS

Section 545(3) and 545(4) are the easiest invalidation provisions to read, understand and apply. "The trustee may avoid the fixing of a statutory lien on the property of the debtor to the extent that such lien   *   *   *

(3) is for rent

(4) is a lien of distress for rent."

Note that the provisions only invalidate STATUTORY landlord liens, i. e., liens for rent arising "solely by force of a statute." If the lease agreement creates an Article 9 security interest in property of the lessee, this contractual lien is not affected by section 545.*

f. DISGUISED PRIORITIES

Section 507 * of the Bankruptcy Code is a priority provision; it sets out the order in which the various unsecured claims against the debtor are to be satisfied. It displaces any state priority statutes.

Section 545 protects this federal priority scheme from disruption by state priority provisions that are "disguised" as statutory liens. Section 545 invalidates spurious statutory liens which are in reality merely priorities.

When is a statutory lien more like a priority than a lien? As noted on page 4, a priority does not arise until distribution of a debtor's assets on insolvency. Accordingly, section 545(1) invalidates all statutory liens which first become effective on the bankruptcy or insolvency of the debtor.

---

* When a landlord requires its tenant to sign a security agreement giving the landlord a security interest in property of the tenant to secure rental payments, the landlord has, of course, obtained a lien. This lien held by the landlord is not, however, a "landlord's lien"; it is a security interest. Not all liens securing claims by landlords are "landlord's liens." Only Chuck Berry would be inclined to call a security interest obtained by Mabel "Mabelline."

* Section 507 is considered infra at pages 272–276.

g. RECLAMATION UNDER SECTION 2–702

When a buyer fails to pay for goods it accepts, the seller has a legal right to recover the contract price, UCC section 2–709. This legal right is of limited practical significance if the buyer is insolvent. Accordingly, the Uniform Commercial Code grants unpaid sellers a right to recover the goods. Section 2–702 of the Uniform Commercial Code empowers a seller to "reclaim" the goods if:

(1) credit sale, *and*

(2) buyer insolvent when goods received, *and*

(3) written misrepresentation of solvency within three months before delivery *or* the demand for reclamation is made within ten days of the buyer's receipt of the goods.

Case law has created a similar right of reclamation for sellers paid with bad checks.*

There has been considerable controversy over the validity of the seller's right to reclamation in a bankruptcy proceeding governed by the Bankruptcy Act of 1898. No provision in the Bankruptcy Act of 1898 deals specifically with the seller's right of reclamation, and cases and commentators are divided as to whether the trustee may

---

* The right of reclamation of a "cash" seller who has been paid by a check that is subsequently dishonored is based on section 2–507. See In re Samuels & Co., Inc., 526 F.2d 1238 (5th Cir. 1976).

use section 60, 67c, 70c, or 70d to invalidate the unpaid seller's reclamation.

There is a provision in the Bankruptcy Reform Act of 1978 that deals with certain reclamation claims. Section 553(c) applies to reclamation by a seller if:

(1) credit sale, *and*

(2) buyer insolvent when the goods are received, *and*

(3) *writte*n demand for reclamation no later than ten days after the buyer's receipt of goods, *and*

(4) in the ordinary course of business.

If a seller has complied with these four requirements, the bankruptcy trustee can not invalidate the seller's right of reclamation under section 544(a) (considered supra at page 208), section 545 (considered supra at page 221), section 547 (considered supra at page 175), or section 549 (considered infra at page 228).** The court may, however, deny reclamation to a seller who

---

** Section 546(c) does not protect the seller's right of reclamation from invalidation based on section 544(b). Section 544(b) is considered supra at pages 203–208. If other unsecured creditors have rights superior to the seller's right of reclamation, the trustee may assert these rights under section 544(b) to defeat the seller's right of reclamation. If a secured creditor has rights superior to the seller's right of reclamation, the trustee may assert these rights only if the trustee is able to avoid the lien of the secured creditor and preserve it for the benefit of the estate.

has met the four requirements of section 553(b) if it protects the seller by either granting its claim arising from the sale of goods an administrative expense priority or securing the claim by a lien.

While both Bankruptcy Reform Act of 1978 section 546(c) and UCC section 2–702 deal with reclamation by unpaid sellers, the scope of application of the two provisions differs in a number of significant respects:

1. Section 546(c) applies to common law rights of reclamation as well as rights of reclamation under statutes such as section 2–702;

2. Section 546(c) requires that the right of reclamation be asserted no later than ten days after the buyer's receipt of the goods; section 2–702 eliminates the ten-day requirement if the buyer made a misrepresentation of solvency;

3. Section 546(c) requires that the seller's demand for the return of the goods be in writing;

4. Section 546(c) also adds an "in the ordinary course of business" requirement.

Accordingly, some reclamation claims will not be protected by section 546(c). The bankruptcy trustee may attack such reclamation claims under sections 544(a), 545, 547, or 549. As noted above, the cases and commentators are divided as to whether the corresponding provisions of the Bankruptcy Act of 1898 invalidate an unpaid seller's right of reclamation.

5. AVOIDANCE OF POST–BANKRUPTCY TRANSFERS

For most purposes, the date of the filing of the bankruptcy petition is the critical date. Subject to limited exceptions noted on page 163, only the property of the debtor as of the date of the filing of the petition becomes property of the estate. Generally, property acquired by the debtor after the bankruptcy petition has been filed remains property of the debtor.

The date of the filing of the petition is significant not only in determining what property becomes property of the estate but also in determining when the property becomes property of the estate. The filing of a bankruptcy petition—voluntary or involuntary—creates the estate.

The date of the filing of the bankruptcy petition is not, however, the date that the trustee takes possession of the debtor's property. While section 701 provides for the appointment of an interim trustee in liquidation cases "promptly after the order for relief," there will be some delay before the trustee takes possession of the property.

During the hiatus between the filing of the bankruptcy petition and the bankruptcy trustee's taking possession of the property of the estate, the debtor will usually have possession and control of the property of the estate. At times, the debtor will, after the filing of the petition, transfer property of the estate to some third party. Assume, for example, that B files a bankruptcy petition on January 10. On January 12, B sells her summer home to X. On January 13, B sells her boat to Y. What should be the effect of those transfers? Should the bankruptcy laws protect X and/or Y?

Section 549 protects X and Y in certain circumstances. Before considering those circumstances, note that section 549's protection is limited to the transferee. The consideration received by the debtor from post-petition transfers is property of the estate.

The transferee will be protected if the post-petition transfer was authorized by the court. Obviously, a post-petition transfer will be effective against the bankruptcy trustee if the transfer was authorized by the bankruptcy court, section 549(a)(2)(B).

Section 549(b) validates transfers by the debtor that occur after the filing of an *involuntary* bankruptcy petition and before the order for relief to the extent that the transferee gave value to the debtor after the filing of the bankruptcy petition. To illustrate,

1. On February 22, D's creditors file an involuntary petition. On February 25, D sells her stove to X for $300. The trustee may *not* recover the stove from X. X is protected by section 549(b).

2. Same facts as # 1 except that D knew of the involuntary petition. Same result. Section 549(b) protects post-petition transfers "notwithstanding any notice or knowledge of the case that the transferee has."

3. On January 10, C lends D $1,000. On February 2, D's creditors file an involuntary petition. On February 15, D transfers his stereo to C in satisfaction of the January 10 debt. The trustee can recover the stereo from C. The stereo was transferred to satisfy a debt that arose before the petition. The transferee did not give value to the debtor after the filing of the bankruptcy petition. The transferee is not protected by section 549(b).

4. On April 4, the creditors of D file an involuntary petition. On April 14, D sells Greenacre to Y for $40,000. The trustee may not recover Greenacre from Y. Section 549(b) protects transferees of both personalty and realty.

Section 549(c) also protects post-petition transfers of realty from trustee avoidance. A transfer of real property by the debtor after the filing of a voluntary petition or after an order for relief in an involuntary case will be effective against the bankruptcy trustee if:

> (1) the real property transferred is situated in a county other than the county in which the bankruptcy proceeding is commenced; *and*

(2) the transfer occurs and is properly recorded before a copy of the bankruptcy petition is filed in the real estate records for the county where the land is located, *and*

(3) the transferee is a purchaser at a judicial sale, or a buyer or lienor for fair equivalent value without knowledge of the petition.

If all three of these requirements are satisfied, the bankruptcy trustee can not recover the real property from the transferee.

Consider the following hypotheticals illustrating the operation of section 549(c):

1.   On January 10, B files a voluntary bankruptcy petition in Hog County. On January 11, B sells land in Hog County to X. The bankruptcy trustee can avoid the transfer because the real property transferred is located in the county where the case was commenced.

2.   On February 2, B files a voluntary petition in Sutton County. On February 3, B sells land in Holtz County to Y for $10,000, the "fair equivalent value" of the land. Y has no "knowledge of the commencement of the case." Y properly files the transfer in the Holtz County real estate records on February 4. A copy of the bankruptcy petition is filed in the real estate records for Holtz County on February 5. The trustee can *not* avoid the transfer. Y is protected by section 549(c).

There is no personal property counterpart to section 549(c). The debtor's * transfers of personal property after the filing of a voluntary petition or after an order for relief in an involuntary case are avoidable by the trustee.

Some post-petition transfers of property of the estate are made by persons holding property of the debtor, not the debtor. For example, on January 11, D files a voluntary bankruptcy petition. As of that date, D has $1,000 in her checking account at B Bank. This checking account becomes property of the estate on January 11. On January 13, B Bank honors a $300 check issued by D to X on January 7 and charges D's account. Can D's bankruptcy trustee recover the $300 from B Bank? Bank of Marin v. England, 385 U.S. 99 (1966) protected the bank under the Bankruptcy Act of 1898; section 542 protects the bank under the Bankruptcy Reform Act of 1978.

---

* A transfer of *personal* property after the filing of a voluntary petition or after an order for relief in an involuntary case is effective against the bankruptcy trustee if:

    (1) the debtor is a business debtor;

    (2) the business of the debtor is authorized to be operated after the filing of the petition; and

    (3) the sale is in the ordinary course of the debtor's business, sections 549(a)(2)(B); 363(c)(1). Such a transfer will usually be made by the trustee or a Chapter 11 debtor in possession, not the debtor. For example, B Fashions, Inc., files a Chapter 7 petition. The bankruptcy court authorizes the bankruptcy trustee to operate the business, section 721. X buys a suit from B Fashions, Inc. The post-petition sale to X by B Fashions, Inc.'s bankruptcy trustee would, of course, be effective against the bankruptcy trustee.

Under section 542(c), a third party who in good faith transfers property of the estate after the filing of the petition is protected from the bankruptcy trustee if the third party had "neither notice nor actual knowledge of the commencement of the case." Accordingly, if B Bank has neither actual knowledge or notice of D's petition, it will not be liable to the bankruptcy trustee. Note that section 542(c) only protects B Bank, the party that transfers the property of the estate; it does not protect X, the transferee. The trustee has a right to recover the $300, property of the estate, from X.

B. DISCHARGE

Most individuals who file voluntary bankruptcy petitions expect that the bankruptcy proceeding will release them from any further liability on their debts. These expectations are not always realized. Bankruptcy "discharges" *certain* debtors from *certain* debts.

Section 727(a) determines which debtors receive a bankruptcy discharge in a Chapter 7 proceeding.* Sections 523 and 727(b) determine which debts are discharged. These provisions are considered below.

---

* Discharge in a Chapter 11 proceeding is considered infra at page 302. Discharge in a Chapter 13 proceeding is considered infra at pages 311–312.

1. OBJECTIONS TO DISCHARGE

In counseling a beleaguered debtor, it is very important to ascertain his or her eligibility for discharge—to determine whether any of the grounds for withholding discharge can be established by the bankruptcy trustee or a creditor. If the debtor is denied a discharge, s/he loses two ways. The debtor will leave the bankruptcy proceeding without his or her section 541 property yet owing the same debts that s/he owed at the time of the filing of the bankruptcy proceeding less any distribution that creditors received from the trustee.

The grounds for withholding a discharge, i. e., objections to discharge, are set out in section 727(a). These ten grounds are exclusive. Unless the bankruptcy trustee or a creditor is able to establish one of these ten objections, the debtor in a Chapter 7 proceeding will receive a bankruptcy discharge.

Section 727(a)(1) denies a discharge to corporations and partnerships.* Only an individual is eligible to receive a discharge in a proceeding

* Section 727(a)(1) is intended to prevent "trafficking in corporate shells and partnerships." Generally, the owners of a bankrupt corporation do not need a bankruptcy discharge. Since the corporation is a separate legal entity, they are protected from personal liability for the corporation's debts.

under Chapter 7 of the Bankruptcy Reform Act of 1978.**

The next six grounds for withholding discharge have as their foundation some form of dishonesty or lack of cooperation by the individual debtor.

A fraudulent conveyance may be the basis for an objection to discharge. Section 727(a)(2) denies a discharge to a debtor who transfers property "with an intent to hinder, delay or defraud" within the twelve months immediately preceeding the filing of the bankruptcy petition or after the filing of the bankruptcy petition.

An objection to discharge may be based on the unjustified failure to keep or preserve financial records, section 727(a)(3). A section 727(a)(3) objection raises the following issues of fact: (1) Has the debtor failed to keep financial records? (2) Is such failure "justified under all of the circumstances of the case"? and (3) Is it still possible to ascertain the debtor's financial condition and business transactions? The standards applied in resolving these fact questions will reflect the nature of the debtor's business and his assets and liabilities.

Section 727(a)(4) lists four acts which tend to deprive the bankruptcy trustee of property of the

---

** A corporation may receive a discharge in a proceeding under Chapter 11 of the Bankruptcy Reform Act of 1978, section 1141(d), considered infra at page 302.

estate or of information necessary to discover or collect property of the estate:

>1. making a false oath or account in connection with the bankruptcy case;

>2. presenting or using a false claim against the estate;

>3. receiving or giving consideration for action or inaction in the bankruptcy proceeding; or

>4. withholding books and records from the bankruptcy trustee.

Proof that the debtor "knowingly and fraudulently" committed one of these acts will bar discharge.†

The fifth ground for denial of discharge is the failure to explain "satisfactorily" any loss or deficiency of assets, section 727(a)(5). Section 727(a)(5) focuses on the truth of the debtor's explanation, not on the wisdom of his or her expenditures.

Under section 727(a)(6), a debtor may be denied discharge if s/he refuses to testify after hav-

---

† Proof that the debtor "knowingly and fraudulently" committed one of these acts will also subject the debtor to criminal sanctions: a fine of not more than $5,000 and/or imprisonment for not more than five years, 18 U.S.C.A. section 152. The standard of proof under 18 U.S.C.A. is beyond a reasonable doubt; section 727(a)(4) merely requires a preponderance of the evidence. Accordingly, section 727(a)(4) focuses on commission of the act, not conviction for the crime.

ing being granted immunity or after improperly invoking the constitutional privilege against self-incrimination.

The seventh ground for withholding discharge is the debtor's commission of any act specified in section 727(a)(2)–(6) no more than a year before the filing of the bankruptcy petition in connection with another bankruptcy case concerning an "insider," section 727(a)(7). The term "insider" is defined in section 101(28). An individual's relatives, partners, partnership and corporation all come within the definition.

Section 727(a)(8) and section 727(a)(9) limit the frequency of discharge relief. If a debtor has received a discharge in a liquidation or Chapter 11 (or XI) proceeding in the past six years, s/he will be denied discharge, section 727(a)(8). If a debtor has received a discharge in a Chapter 13 (or XIII) proceeding within the past six years s/he will be denied a discharge unless (a) payments under the plan totalled at least 100% of the allowed unsecured claims, *or* (b) payments under the plan totalled at least 70% of the allowed unsecured claims *and* the plan was proposed in good faith *and* was the debtor's "best effort," section 727(a)(9).

The six years are measured from filing date to filing date. So, if X obtains a bankruptcy discharge on April 5, 1979, in a bankruptcy proceeding filed on December 7, 1978, section 727(a)(9) would not bar X's bankruptcy discharge in a Chapter 7 case filed on December 8, 1984.

Section 727(a)(8) and section 727(a)(9) only limit the availability of a bankruptcy discharge. They do not affect the debtor's right to file a voluntary petition or creditors' right to file involuntary petitions.

Section 727(a)(10) recognizes certain waivers of discharge. A debtor's waiver will bar discharge only if it is:

>   (1) in writing, and

>   (2) executed after the filing of the bankruptcy petition, after the order for relief, and

>   (3) approved by the court.

Remember that section 727(a) is not self-executing. The bankruptcy trustee or a creditor must object to discharge, section 727(c)(1). The time for and form of objection will be governed by the new rules.

2. EXCEPTIONS TO DISCHARGE

Even when the debtor receives a bankruptcy discharge s/he is not necessarily freed for all creditors' claims. A discharge in a Chapter 7 proceeding only relieves the debtor from personal liability for debts that are (1) incurred prior to the date of the filing of the bankruptcy petition, section 727(b), and (2) not within one of the exceptions to discharge set out in section 523(a).

It is very important to understand the difference between section 727(a) objections to discharge and section 523(a) exceptions to discharge. If an objection to discharge has been established, all creditors may attempt to collect the unpaid balance of their claims from the debtor. If a creditor establishes an exception to discharge, only that creditor may attempt to collect the unpaid portion of its claim from the debtor; all other pre-petition claims remain discharged. Proof of an objection to discharge benefits all creditors; proof of an exception to discharge benefits only the creditor that establishes the exception.

Section 523(a) sets out nine exceptions to discharge.

Bankruptcy affords very little relief to the delinquent tax payer. Most taxes are not discharged in bankruptcy. Section 523(a)(1) excepts from the bankruptcy discharge all income and excise taxes for the three tax years immediately preceding bankruptcy.* And, taxes more than three years old are non-dischargeable if (a) a return was not filed, or (b) a return was filed within two years of the filing of the bankruptcy petition, or (c) a "fraudulent return" was filed.

---

* Taxes that are entitled to a priority are excepted from discharge, section 523(a)(1)(A). Section 507(a)(6)(A) provides a sixth priority for taxes for "a taxable year ending on or before the date of the filing of the petition for which a return, if required, is last due, including extensions after three years before the date of the filing of the petition."

DISCHARGE

Section 523(a)(2) excepts from discharge debts for money, property, or services obtained through fraud, false pretenses, or false representations. Section 523(a)(2) replaces section 17(a)(2) of the Bankruptcy Act of 1898. Section 17(a)(2) was the most frequently invoked exception to discharge, usually by lending institutions, finance companies, credit unions, or credit sellers contending that the debtor obtained money or goods through fraud in that s/he failed to disclose *all* existing debts in the financial data form s/he submitted when s/he applied for credit.

Section 523(a)(2)(B) deals specifically with false financial statements. A creditor seeking an exception to discharge based on the debtor's providing false or incomplete financial information must establish:

(1) materially false written statement respecting the financial condition of the debtor or an "insider",

(2) its *reasonable* reliance on the statement; **

** In consumer loan refinancings, a creditor may have relied on the false financial data only with respect to part of the debt. For example, D owes Friendly Finance $1,200. D wants to borrow an additional $300. To induce, Friendly Finance to lend $300 more, D submits a false financial statement. Friendly Finance combines the $300 of fresh cash with a renewal of the $1,200 of existing debt into a single new note with consolidated payments. If D files a bankruptcy petition, how much of Friendly Finance's

(3) the debtor's intent to deceive.

Section 523(a)(2)(B) presents hard problems of proof for a creditor. Merely establishing the falsity of the debtor's financial data will not be sufficient. The creditor will also have to establish its reliance, the reasonableness of such reliance, and, most difficult of all, the debtor's intent to deceive. If a creditor asserts a section 523(a)(2) exception from discharge against a consumer debtor and is unable to prove the required facts, it will be liable to the debtor for the debtor's costs and attorney's fees unless "clearly inequitable," section 523(d).

Unscheduled debts are excepted from discharge by section 523(a)(3). A creditor needs to know that its debtor is involved in a bankruptcy proceeding. Only a creditor that timely files a proof of claim shares in the distribution of the "property of the estate." How does a creditor learn that its debtor is in bankruptcy? Section 521 requires

$1,500 claim will be excepted from discharge under section 523(a)(2)?

In re Danns, 558 F.2d 114 (2d Cir. 1977) excepted only the claim for the new credit saying that there was no evidence that the original loan was renewed in reliance on the false representation. *Danns* does not establish the rule that only the "fresh cash" claim is excepted for discharge. If the creditor is able to establish that it relied on the false financial data in refinancing the original loan, the entire claim will be excepted from discharge.

According to Senator DeConcini, section 523(a)(2)(B) "codifies the reasoning expressed by the Second Circuit in *In re Danns*." Congressional Record, October 6, 1978, S. 17412.

the debtor to file a schedule of liabilities, and the bankruptcy court sends a notice to each creditor on the list. A creditor whose debt was not scheduled will not receive any notice; a creditor that does not receive the notice will not file a proof of claim unless it knows of the bankruptcy proceeding; a creditor that does not file a proof of claim will not be paid from the property of the estate. Accordingly, section 523(a)(3) excepts from discharge a debt not timely scheduled unless the creditor had notice or actual knowledge of the bankruptcy case.

Section 523(a)(4) excepts from bankruptcy discharge liabilities from "fraud or defalcation while acting in a fiduciary capacity." It also makes nondischargeable all embezzlement and larceny liabilities, whether the debtor is a fiduciary or not.

Section 523(a)(5) makes certain domestic obligations nondischargeable: child support and alimony for the maintenance or support of a spouse. The debt may have been incurred in connection with a property settlement so long as it is actually in the nature of alimony, maintenance, or child support. Liabilities which are a part of a property settlement which are not in the nature of alimony, maintenance or child support are dischargeable.

A section 523(a)(5) exception may be asserted only by the debtor's spouse or child. The exception may not be invoked by an assignee.

Section 523(a)(6) excepts from the operation of the bankruptcy discharge any debt arising from the debtor's "willful and malicious"

1. injury to the person of another
2. injury to the property of another
3. destruction of property of another
4. conversion of property.

There is considerable confusion as to the meaning of the limiting phrase "willful and malicious." The exact same phrase was used in the exception to discharge provisions in the Bankruptcy Act of 1898. The Supreme Court in Tinker v. Colwell, 193 U.S. 473 (1904), held that those provisions excepted a criminal conversation judgment stating that "a *willful disregard* of what one knows to be his duty, * * * which necessarily causes injury and is done intentionally may be said to be done willfully and maliciously."

Since section 523(a)(6) uses the same language as the Bankruptcy Act of 1898, it would seem that *Tinker v. Colwell* would be authority for the meaning of "willful and malicious" in section 523(a)(6). However, the Committee reports that accompanied a late draft of the Bankruptcy Reform Act of 1978 expressly reject *Tinker v. Colwell,* "Under this paragraph 'willful' means deliberate and intentional and to the extent that *Tinker v. Colwell* held that a looser standard is intended, and to the extent that other cases have relied on *Tinker* to apply a 'reckless disregard' standard, they are overruled." H.R. Rep. 95–595, p. 365; S.R. Rep. 95–989, p. 79.

Fines, penalties, or forfeitures that the debtor owes to a governmental entity are nondischargeable unless the debt is compensation for an actual pecuniary loss or a tax penalty on a dischargeable tax,* section 523(a)(7). Section 523(a)(8) contains an exception to discharge for certain educational debts: the debtor's obligations on a student loan made or guaranteed by a governmental unit or a nonprofit institution may be discharged in bankruptcy only if the bankruptcy petition was filed more than five years after the commencement of the repayment period unless the court finds that repayment of the loan will "impose undue hardship on the debtor and the debtor's dependents." Section 523(a)(9) excepts from discharge debts that were or could have been listed in a prior case in which the debtor did not receive a discharge.

Exceptions to discharge based on section 523(a)(2), (4) or (6) must be "timely" ** asserted in bankruptcy court, section 523(c); unless

---

* Claims for fines, penalties, and forfeitures have a very low priority in bankruptcy, section 726(a)(4).

** The time for filing requests for exceptions to discharge will be controlled by the new bankruptcy rules. Obviously, the bankruptcy judge will consider objections to discharge before s/he considers exceptions to discharge. If the bankruptcy judge sustains an objection to discharge, it will, of course, not be necessary to determine which debts are discharged.

the creditor's "request" is timely made, the debt is discharged. When a creditor is relying on section 523(a)(1), (3), (5), (7), (8), or (9), there is no requirement that the matter be heard in bankruptcy court. If no request is filed with the bankruptcy court, the dischargeability issue may arise in connection with the creditor's collection efforts in a non-bankruptcy forum. For example, D owes C $1,000. D files a bankruptcy petition. D fails to list her debt to C on her schedule of liabilities. D receives a bankruptcy discharge. Six months later, C sues D in state court for the $1,000. If D asserts her bankruptcy discharge as a defense, C can counter by asserting a section 523(a)(3) exception to discharge.

In determining the dischargeability of claim previously reduced to judgment, a bankruptcy court is not limited to a review of the judgment and the record in the prior non-bankruptcy proceeding. Brown v. Felsen, 99 S.Ct. 2205 (1979). Assume, for example, that X lends B $2,000 in reliance on a materially false financial statement. B defaults. X obtains a default judgment against B by proving B's obligation to pay and B's failure to pay. X does not offer proof of the false financial statement, and the judgment makes no mention of B's use of a false financial statement. B subsequently files a bankruptcy petition. B's schedule of liabilities includes X's $2,000 judgment. X timely files a request in bankruptcy court that its $2,000 claim be excepted from discharge under section 523(a)(2). In ruling on X's request, the bankruptcy court may consider "new" evidence of B's use of a false financial statement—it is not limited to the record in the prior state court proceeding.

3. EFFECT OF DISCHARGE

A discharge protects the debtor from any further personal liability on discharged debts. Section 524(a) provides that a discharge voids judgments on discharged debts and enjoins any legal action to collect such debts from the debtor or from the property of the debtor. It also bars extrajudicial "acts" such as dunning letters or calls to collect discharged debts.

Section 524(c) and (d) protect debtors from reaffirmation agreements.* A reaffirmation agreement is an agreement to pay a debt discharged in bankruptcy. Under contract law principles, an express promise to pay a debt that has been discharged in bankruptcy is enforceable even though there is no consideration or detrimental reliance to support the promise. Section 524(c) and (d) severely limit the use of reaffirmation agreements by:

* Section 727(a)(10) permits a debtor to waive discharge. Such a waiver would leave the debtor personally liable on all of his unsatisfied prepetition debts. A reaffirmation agreement only makes the debtor personally liable for the debt(s) reaffirmed.

1. requiring that the agreement be executed before the discharge is granted, section 524(c)(1); *and*

2. providing a hearing at which the bankruptcy court advises the debtor that s/he is not required to reaffirm discharged debts and of the consequences of reaffirmation, section 524(d); ** *and*

3. giving the debtor a right to rescind the reaffirmation agreement for 30 days,† section 524(c)(2); *and*

4. if the debt reaffirmed is a "consumer debt" not secured by real property, requiring that the bankruptcy court approve the agreement by finding either that (A) the agreement does not impose undue hardship and is in the debtor's best interests *or* (B) the agreement is a good faith settlement of dischargeability litigation under section 523 or of a redemption under section 772, section 524(c)(3).

Section 525 protects debtors from governmental pressures to pay discharged debts. Subject to

** The debtor is statutorily required to attend this section 524(d) hearing, section 521(4).

† Section 524(c)(2) provides that the debtor may rescind within "30 days after the agreement becomes enforceable." The agreement is only enforceable if there is a hearing under section 524(d). Accordingly, it would seem that the 30 days would begin to run after the section 524(d) hearing.

limited exceptions, "a governmental unit" may not deny the debtor a license or a franchise or otherwise discriminate against a debtor "solely because" the debtor has received a bankruptcy discharge and refuses to pay discharged debts. Note the limitations on the protection afforded by section 525. Section 525 applies only to "governmental units" not private employers or a quasi-governmental organization such as a state bar association. And, it only prohibits actions based "solely" on bankruptcy. It does not prohibit the consideration of factors such as future financial ability or responsibility.

Section 524(e) limits the protection of the bankruptcy discharge to the debtor. A bankruptcy discharge does not affect the liability of other parties such as co-debtors or guarantors. For example, if an insurance company is liable to the plaintiff in a personal injury action, as a matter of state tort law, the subsequent bankruptcy discharge of the insured defendant does not alter the obligation of the insurance company.

4. REVOCATION OF DISCHARGE

A debtor may lose his or her bankruptcy discharge. Under section 727(d), a creditor or the bankruptcy trustee may request the bankruptcy court to revoke the debtor's discharge. Section 727(d) sets out three statutory grounds for revoking a discharge. A request for revocation of discharge based on section 727(d)(1) must be made within one year of the granting of the discharge; a request for revocation of discharge based on section 727(d)(2) or 727(d)(3) must be made within one year of the granting of the discharge or the dismissal of the case, section 727(e).

Under section 727(d)(1), fraud may be the basis for revoking a discharge if (1) the fraud enabled the debtor to obtain the discharge and (2) the person requesting that the discharge be revoked first learned of the fraud after the discharge was granted. Under section 727(d)(2), discharge may be revoked because of the debtor's failure to report acquisition of property of the estate * if the debtor's failure was "knowingly and fraudulently." Under section 727(d)(3), the court may revoke a discharge if the debtor fails to obey any lawful order of the court or refuses to testify after having been granted immunity or refuses to testify after improperly invoking the constitutional privilege against self-incrimination.

The revocation of a bankruptcy discharge makes the discharge a nullity. All of the debtor's pre-petition creditors whose claims were not fully satisfied by the distribution of the property of the estate may attempt to collect the balance of their claims from the debtor and his property.

---

* "Property of the estate" consists primarily of the debtor's pre-petition property. However, certain bequests and other property acquired after the filing of the bankruptcy petition is included in section 541's list of "property of the estate." See page 163 supra.

IX. CHAPTER 7 AND SECURED CLAIMS

A. WHAT IS A SECURED CLAIM

The Bankruptcy Reform Act of 1978 classifies claims, not creditors. Accordingly, under BRA, there will be creditors with secured claims, not secured creditors.

A creditor has a secured claim if it holds a lien * on property of the estate.** The claim is a secured claim only to the extent of the value of "such creditor's interest in the estate's interest in the property." To illustrate,

(1) S & M Leather Goods, Inc. files a Chapter 7 petition:

> S & M Leather Goods, Inc. owes C $11,000.

> The debt is secured by a lien on S & M's equipment. The equipment has a value † of $2,000.

> Accordingly, C has a $2,000 secured claim and a $9,000 unsecured claim.

---

* Section 101 recognizes three distinct forms of liens:

(1) judicial liens defined in section 101(27)

(2) security interests defined in section 101(37)

(3) statutory liens defined in section 101(38).

** Property of the estate is determined under section 541. Section 541 is considered supra at pages 161–164.

† "Value" is to be determined by the court on a case by case basis in light of the purpose of the valuation and of the proposed disposition of the property, section 506(a).

(2) J. R. Ewing files a Chapter 7 petition.

J. R. owes Dallas Bank $20,000.

Dallas Bank has a judgment lien on Redacre.

J. R. and his brother Bobby each own an undivided one half interest in Redacre.

Redacre has a value of $12,000.

Accordingly, the value of the "estate's interest in the property" is only $6,000.

Accordingly, Dallas Bank has a $6,000 secured claim and a $14,000 unsecured claim.

B. INVALIDATION OF LIENS

Some liens that are valid outside of bankruptcy are invalid in a bankruptcy proceeding. Section 522(f) considered supra at pages 167, 170 empowers the debtor to invalidate certain liens on certain exempt property. Sections 544, 545, 547, 548, and 549, considered supra at pages 175, 232 empower the bankruptcy trustee to invalidate certain transfers that create liens.

To illustrate, assume that S lends D $10,000 and obtains a security interest in D's inventory. S does not file a financing statement or otherwise perfect its security interest. Under section 9–203 of the Uniform Commercial Code, S has a valid security interest. Under section 9–201, this unperfected security interest is effective between S and D and is effective against most third parties. For example, S's right to D's inventory is superior to the rights of any of D's unsecured creditors. If, however, D files a bankruptcy petition, S's unperfected security interest may be invalidated by the trustee under section 544(a) * so that S will simply have a general claim for $10,000.

Note the effect of lien invalidation. All that is eliminated is the lien. The creditor's claim remains. Lien invalidation converts a secured claim into an unsecured claim.

C. RIGHTS OF A CREDITOR WITH A VALID LIEN

In a proceeding under Chapter 7 of the Bankruptcy Reform Act of 1978, claims secured by valid in bankruptcy liens on property of the estate are satisfied before unsecured claims, section 725. To illustrate, assume that D Co. files a Chapter 7 petition. D Co. owes X, Y, and Z $10,000 each. D Co. owns machinery valued at $10,000 and miscellaneous other property worth $750. X has a lien on D Co.'s machinery. Y and Z merely have general claims. If X's lien is valid in bankruptcy,

---

* Section 544(a) gives the bankruptcy trustee the rights and powers of a creditor who obtain a judicial lien at the time the bankruptcy petition was filed. At the time the bankruptcy petition was filed, S's security interest was unperfected. An unperfected security interest is ineffective as against a creditor with a judicial lien, UCC section 9–301. Accordingly, S's unperfected security interest is ineffective as against the bankruptcy trustee. Section 544(a) is considered supra at pages 208, 213.

X will receive the $10,000 machine or the proceeds from the sale thereof.*

How does a creditor with a valid in bankruptcy lien on property of the estate obtain the collateral or the proceeds from its sale?

In a Chapter 7 case, all property of the estate is to be administered by the bankruptcy trustee. Anyone holding property of the estate at the time of the filing of a bankruptcy petition is required to turn over the property to the bankruptcy trustee, section 542.** Accordingly, if X repossessed the machinery of D Co. prior to the filing of the bankruptcy petition, section 542 requires that X turn over the machinery to the bankruptcy trustee.

---

* Y and Z will share pro rata in the remaining $750. If the net value of the machine was only $5,000, X would receive that $5,000 and the remaining $750 would be paid as follows:

    $300 to Y
    $300 to Z
    $150 to X.

The rights of creditors with general claims are considered infra at pages 259–278.

** Section 542 requires the turnover of "property that the trustee may use, sell, or lease under section 363." Under section 363(b), the trustee may "use, sell, or lease" "property of the estate." Property of the estate includes "all legal or equitable interests of the debtor in property as of the commencement of the case," section 541(1). Under UCC section 9–506, the debtor has a right to redeem property repossessed by the secured party. Accordingly, it would seem that even property repossessed by the secured party on the default of the debtor is "property of the estate." Accordingly, it would seem that a secured party in possession of collateral is subject to section 542's turnover requirement.

To satisfy a secured claim by repossessing the encumbered property from the bankruptcy trustee, it is necessary to obtain relief from the automatic stay. The automatic stay and relief therefrom is considered supra at pages 150–160.

Section 554 authorizes the bankruptcy trustee to abandon property of the estate that is "burdensome to the estate or that is of inconsequential value to the estate." If property is subject to valid liens that secure claims that are greater than the value of the property, the bankruptcy trustee will usually abandon the property, and the creditors with valid liens may then proceed against the property.

If, however, the bankruptcy court does not modify the automatic stay to permit the creditor to foreclose its lien or abandon the encumbered property, the encumbered property will be sold by the bankruptcy trustee, section 704(1). The trustee will usually sell the property free and clear of liens.† Section 363(f) authorizes the trustee to sell property of the estate free and clear of the lien of a secured creditor if:

(1) Applicable nonbankruptcy law permits it; *or*

(2) The secured creditor consents; *or*

† In the unlikely event that the encumbered property is sold subject to liens, the creditor with a secured claim may enforce its lien against the encumbered property in the hands of the buyer.

(3) The sales price of the encumbered property is greater than the amount of the secured claim; *or*

(4) The secured creditor could be compelled to accept a money satisfaction of the lien in a legal or equitable proceeding. If encumbered property is sold free and clear of liens, the creditor with a secured claim receives the proceeds from the sale less the costs that the bankruptcy trustee incurs in preserving and selling the property, sections 725, 506(c). In the unlikely event that the net proceeds of such a sale exceeds the amount of the creditor's claim, the creditor may also recover interest and reasonable fees, costs, or charges provided under the agreement out of which the secured claim arises, section 506(b).

D. POSTPONEMENT OF TAX LIENS

A government's claim for taxes is generally secured by a statutory lien.* These statutory tax liens are not always valid in bankruptcy. For example, an unfiled federal tax lien can be invalidated by the bankruptcy trustee under section 544(a).** If a claim for taxes is unsecured, it is

---

* Federal tax liens are considered supra at pages 104–114.

** An unfiled federal tax lien is not valid as against a creditor with a judicial lien, IRC 6323(a). Section 544(a) gives the bankruptcy trustee the rights and powers of a creditor that obtained a judicial lien as of the date that the bankruptcy petition was filed. Accordingly, if the federal

governed by section 507(a)(6) and may be entitled to a "sixth priority." †

In a Chapter 7 proceeding, if a claim for taxes is secured by a lien that is valid in the bankruptcy, it is governed by section 724(b). Senator De Concini has described the effect of section 724(b) as follows: "In effect, a tax claim secured by a lien is treated as a claim between the fifth and sixth priority in a case under Chapter 7, rather than as a secured claim." Congressional Record, October 6, 1978, S. 17415.

Section 724(b) postpones payment of an indefeasible tax lien until after the complete payment of all claims entitled to priority under section 507(a)(1)–(5). The following problems illustrate the application of section 724(b).

1. The debtor has property worth $4,000. This property is subject to a properly recorded tax lien for $3,000. The debtor also has $3,000 of debts entitled to priority under section 507(a)(1)–(5) and $5,000 of general unsecured debts. The distribution in Chapter 5 would be

$3,000 to the section 507(a)(1)–(5) claimants

$1,000 to the tax lienor.

tax lien has not been filed prior to bankruptcy, the bankruptcy trustee may invalidate the lien under section 544(a). Section 544(a) is considered supra at pages —, —.

† The priority provisions of section 507 are considered infra at pages 272–276.

2. Same facts as # 1 except that the property is also subject to a $2,000 security interest. Under non-bankruptcy law, the security interest is junior in right to the nonpossessory tax lien. The distribution in Chapter 7 would be

$3,000 to 507(a)(1)-(5) claimants

$1,000 to the junior security interest

[See section 724(b)(4). Note that the junior secured creditor is receiving exactly the same amount that it would have received if section 724(b) had not been applicable. Section 724(b) results in different claims being paid prior to the junior indefeasible lien, but the amount so paid is not affected by section 724(b).]

3. Same facts as # 2 except that the amount of the claims entitled to a section 507(a)(1)-(5) priority is $6,000. The distribution in Chapter 7 would be

$3,000 to section 507(a)(1)-(5) claimants

$1,000 to the junior security interest

4. Same facts as # 2 except that the amount of the claims entitled to a section 507(a)(1)-(5) priority is only $1,400. The distribution in Chapter 7 would be

$1,400 to section 507(a)(1)-(5) claimants

$1,600 to the tax lienor

$1,000 to the junior security interest
[See section 724(b)(3).]

5. Same facts as # 1 except that the property is real property and is also subject to a $3,000 mortgage. Under non-bankruptcy law, this mortgage is senior in right to the tax lien. The distribution in bankruptcy would be

$3,000 for the senior mortgage

$1,000 to section 507(a)(1)–(5) claimants [See section 724(b)(1).]

The above combinations do not exhaust all possible section 724(b) problems. In resolving other section 724(b) problems remember that the amount distributed to a claim secured by an indefeasible non-tax lien is neither increased nor decreased by the application of section 724(b); such creditors should receive the same distribution they would receive if section 724(b) were not applicable.

E. OTHER PROVISIONS AFFECTING SECURED CLAIMS

There are a number of other provisions in the Bankruptcy Reform Act of 1978 that affect the rights of creditors with secured claims.

Section 363 empowers the bankruptcy trustee to use property subject to a valid in bankruptcy lien.

Section 554 limits a floating lien to property acquired by the debtor before the filing of the bankruptcy petition, the proceeds thereof, and the rents and profits therefrom. Even if the security agreement creating the lien contains a comprehensive after-acquired property clause, the security interest does not reach additional property obtained by the debtor after the filing of the bankruptcy petition.

Under section 364, the bankruptcy court may authorize the trustee to incur debt secured by liens that will have a priority over all pre-bankruptcy liens.

These provisions are of real practical significance only if the business of the debtor continues in operation. While the trustee may be authorized to continue operating a business in a Chapter 7 proceeding,* operation of business problems under sections 363, 554, and 364 arise primarily in Chapter 11 proceedings. Accordingly, these provisions are discussed in connection with Chapter 11 on pages 285–290.

---

* Under section 721, the court may authorize the trustee to operate the business for a limited period if it is in the best interests of the estate.

X. CHAPTER 7 AND GENERAL CLAIMS

A. WHAT IS A GENERAL CLAIM?

A creditor has a claim if it has a "right to payment, whether or not such right is reduced to judgment, liquidated, unliquidated, fixed, contingent, matured, unmatured, disputed, undisputed, legal, equitable, secured, or unsecured," section 101(4). The creditor's claim is a general claim if the creditor has not obtained a consensual, judicial or statutory lien or if the value of the property subject to the creditor's lien is less than the amount of the creditor's claim, section 506(a).

Consider the following examples of general claims:

1. X tortiously injures Y. Y sues X. X files a bankruptcy petition while the tort litigation is pending. Y is a creditor with a general claim.

2. A provides diaper service to B. B files a bankruptcy petition. At the time of the bankruptcy petition, B owes A $200 for diaper service. A is a creditor with a general claim.

3. D borrows $30,000 from S. S obtains and records a mortgage on real property owned by D to secure the loan. D files a bankruptcy petition. At the time of the petition, D still owes S $30,000, and the encumbered real property has a

value of $13,000. S is a creditor with a general claim.*

B. COLLECTION OF GENERAL CLAIMS FROM THE DEBTOR

Under section 362, the filing of a Chapter 7 petition operates as a "stay." This automatic stay prevents a creditor from collecting its unsecured claim from the debtor until the bankruptcy case is closed. The automatic stay and relief therefrom is considered on pages 150–160, supra.

Under section 727, the bankruptcy court generally grants the debtor a "discharge." This discharge prevents a creditor from collecting its claim from the debtor after the bankruptcy case is closed. The discharge and exceptions thereto is considered supra on pages 232–248.

The section 362 stay coupled with the section 727 discharge makes it necessary for most holders of general claims to look to the "property of the estate" for the satisfaction of their claims.

---

* S is also a creditor with a secured claim. The rights of holders of secured claims in a Chapter 7 proceeding are considered supra at pages 249–258.

C. COLLECTION OF GENERAL CLAIMS FROM THE PROPERTY OF THE ESTATE

1. WHAT PROPERTY IS DISTRIBUTED TO HOLDERS OF GENERAL CLAIMS

The bankruptcy trustee has a statutory duty to sell the "property of the estate," * section 704(1). The net proceeds received from the liquidation of the "property of the estate" is to be distributed to the holders of unsecured or general claims. Such claimants do not, however, receive the net proceeds from the sale of all of the "property of the estate":

1. Some "property of the estate" will be turned over to the debtor as exempt property, section 522.

2. Some "property of the estate" will be transferred after the filing of the bankruptcy petition to third parties protected by section 549.

---

* Property of the estate is controlled by section 541. Section 541 is considered supra at pages 161–164. Remember that property of the estate includes:

    1. The non-exempt property interests of the debtor at the time of the filing of the bankruptcy petition;

    2. Property recovered by the trustee as a result of invalidating pre-petition transfers

    3. Property recovered by the trustee as a result of invalidating pre-petition transfers;

Subject to the limited exceptions noted on page 163, property of the estate does not include property acquired by the debtor after the filing of the bankruptcy petition.

3. Some "property of the estate" will be subject to liens that are valid in bankruptcy. Encumbered property or the proceeds thereof must be first used to satisfy the holders of secured claims, section 725.

4. Some "property of the estate" must be used to satisfy the administrative expenses of the bankruptcy proceeding.

Subject to these four exceptions, holders of general claims receive the net proceeds from the bankruptcy trustee's sale of the "property of the estate."

2. WHICH HOLDERS OF GENERAL CLAIMS PARTICIPATE IN THE DISTRIBUTION OF PROPERTY OF THE ESTATE

a. PROOF OF CLAIM

In a case under Chapter 7 of the Bankruptcy Reform Act of 1978, the debtor will file a list of creditors, section 521. The court will then send notice of the Chapter 7 proceeding to the listed creditors, section 342. The creditors that wish to participate in the distribution of the proceeds of the liquidation of the "property of the estate" will file a proof of claim, sections 501, 726.

Under the Bankruptcy Act of 1898, most of the requirements as to form, content and procedure for proofs of claim are found in the Bankruptcy Rules. This is also the approach of the Bankruptcy Reform Act of 1978. For example, there is no statutory language governing the time for filing a proof of claim. Section 501 simply speaks of "timely filing." Remember that by virtue of section 405 (d) of Title IV, the current rules will continue to be applicable to cases under the new act until new rules are presented to the Supreme Court. Thus, until new Bankruptcy Rules have been promulgated, the six months after the first date for the first creditors' meeting time requirement of Rule 302 (e) will control.

Section 501 (e) authorizes the debtor to file a proof of claim for a creditor who does not timely file. This provision is primarily intended to protect the debtor if the claim of the creditor is nondischargeable. When no proof of claim is filed, there will be no bankruptcy distribution to the holder of the claim. If no bankruptcy distribution is made to the holder of a claim excepted from discharge, the debtor will have to pay the claim in full after the bankruptcy case is closed. If, however, the debtor files a proof of claim, the holder of the nondischargeable claim will participate in the bankruptcy distribution and the post-bankruptcy liability of the debtor to the creditor will be reduced by the amount of distribution.

To illustrate, assume that Richard Fetter of Fort Lee, New Jersey files a Chapter 7 petition. He owes New Jersey Bank $10,000. New Jersey Bank made the loan to Fetter because of a false financial statement; its claim against Fetter is excepted from discharge.* If no proof of claim is filed by or for New Jersey Bank, it will have a $10,000 claim against Fetter after the close of the Chapter 7 proceeding. If, however, Fetter files a proof of claim for New Jersey Bank, its post-bankruptcy claim against him will be reduced by the amount it receives in the bankruptcy distribution.

b. ALLOWANCE

In a Chapter 7 proceeding, the proceeds of the liquidation of the property of the estate is not distributed to all holders of unsecured claims against the debtor. Rather, the distribution is only made to unsecured creditors whose claims are "allowed," section 726.**

If a proof of claim has been filed, the claim is deemed allowed "unless a party in interest objects," section 502(b). The statute does not define "party in interest"; clearly, another creditor

---

* Section 523(a)(2) excepts from discharge claims based on credit extended in reliance on a false financial statement. Section 523(a)(2) is considered supra at page 239.

** Under the Bankruptcy Act of 1898, only claims that were both allowable and *provable* were permitted to participate in the bankruptcy distribution. The requirement of provability excluded certain tort claims and certain other contingent and unliquidated claims from sharing in the distribution of the proceeds from the liquidation of the bankrupt estate, section 63. The Bankruptcy Reform Act of 1978 eliminates the requirement of provability. Tort claims and other contingent and unliquidated claims may participate in the bankruptcy distribution, of sections 502(b)(1), 502(c).

or the bankruptcy trustee is a "party interest" for purposes of objections to allowance of a claim.

The statute does set out nine grounds for disallowing claims in section 502(b):

1. If the claim is unenforceable against the debtor or the property of the debtor by reason of any agreement or applicable law, it will not be allowed, section 502(b)(1).

[A non-recourse loan is an example of an agreement which makes a claim unenforceable; UCC section 2–302 is an example of a law which makes a claim unenforceable.]

2. A claim for unearned interest will be disallowed, section 502(b)(2).

3. The claim will be disallowed if it may be offset under section 553 as a debt owing to the debtor,*** section 502(b)(3).

4. If a claim is for an ad valorem property tax, it will not be allowed to the extent that the claim exceeds the value of the estate's interest in the property, section 502(b)(4).

5. If the claim is for services of debtor's attorney or an "insider," † it will be disallowed to the extent the claim exceeds the reasonable value of such services, section 502(b)(5).

*** Setoffs are considered supra at pages 189–196.

† "Insider" is defined in section 101(25). "Insider" includes the relatives of an individual debtor; the partners of a partnership debtor; the officers, directors, and other control persons of a corporate debtor.

6. If the claim is for post-petition alimony or child support, it will not be allowed, section 502(b)(6).††

7. If the claim is that of a landlord for future rent, it will be limited to the greater of one year's payments or 15% of the payments for the balance of the lease, not to exceed three years' payments in total, section 502(b)(7).

(Note that section 502(b)(7) only limits the allowance of claims for future rentals by a lessor of *real* property.* It does not affect a claim for

†† These claims are excepted from discharge under section 523(a)(5). The following hypothetical illustrates the application of sections 502(b)(6) and 523(a)(5).

H and W are divorced in January of 1979. The divorce decree orders H to pay alimony of $1,000 a month. H files a bankruptcy petition on December 31, 1979. He owes W $2,000 for November and December alimony.

W's claims for $2,000 of unpaid 1979 alimony is allowable. Section 502(b)(6) only disallows a claim for alimony that is "unmatured on the date of the filing of the petition." Accordingly, W's claim for 1980, 1981, * * * alimony is disallowed.

If W's claim for $2,000 of unpaid 1979 alimony is not fully satisfied by the bankruptcy distribution, W may attempt to collect any deficiency from H personally. Section 523(a)(5) excepts alimony claims from the bankruptcy discharge. Accordingly, H's bankruptcy discharge will not affect W's right to collect 1980, 1981, * * * alimony from H personally.

* Section 502(b)(7) does not limit the amount of a claim for future rents of personal property. Section 547(e) suggests that the Bankruptcy Reform Act of 1978 considers "fixtures" to be real property. If so, section 502(b)(7) would apply to a claim by a lessor of equipment that was installed in such a manner as to become a fixture under state law.

rentals due on or before the filing of the bankruptcy petition. It does not affect a claim for rentals under a lease of personal property.

Note also that section 502(b)(7) does not guarantee an allowable claim for back rent plus a minimum of one year's rent; rather, it places a ceiling on the allowance of rent claims.

The following three hypotheticals illustrate the application of section 502(b)(7):

1. D rented Redacre from L under a 20-year lease at a monthly rental of $1,000 a month. At the time D filed her Chapter 7 petition, the lease had 60 months to run. The bankruptcy trustee rejected the lease.** In his proof of claim, L contended that Redacre had a rental value at the time of the filing of the bankruptcy petition of only $600 a month. L thus claims damages for future rentals of $24,000 [60 × ($1,000 − $600)]. Section 502(b)(7) limits L's claim for future rents to one year's rent, $12,000.

2. Same facts as #1 except that at the time that D filed her Chapter 7 petition, the lease had 120 months to run. Section 502(b)(7) limits L's claim for future rents to $18,000. [15% × ($1,000 × 120)].

3. Same facts as # 1 except that when the bankruptcy trustee rejected the lease, L leased

** Rejection of leases by the bankruptcy trustee is considered supra at pages 170–174.

Redacre to T for 60 months at $2,000 a month. L has no claim for future rents.)

8. If the claim is for damages resulting from the breach by the debtor of an employment contract, recovery of compensation under the contract will be limited to the amount due for one year following the earlier of the date of the petition or the date of termination of employment, section 502(b)(8).

9. If the claim is a federal tax claim which arises because the state unemployment tax is paid late and so no federal tax credit is allowed, the federal claim will be treated the same as if the credit had been allowed in full in the federal return, which means the federal tax claim would be disallowed, section 502(b)(9).

The fact that a claim is contingent or unliquidated at the time that the bankruptcy petition is filed does not affect its allowance, section 502(b)(1). The bankruptcy court may either delay bankruptcy distribution until the claim is fixed in amount, or, if liquidation of the claim would "unduly delay the closing of the case," estimate the amount of the claim, section 502(c). Assume, for example, that V files a $100,000 tort suit against T. T immediately files a bankruptcy petition. V then files a proof of claim. V's claim is allowable. The bankruptcy court may either delay distribution to T's creditors and the closing of T's bankruptcy case until V's tort claim has been litigated or estimate the amount of V's claim.

Generally, only claims that arise before the bankruptcy petition are allowable. If, for example, D files a voluntary bankruptcy petition on January 11, and C lends D $100 on February 2, C's claim is not allowable.

There are four exceptions to the rule that only claims that predate the bankruptcy petition are allowable:

1. In an involuntary case, claims arising in the ordinary course of the debtor's business after the commencement of the case but before the earlier of the appointment of a trustee or the order for relief will be allowed as if the claim had arisen before the bankruptcy petition, section 502(f).

2. Claims arising from the rejection of an executory contract or unexpired lease of the debtor are allowed as if the claim had arisen before the date of the filing of the petition, section 502(g).

3. A claim arising from the recovery of property because of a voidable preference or fraudulent conveyance or setoff will be determined and allowed as though it were a pre-petition claim, section 502(h).*

---

* To illustrate, assume that on January 11, D repays C the $1,000 he owes her. On February 2, D files a bankruptcy petition. On May 5, D's bankruptcy trustee recovers the $1,000 from C as a section 547 preference. Under section 502(h), C has an allowable claim for $1,000.

4. A claim that does not arise until after the commencement of the case for a tax entitled to the sixth priority shall be treated as if the claim had arisen before the date of the filing of the petition, section 502(i).

Before a case is closed, a claim that has been allowed may be reconsidered for cause and reallowed or disallowed according to the equities of the case, section 502(j).

3. ORDER OF DISTRIBUTION

There are a number of statements in reported cases, law review articles, and legal texts praising the theme of equality of distribution to creditors in bankruptcy proceedings. Such statements must be using the term "equality" in the *Animal Farm* sense; in bankruptcy, some creditors are clearly "more equal" than others. Some unsecured claims must be fully satisfied before any distribution is made to other unsecured claims.

Section 726 establishes the rules for distribution in a Chapter 7 proceeding to the holders of unsecured claims. Basically, the distribution is to be as follows:

(1) priorities under section 507 (section 507 is considered below)

(2) allowed unsecured claims which were either timely filed or tardily filed by a creditor who did not know of the bankruptcy

(3) allowed unsecured claims which were tardily filed by creditors with notice or actual knowledge of the bankruptcy

(4) fines and punitive damages

(5) post-petition interest on pre-petition claims.

Each claim of each of the five classes must be paid in full before any claim in the next class receives any distribution. Each claimant within a particular class shares pro rata if the proceeds from the liquidation of the property of the estate is insufficient to satisfy all claims in that class.

Assume, for example, that there is $20,000 available to pay to holders of general claims and the following general claims:

$11,000—claims entitled to priority under section 507

$4,800—claim by X that was timely filed

$7,200—claim by Y that was timely filed

$3,000—claim by Z that was not timely filed even though Z knew of the bankruptcy proceedings.

The distribution would be:

$11,000 to holders of priority claims

$3,600 to X *

$5,400 to Y.

---

* The first $11,000 must be used to pay priority claims. The remaining $9,000 ($20,000 – $11,000) must be

CHAPTER 7 AND GENERAL CLAIMS

In the very unlikely event that the sale of the "property of the estate" yields enough to satisfy each claim in each of the five "classes" listed above, the surplus is paid to the debtor.

a. PRIORITIES

The task of distributing the proceeds from the sale of the property of the estate is complicated by the fact that claims do not come neatly labelled "claims entitled to priority under section 507." Instead, it is necessary to recognize which claims are entitled to priority under section 507.

In the typical Chapter 7 proceeding, administrative expenses allowed under section 503(b) and fees and charges assessed against an estate under Chapter 123 of Title 28 are accorded first priority,* section 507(b)(1). Administrative ex-

distributed pro rata to $12,000 ($4,800 + $7,200) of timely filed claims. Accordingly, each timely filed claim will be paid at the rate of 75¢ on the dollar. ($9,000/$12,000). Accordingly, X will receive $3,600 for its $4,800 claim.

* Section 364(c) empowers the bankruptcy court to authorize a bankruptcy trustee or debtor in possession to obtain credit or incur debt that has a priority over all administrative expenses. Section 364(c) is considered infra at page 286.

Section 507(b) grants a holder of a secured claim whose "adequate protection" proved to be less than adequate a "superiority" over all administrative expenses. "Adequate protection" is considered supra at pages 155, 158; section 507(b) is considered supra at page 157.

These provisions apply only if the bankruptcy trustee or a Chapter 11 debtor in possession is authorized to operate the business. In the typical Chapter 7 case, the bankruptcy trustee is *not* authorized to operate the business. Ac-

penses include the costs of maintaining, repairing, storing, and selling the property of the estate; taxes the trustee incurs in administering property of the estate; the trustee's fee; the debtor's attorney's fees; the trustee's attorney's fee; and limited expenses of certain creditors.

In the typical Chapter 7 proceeding,** each section 507(b)(1) administrative expense claimant shares pro rata if the proceeds from the sale of the property of the estate is less than the total amount of all claims entitled to this priority. If the proceeds from the sale of the property of the estate is more than the total amount of all claims entitled to a first priority, second priority claims are next paid.

In an involuntary case, the second priority is accorded to claims arising in the ordinary course of the debtor's business after the commencement of the case but before the earlier of the appointment of a trustee or the order for relief. For example, the creditors of an all-night Chinese res-

cordingly, in a typical Chapter 7 case, sections 364(c) and 507(b) do not apply. Accordingly, in a typical Chapter 7 case, administrative expenses are accorded a first priority after indefeasible liens.

** Some Chapter 7 cases start as Chapter 11 or Chapter 13 cases and are converted to Chapter 7, sections 1112, 1307. In such a proceeding, the administrative expenses incurred in the Chapter 7 liquidation are paid in full before any payment is made for the administrative expenses incurred while the case was under Chapter 11 or 13, section 726(b).

taurant, Wok Around the Clock, Inc., file an involuntary Chapter 7 petition on January 11. On January 12, T. Hee makes his usual weekly delivery of Chinese vegetables to Wok Around the Clock, Inc. Mr. Hee's claim will be entitled to a second priority under section 507(b)(2).

Section 507(b)(2) only applies in involuntary bankruptcy cases. If the Chapter 7 proceeding was debtor-initiated, or if all second priority claims are satisfied, it is necessary to look to the third priority.

Section 507(b)(3) grants a third priority to wage claims. This third priority includes claims for vacation pay, severance pay, and sick leave pay. It is subject to two limitations:

(1) Time—only compensation earned within 90 days before the bankruptcy petition. (If the debtor's business ceased operations before the bankruptcy petition, the 90 day period is measured from the cessation of business operations.)

(2) Amount—only $2,000 per employer.

Assume, for example, that Temple Beth Putz files a Chapter 7 petition on December 31. It owes its rabbi, Baruch Korff, $5,000 for November and December salary. $2,000 of Rabbi Korff's wage claim would be entitled to a third priority under section 507(b)(3); the remaining $3,000 of his claim would be a general claim.

Claims for contributions to employee benefit plans receive a fourth priority under section 507(b)(4). This priority for fringe benefits is also subject to time and amount limitations:

(1) Time—only for services rendered within 120 days of the bankruptcy petition. (If the debtor's business ceased operations before the bankruptcy petition, the 120 days is measured from the cessation of business operation.)

(2) Amount—[$2,000 × number of employees] − total payment to employees under section 507(a)(3) + total payments to other employee benefit plans.]

Note that payments under section 507(a)(4) will be made to the benefit plan, not directly to individual employees. Note also that section 507(a)(4) focuses on the aggregate of other payments to all employees covered by the plan, not the payments to an individual employee.

Section 507(b)(5) grants a fifth priority to consumers who made a money deposit for property or services that were never provided. If, for instance, D pays $2,500 for five years of dance lessons at C Dance Studios, Inc., and C files a Chapter 7 petition before providing dance lessons, $900 of D's claim will be entitled to a fifth priority. The fifth priority is limited in amount to $900 per claimant.

Certain specified tax claims enjoy a sixth priority.* Taxes entitled to this sixth priority include:

> (1) income taxes for the three tax years immediately preceding the filing of the bankruptcy petition,** and

> (2) property taxes assessed before the filing of the bankruptcy petition and last payable without a penalty one year before that date, and

> (3) if the debtor is an employer, taxes withheld from employees' paychecks.

To review, section 507(b) establishes six classes of priority claims. Each claim of a class must be paid in full before any claim in the next class receives any distribution. After all of the priority claims have been fully satisfied, distributions are made to general claims that are timely filed, section 726(a)(2).

---

* Remember that under section 724(b), a tax claim secured by an indefeasible lien is paid after fifth priority claims but before sixth priority claims. Section 724(b) is considered supra at pages 255–257.

** The three-year period is measured from the last date including extensions for filing a return to the date of the bankruptcy petition. If, for example, D files a bankruptcy petition on April 15, 1980, claims for taxes for 1979, 1978, and 1977 would be entitled to a priority. If, however, D files a bankruptcy petition on December 7, 1980, only claims for taxes for 1979 and 1978 would be entitled to a priority.

b. SUBORDINATION

Section 507, the priority provision, has the effect of moving certain specified claims to the head of the line. Section 510, the subordination provision, has the effect of moving some claims further back in the line.*

Section 510 requires subordination in two instances:

> (1) when there is a subordination agreement that would be enforceable under nonbankruptcy law, section 510(a)
>
> (2) when a seller or purchaser of equity securities seeks damages or rescission, section 510(b).

Additionally, the court has the discretion after notice and hearing to subordinate any claim to other claim or claims "under principles of equitable subordination," section 510(c). According to legislative history, these equitable principles are defined by case law. A student note summarized the case law on equitable subordination as follows:

"The federal courts have employed equity powers to subordinate claims valid under state law in two broad classes of cases. Where a claimant has engaged in inequitable conduct toward other

---

* Section 726 which governs the order of distribution in a Chapter 7 case is prefaced "Except as provided in section 510."

claimants, the bankruptcy court will often subordinate his claim. * * * Secondly, courts have subordinated valid claims of persons holding positions of control whose actions have caused damage to the estate." Note, Bankruptcy: Power to Subordinate on Equitable Grounds Claims Valid Under State Law, 67 Colum.L.Rev. 583, 586–7 (1967).

XI. CHAPTER 11

The Bankruptcy Act of 1898 contains four separate chapters for the reorganization of businesses: Chapter VIII which deals with railroad reorganizations; Chapter IX which covers corporate reorganizations; Chapter XI for the arrangement of unsecured debts by corporations, partnerships and individuals; and Chapter XII which is available to non-corporate debtors who own encumbered real estate. Chapter 11 of the Bankruptcy Reform Act of 1898 replaces these four chapters.* It contains some principles from each of the above chapters and some new concepts.

A. COMMENCEMENT OF THE CASE

1. FILING THE PETITION

A case under Chapter 11 is commenced by the filing of a petition. The petition may be filed by either the debtor or creditors.

Insolvency is not a condition precedent to a voluntary Chapter 11 proceeding. With two exceptions, any person that is eligible to file a voluntary bankruptcy petition under Chapter 7 is also eligible to file a petition under Chapter 11. The first exception is stockbrokers and commodi-

---

* Chapter 13 is also available to certain business debtors, i. e., "individuals with a regular income" and less than $100,000 of unsecured debts and $350,000 of secured debts. Chapter 13 is considered infra at pages 303–315.

ty brokers: they are eligible for Chapter 7, but not Chapter 11. The second exception is railroads: railroads are eligible for Chapter 11, but not Chapter 7.

If the Chapter 11 petition has been filed by an eligible debtor, no formal adjudication is necessary. The filing of the petition operates as an "order for relief," section 301.

The requirements for a creditor-initiated Chapter 11 case are the same as the requirements for an involuntary Chapter 7 case, section 303. These requirements are discussed supra at pages 146–149.

2. NOTIFYING AND ORGANIZING THE CREDITORS

How will creditors learn of a Chapter 11 proceeding? Sections 521 and 342 provide a partial answer. The new rules will furnish the rest of the answer.

Section 521 obligates the debtor to file a list of creditors. Section 342 requires appropriate notice of the order for relief. The Rules will prescribe to whom the notice should be sent and in what manner the notice must be given. It is safe to assume that the Rules will require that all creditors scheduled by the debtor be informed of the Chapter 11 case.

Generally, a creditor whose claim is included on a Chapter 11 debtor's list of creditors will not have to file a proof of claim. Unless the claim is scheduled as disputed, contingent or unliquidated, a proof of claim is "deemed" filed by section 1111(a). A creditor holding a claim that is scheduled as disputed, contingent, or unliquidated does have to file a proof of claim. The rules will establish the time for filing such proofs of claim.

The Bankruptcy Reform Act of 1978 requires a meeting of creditors "within a reasonable time after the order for relief," section 341. The Act provides little information about the purposes of and procedures for such a meeting. Section 343 indicates that the debtor is to be examined under oath at the meeting. Section 341(c) prohibits the bankruptcy judge from presiding at or attending the meeting.* Other details will be provided by the Rules.

In most Chapter 11 cases, the debtor has hundreds if not thousands of creditors. In these cases, it would not be practical for the debtor to attempt to negotiate with each creditor individually. Accordingly, section 1102 directs the bankruptcy court to appoint a committee of unsecured creditors as soon as practicable after the order for relief.** A pre-petition creditors' committee

---

* This prohibition is consistent with the Bankruptcy Reform Act of 1978's goal of limiting the judge to adjudicatory functions. At a creditors' meeting, the judge might obtain a great deal of extraneous information without the constraints of adversarial trial procedure.

** Under Chapter XI of the Bankruptcy Act of 1898, creditors' committee were elected, not appointed. Profes-

will be continued if it was "fairly chosen and is representative of the different kinds of claims to be represented," section 1102(b)(1). In the absence of any such pre-petition committee, the court is instructed to appoint the seven largest unsecured creditors willing to serve, section 1102(b)(2). On request of a party in interest and after notice and hearing, the court may change the membership or size of a committee if it is not sufficiently representative, section 1102 (c).

A creditors' committee performs a number of functions. It may:

(1) consult with the trustee or debtor in possession† concerning the administration of the case

(2) investigate the debtors' acts and financial condition

(3) participate in the formulation of the plan

sor King suggests the following explanation and criticism of the change: "Too often in the past, attorneys sought creditor clients to obtain control of the election and to have themselves retained by the committee. Since election frequently served only the purposes of the attorneys, rather than the democratic process, changing to an appointment system was thought to be more appropriate. Unfortunately, section 1102(b)(1) leaves the door open to questionable practices by permitting the continuance of a pre-petition committee if it was fairly chosen and is 'representative of the different kinds of claims to be represented.'" King, *Chapter 11 of the 1978 Bankruptcy Code*, 53 Am. Bankr.L.J. 107, 112 (1979).

† Debtor in possession is considered infra at page 283.

(4) request the appointment of a trustee ††

(5) "perform such other services as are in the interest of those represented," section 1103(c). The creditors' committee may also appear at various hearings as a party in interest, section 1109(b). And, the committee may file a plan in those situations where the debtor ceases to have the exclusive right to do so, section 1121.*

B. OPERATION OF THE BUSINESS

Successful rehabilitation of a business under Chapter 11 generally requires the continued operation of the business. No court order is necessary in order to operate the debtor's business after the filing of a Chapter 11 petition. Section 1108 provides: "Unless the court orders otherwise, the trustee may operate the debtor's business."

1. WHO OPERATES THE BUSINESS

Notwithstanding section 1108's use of the word "trustee," the debtor will remain in control of the business in most Chapter 11 cases. Pre-bankruptcy management will continue to operate the business as a "debtor in possession" unless a request is made for the appointment of a trustee

††The appointment of a trustee in a Chapter 11 case is considered infra at page 284.

* The question of who may file a Chapter 11 plan is considered infra at page 290.

and the court, after notice and a hearing grants the request.

Section 1104 sets out the grounds for the appointment of a trustee. A trustee is to be appointed if there is cause (fraud, dishonesty, mismanagement, or incompetence) or if the appointment of a trustee is "in the interests of creditors, any equity security holders, and other interests of the estate." Section 1104 specifically instructs the court to disregard the number of shareholders or the amount of assets and liabilities of the debtor in deciding whether to appoint a trustee.

If a trustee is appointed, s/he must be "disinterested," as defined in section 101(13). The duties of a trustee are enumerated in section 1106. Essentially, the trustee has responsibility for the operation of the business and formulation of the Chapter 11 plan.

If a trustee is not appointed, the court may appoint an "examiner." Section 1104(b) sets out the requirements for the appointment of an examiner:

(1) a trustee was not appointed, *and*

(2) appointment of an examiner was requested by a party in interest, *and*

(3) the debtor's nontrade, nontax, unsecured debts exceed $5,000,000, *or* "such appointment is in the interests of creditors, any equity security holders, and other interests of the estate."

[284]

An "examiner" does not operate the business. Rather s/he investigates the competence and honesty of the debtor and files a report of the investigation, sections 1104(b), 1106(b).

2. OBTAINING CREDIT

One of the first problems confronting a debtor in possession or a Chapter 11 trustee is financing the operation of the business pending the formulation and approval of a plan of rehabilitation. Obtaining credit is essential to almost every Chapter 11 proceeding. Section 364 deals with obtaining credit. It provides a number of inducements to third parties to extend credit to a debtor that has filed a Chapter 11 petition.

A post-petition unsecured credit transaction in the Chapter 11 debtor's "ordinary course of business automatically has administrative expense priority* over pre-petition creditors, section 364(a). The court may, after notice and hearing, provide administrative expense priority for credit transactions that are not in the ordinary course of business, section 364(b).

If priority over pre-petition unsecured creditors is not a sufficient inducement, the bankruptcy court may, after notice and hearing, authorize obtaining credit with:

> (1) priority over other administrative expenses, *or*

---

* The priority afforded administrative expenses is considered supra at pages 272–273.

(2) a lien on the debtor's unencumbered property, *or*

(3) a lien on the debtor's encumbered property, section 364(c).

Section 364(d) is the "last resort" provision. If the debtor is unable to otherwise obtain credit, the court may authorize the debtor to grant its post-petition creditors a "superpriority," i. e., a lien on encumbered property that is equal or senior to existing liens. The court may authorize such a "superpriority" only if there is "adequate protection" of the pre-petition secured creditor's interest. "Adequate protection" is considered supra at pages 155–157.

3. USE OF ENCUMBERED PROPERTY

In the typical Chapter 11 proceeding, most of the personal and real property that the debtor owns at the time of the filing of the Chapter 11 petition is encumbered by liens.

The personal and real property that the debtor acquires after the filing of the Chapter 11 petition is protected from pre-petition liens. Property acquired by the debtor after it files a Chapter 11 petition will not be "subject to any lien resulting from any security agreement entered into by the debtor before the commencement of the case," section 552(a). After-acquired property clauses are not recognized in proceedings under the Bankruptcy Reform Act of 1978.

Assume, for example, that Reems Organ Co. files a Chapter 11 petition. If First Bank has contracted for a security interest in "all of Reems' inventory, now owned or hereafter acquired," section 552(a) will limit First's lien to organs manufactured by Reems before the Chapter 11 petition was filed.

First Bank's lien will probably also reach the proceeds from the sale of such pre-petition organs. The Bankruptcy Reform Act of 1978 does recognize a right to "products, proceeds, offsprings, rent, and profits," section 552(b). Under section 552(b), a pre-petition security interest continues to reach proceeds acquired after the bankruptcy proceeding was filed "except to the extent that the court, after notice and hearing based on the equities of the case orders otherwise." *

Section 362(a), considered supra at page 151, stays a creditor with a lien on the property of a Chapter 11 debtor from repossessing the encumbered property. Section 362(d), considered supra at page 153, provides for relief from the stay in limited situations.

Section 363 empowers the debtor in possession or trustee to continue using, selling, and leasing

---

* The "equities of the case" exception covers situations where property of the estate is used in converting the collateral into proceeds. If, for example, Reems incurs costs of $1,000 in selling organs for $7,000, the court may limit First Bank's lien on the proceeds to $6,000.

encumbered property. The interest of the lien creditor is safeguarded by section 363's requirement of "adequate protection," section 363(e). (The concept of "adequate protection" is dealt with by section 361. Section 361 is dealt with on pages 155–157.)

Encumbered property that is not "cash collateral" as defined in section 363(a) may be used, sold, or leased in the ordinary course of business without a prior judicial determination of "adequate protection," section 363(c)(1).** On "request" of the lien creditor, the court shall condition the use, sale, or lease of encumbered property so as to provide "adequate protection," section 363(e). In other words, if Calderwood Department Stores, Inc. files a Chapter 11 petition and Port Phillips Bank has a perfected security interest in Calderwood's inventory, Calderwood may continue to sell inventory in the ordinary course of business. Calderwood will not have to obtain court permission in order to make such sales; rather, Port Phillips Bank will have the burden of requesting the court to prohibit or condition such sales so as to provide "adequate protection" of the Bank's security interest.

** Section 363(c)(1) is applicable only if "the business of the debtor is authorized to be operated." In a Chapter 11 case, the trustee or debtor in possession is authorized to operate the business "unless the court orders otherwise," section 1108.

Notice and a hearing † on the issue of "adequate protection" is required before a Chapter 11 debtor uses, sells, or leases encumbered property in a manner that is *not* in the ordinary course of business, section 363(b). If for example, Calderwood Department Store, after filing its Chapter 11 petition, decides to discontinue its furniture department and wants to make a bulk sale of its furniture inventory, Port Phillips Bank must be first given notice and the opportunity for a hearing on the issue of "adequate protection."

Encumbered "cash collateral" may only be used if the court after notice and hearing on adequate protection authorizes such use, section 363(c)(2). "Cash collateral" is defined in section 363(a): "cash, negotiable instruments, documents of title, securities, deposit accounts, or other cash equivalents." A bank account is "cash collateral"; accounts receivable are not. Accordingly, Calderwood Department Store may not withdraw funds from its bank account to pay employees or the utilities without bankruptcy court authorization. And, Calderwood Department Store may not spend the cash it receives from post-petition sales of inventory without such authorization. Unless the debtor in possession or trustee is authorized to use cash collateral, all such cash collateral

---

†Remember that "notice and hearing" means "such notice as is appropriate in the particular circumstances and such *opportunity* for a hearing as is appropriate in the particular circumstances," section 102(1)(a).

coming into the debtor in possession or trustee's possession must be segregated and accounted for, section 363(c)(4).

C. PREPARATION OF THE PLAN OF REHABILITATION

1. WHO PREPARES THE PLAN

A Chapter 11 plan may be filed at the same time as the petition or any time thereafter. Unless a trustee has been appointed, the debtor has the exclusive right to file a Chapter 11 plan. "Only a debtor may file a plan until after 120 days after the date of the order for relief under this chapter," section 1121(b). If the debtor does file a plan within this 120 day period, no other plan may be filed during the first 180 days of the case, section 1121(c)(3).* Section 1121(d) empowers the bankruptcy court to extend or reduce the 120 day and 180 day periods. For example, in a complex case such as W. T. Grant these times may not be sufficient.

If a trustee is appointed, the trustee, the debtor, a creditor, the creditors' committee, and any other party in interest may file a plan, section 1121(c). More than one plan may be filed. Sim-

---

* Note that the time is to be measured from the date of the order of relief, not the date that the Chapter 11 plan was filed. Assume, for example, that D files a Chapter 11 petition on January 12, and files its Chapter 11 plan on February 22. No other plan may be filed until after July 11 (180 days from January 12).

ilarly, if the debtor fails to file a plan and obtain creditor acceptances** within the specified time periods, any party in interest may file a plan and more than one plan may be filed.

Regardless of who files the plan, the creditors' committee will probably play a major role in formulating the plan, cf. section 1103(c)(3).

2. TERMS OF THE PLAN

Section 1123 governs the provisions of a Chapter 11 plan. Subparagraph (a) sets out the mandatory provisions of a Chapter 11 plan ("shall"); subparagraph (b) of section 1123 indicates the permissive provisions of a Chapter 11 plan ("may").

A Chapter 11 plan may alter the rights of unsecured creditors, secured creditors, and/or shareholders. A Chapter 11 plan will not treat each creditor the same. Section 1123 contemplates that the plan will divide creditors' claims into classes and treat each claim in a particular class the same.

Section 1122 indicates that claims in the same class will be "substantially similar." Small claims may be put in a separate class for the purpose of providing in payment, in full, section 1121(b).*

** Acceptance of a Chapter 11 plan by creditors is considered infra at pages 293–298.

* A Chapter 11 debtor will often find it advantageous to pay small claims in full. A class of claims that receives full cash payment on the effective date of the plan is not

If creditor X has a mortgage on Redacre and Creditor X a security interest in equipment, Creditor X will be in a different class from Creditor Y. If, however, Banks A, B, and C participate in a loan to D secured by a lien on Redacre, then A, B, and C will be in the same class.

3. FUNDING FOR THE PLAN

Compliance with the requirements of section 1123 is not the difficult part of preparing a plan for the rehabilitation of a business under Chapter 11. Rather, the hard questions are how much will creditors be offered by the plan and how will the plan be effectuated.

Chapter 11 debtors often use money borrowed from third parties to make distributions to creditors under Chapter 11 plans. Sale of assets is another major source for Chapter 11 payments.

A Chapter 11 plan may provide for the sale of all or substantially all of the debtor's assets, section 1123(b)(4). Under most states' corporate codes, a sale of all or substantially all of the assets requires board of director and shareholder approval. Section 1142 seems to excuse compliance with such state law requirements in carrying out a Chapter 11 plan.

"impaired," section 1124(a)(3). "A class that is not impaired under the plan is deemed to have accepted the plan, and solicitation of acceptances with respect to such class * * * is not required," section 1126(f).

Often, a Chapter 11 plan offers creditors the debtor's debt or equity securities, rather than cash. Generally, the issuance of a security requires expensive and time-consuming federal and state registration. Section 1145(a)(1) exempts the issuance of the debtor's securities under a Chapter 11 plan from federal and state registration requirements. A creditor's resale of a security received under a Chapter 11 is also exempted from federal and state registration requirements, section 1145(b).*

D. ACCEPTANCE

1. DISCLOSURE

"The premise underlying * * * Chapter 11 * * * is the same as the premise of the securities law. If adequate disclosure is provided to all creditors and stockholders whose rights are to be affected, then they should be able to make an informed judgment of their own, rather than having the court or the Securities and Exchange Commission inform them in advance whether the proposed plan is a good plan," H.R. 95–595, p. 226. Accordingly, the bankruptcy court does not review a Chapter 11 plan before it is submitted to creditors and shareholders for vote. Instead, the

* Section 4(1) of the Securities Act of 1933 states in essence that transactions by any person who is not an "issuer, underwriter, or dealer" need not be registered. Section 1145(b)(2) provides an exemption to creditors who resell securities obtained under a Chapter 11 plan by indicating that such creditors are not "underwriters."

bankruptcy court reviews the information provided to creditors and shareholders to insure that their judgment is an "informed judgment."

Section 1125 requires full disclosure before post-petition solicitation of acceptances of a Chapter 11 plan. Creditors and shareholders must be provided:

> (1) a copy of the plan or a summary of the plan, and

> (2) "a written disclosure statement approved, after notice and a hearing, by the court as containing adequate information."

Section 1125(b).

"Adequate information" is defined in section 1125(a) as information which it is "reasonably practicable" for this debtor to provide to enable a "hypothetical reasonable investor" who is typical of the holder of the claims or interests to make an informed judgment on the plan. What constitutes "adequate information" thus depends on the circumstances of each case—on factors such as (1) the condition of the debtor's books or records, (2) the sophistication of the creditors and stockholders, and (3) the nature of the plan.

The Bankruptcy Rules will provide the details about the time and form of the hearing on the disclosure statement. If the debtor is a large, public corporation, the Securities and Exchange Commission will probably participate in the disclosure hearing, sections 1109(a), 1125(d).

ACCEPTANCE

Section 1125(d) exempts Chapter 11 disclosure statements from the requirements of federal securities laws such as the proxy rules of Section 14 of the Securities Exchange Act of 1934 and from similar state securities laws. Section 1125(e) protects those who prepare disclosure statements and solicit acceptances in "good faith and in compliance with the applicable provisions of (the bankruptcy act)" from liability under the federal securities law or other non-bankruptcy laws.

Non-bankruptcy law is more relevant to *pre*-petition solicitations. Non-bankruptcy workout agreements frequently contain provisions similar to the following:

> "In the event that the debtor becomes a debtor in a proceeding under Chapter 11 of the Bankruptcy Code and proposes a plan of arrangement with terms as favorable or more favorable to creditors than the terms contained herein, then the creditors who have accepted this agreement shall be deemed to have accepted said plan of arrangement without the need for further separate written acceptance."

Section 1126(b) governs pre-petition acceptances. An acceptance obtained before the Chapter 11 proceeding was commenced will be counted only if:

> (1) some non-bankruptcy law such as the federal proxy rules governed the adequacy of

information furnished to creditors and shareholders, and such law was satisfied, or

(2) there is no such applicable non-bankruptcy law but creditors and shareholders were furnished "adequate information" as defined in section 1125(a) before their acceptances were solicited, section 1126(b).

2. WHO VOTES

According to section 1126(a), creditors with claims "allowed under section 502" and shareholders with interests "allowed under section 502" vote on Chapter 11 plans. The statutory requirement of "allowed under section 502" is generally satisfied by the Bankruptcy Reform Act of 1978's "double-deeming." In a Chapter 11 case, section 1111 deems filed a claim or interest that is scheduled and is not shown as disputed, contingent, or unliquidated. And, as noted on page 264, section 502 deems allowed any claim that is filed and not objected to by a party in interest.

Statutory "deeming" also eliminates voting by two classes of claims or interests. First, if a class is to receive nothing under the plan, it is deemed to have rejected the plan, and its vote need not be solicited, section 1126(g). Second, if a class is not "impaired" under the plan, the class is deemed to have accepted the plan and again its vote need not be solicited, section 1125(f).

Section 1124 establishes standards for determining whether a class of claims or interests is impaired under the plan. It provides that a class is not impaired if:

(1) the legal, equitable, and contractual rights of the holder are left unaltered by the plan; *or*

(2) the only alteration of legal, equitable, or contractual rights is reversal of an acceleration on default by curing the default and reinstating the debt; *or*

(3) cash payment to a creditor on the effective date of the plan is equal to the allowed amount of the claim; *or*

(4) cash payment to a shareholder on the effective date of the plan is equal to the greater of the share's redemption price and its liquidation preference.

3. NEEDED MAJORITIES

A class of claims has accepted a plan when more than one half in number and two thirds in amount of the allowed claims actually voting on the plan approve the plan, section 1126(c). The following hypothetical illustrates the application of section 1126(c):

D files a Chapter 11 petition. D's schedule of creditors shows 222 different creditors and $1,000,000 of debt. D's Chapter 11 plan divides creditors into four classes. Class 3 consists of 55 creditors, with claims totalling $650,000. Only 39 of the creditors in Class 3 vote on the plan. Their claims total $450,000. If at least 20 Class 3 creditors (more than $\frac{1}{2}$ of 39) with claims totalling at least $300,000 ($\frac{2}{3}$ of 450,000) vote for D's plan, the plan has been accepted by Class 3.

A class of interests has accepted a plan when at least two thirds in amount of the allowed interests actually voting on the plan approve the plan, section 1126(d).

E. CONFIRMATION

Section 1128 requires that the bankruptcy court hold a hearing on confirmation and give parties in interest notice of the hearing so that they might raise objections to confirmation. Even though the SEC is not a "party in interest," it may also raise objections to confirmation, section 1109(a).

While it is possible for more than one plan to be filed and accepted, only one plan may be confirmed. If more than one plan meets the confirmation standards of section 1129, the court "shall consider the preferences of creditors and equity security holders in determining which plan to confirm," section 1129(d).

Subparagraphs (a), (b), and (d) of section 1129 contain the confirmation standards. Section 1129(d) prohibits confirmation of a plan whose "principal purpose" is the avoidance of taxes or the avoidance of registration of securities. Subparagraph (a) and (b) are discussed below.

1. STANDARDS FOR CONFIRMATION

a. PLANS ACCEPTED BY EVERY CLASS

Subject to the limited exception of section 1129(d), a plan that has been accepted by every class of claims and every class of interests must be confirmed by the bankruptcy court if the 11 enumerated requirements of section 1129(a) satisfied. Section 1129(b) does not apply to plans that have been accepted by every class of claims and every class of interests.

Most of the requirements of section 1129(a) are easy to understand, easy to apply. Two of the requirements are somewhat complex. Section 1129(a)(7) creates a "best interests of creditors" test. It requires that each dissenting member of a class—even dissenting members of classes that approve the plan—receive at least as much under the plan as it would have received in a Chapter 7 liquidation.*

Section 1129(a)(9) provides special treatment for priority claims. A holder of an administrative expense claim or a claim for certain postpetition expenses in an involuntary case must be paid

---

* Section 1129(a)(6) looks to the value of the distribution under the plan as of the effective date of the plan. If for example the plan calls for payment to Creditor X of $100 a month for 20 months, the value of the payment to X "as of the effective date of the plan" is clearly less than $2,000.

in cash on the effective date of the plan unless the *claim holder* otherwise agrees, section 1129(a)(9)(A). Wage claims, claims for fringe benefits, and certain claims of consumer creditors must be paid in cash on the effective date of the plan unless the *class* agrees to accept deferred cash payments that have a present value equal to the amount of the claims, section 1129(a)(9)(B). Each priority tax claim must receive deferred cash payments that have a present value equal to the amount of the claim, section 1129(a)(9)(C).

b. PLANS ACCEPTED BY LESS THAN EVERY CLASS

A plan can not be confirmed unless at least one class of claims has accepted the plan, section 1129(a)(10). A plan can be confirmed even though one or more classes of claims or interests fail to accept the plan. Confirmation of plan over the objections of one or more classes of claims or interests is commonly referred to as a "cram down."

The bankruptcy court is required to confirm a plan that has been accepted by some classes of claims if the plan meets the other requirements of section 1129(a), section 1129(b), and section 1129(d). Section 1129(b)(1) requires that the plan be "fair and equitable." Section 1129(b)(2) sets out three different tests for determining whether a plan is "fair and equitable" depending on whether the dissenting class of secured claims, unsecured claims, or ownership interests. A detailed discussion of these provisions is beyond the scope of this basic student text. For a comprehensive consideration of section 1129's "fair and equitable" standard, see Klee, *All You Ever Wanted to Know About the Cram Down Under the New Bankruptcy Code,* 53 Am.Bank.L.J. 133 (1979).

2. EFFECT OF CONFIRMATION

After confirmation of a Chapter 11 plan, the debtor's performance obligations are governed by the terms of the plan. The provisions of a confirmed Chapter 11 plan bind not only the debtor but also the debtor's creditors and shareholders "whether or not such creditor, equity security holder, or general partner has accepted the plan," section 1141(a). Subject to limitations noted below, confirmation of a Chapter 11 plan operates as a discharge, section 1141(d). The following hypothetical illustrates the possible application of section 1141(a) and section 1141(d).

> D's confirmed Chapter 11 plan provides for monthly payments to creditors. Each creditor in Class 2 is to receive 5% of its claim each month for 15 months. After making two payments under the plan, D defaults. At the time of the filing of the petition D owed C $10,000. C has received $1,000 under the plan. C's claim against D is now limited to $6,500. (75% × $10,000 − 1,000).

CHAPTER 11

Chapter 11 withholds discharge from some debtors and some debts. The plan may limit discharge, section 1141(d)(1). The order of confirmation may limit discharge, section 1141(d)(1). The exceptions to discharge in section 523 are applicable to individual debtors, section 1141(d)(2). The objections to discharge in section 727 are applicable only if (1) the plan provides for the sale of all or substantially all of the debtor's property, *and* (2) the debtor does not engage in business after the consummation of the plan, section 1141(d)(3).

The following chart compares Chapter 11 discharge rules with those of Chapter 7, considered supra at page 232.

	Chapter 7	Chapter 11
Corporations, Partnerships	Not eligible for discharge	Eligible for discharge unless plan is a liquidating plan and the debtor terminates business
Section 523	Applicable to individuals	Applicable to individuals
Grounds for withholding discharge	Section 727	1. provision in plan, 2. provision in confirmation order, 3. Section 727 *if* a. liquidating plan, and b. termination of business operations

[C516]

XII. CHAPTER 13

A. COMMENCEMENT OF THE CASE

Chapter 13 of the Bankruptcy Reform Act of 1978 replaces Chapter XIII of the Bankruptcy Act of 1898. Chapter XIII was limited to a "wage earner", i. e. "an individual whose principal income is derived from wages, salary, or commissions."

Chapter 13 is open to more debtors. Subject to limited exceptions,* the source of income is not an eligibility test. A debtor may file for Chapter 13 relief if s/he:

(1) *is an individual, and*

[Chapter 13 is not available to corporations or partnerships.]

(2) *has a "regular income", and*

[The phrase "individual with a regular income" is statutorily defined in section 101(24) as "an individual whose income is sufficiently stable and regular to enable such individual to make payments under a plan under Chapter 13 of this title."]

(3) *has fixed unsecured debts of less than $100,000 and fixed secured debts of less than $350,000,* section 109(e).

---

* Neither a stockbroker nor a commodity broker may file a petition under Chapter 13, section 109(e).

[Note that the debt limitation does not include contingent, unliquidated claims. For example, Dr. Frank Burns is sued for $400,000 for malpractice on April 4. He could still file a Chapter 13 petition on April 5.]

Chapter 13 is similar to Chapter 7 and Chapter 11 in that the proceeding begins with the filing of a bankruptcy petition, section 301. Chapter 13 is different from Chapter 7 and Chapter 11 in that only the debtor may file a Chapter 13 petition. There are no involuntary, i. e., creditor-initiated, Chapter 13 proceedings.

The filing of a Chapter 13 petition triggers the automatic stay of section 362. Section 362 is discussed supra at pages 150–160. A Chapter 13 petition also stays civil collection activities directed against codebtors of the individual who filed the petition, section 1301.

B. CODEBTOR STAY

Section 1301 restrains a creditor from attempting to collect a debt from the codebtor of a Chapter 13 debtor.

The following hypothetical illustrates the application of section 1301's codebtor stay: Amy borrows money from Capital Credit to buy a pair of contact lenses. Her mother, Rosalynn, signs the note as a comaker. Amy later incurs financial problems and files a Chapter 13 petition. Section

362 stays Capital Credit from attempting to collect from Amy; section 1301 stays Capital Credit from attempting to collect from Rosalynn.

Section 1301's stay of collection activities directed at codebtors is applicable only if:

> (1) the debt is a consumer debt, and

> (2) the codebtor is not in the credit business.

This codebtor stay automatically terminates when the case is closed, dismissed, or converted to Chapter 7 or 11.

Section 1301(c) sets out three grounds for relief from the codebtor stay. Section 1301(c) requires notice and hearing and requires the court to grant relief if any of the three grounds are established.

First, the stay on collection from the codebtor will be lifted if the codebtor, not the Chapter 13 debtor, received the consideration for the claim, section 1301(c)(1). For example, if in the above hypothetical, Rosalynn, not Amy, filed for Chapter 13 relief, Capital Credit could petition for relief under section 1301(c)(1) so that it could attempt to collect from Amy. Section 1301(c)(1) also covers the situation in which the Chapter 13 debtor is merely an accommodation endorser.

Second, when the Chapter 13 plan has been filed, a creditor may obtain relief from the codebtor stay to the extent that "the plan filed by the debtor proposes not to pay such claim," section 1301(c)(2). Assume, for example, that Amy still owes Capital $200. Amy proposes to pay each holder of an unsecured claim 70 cents on the dollar. As soon as this plan is filed, Capital can obtain relief from the codebtor stay so that it can attempt to collect $60 from Rosalynn.

Third, section 1301(c)(3) requires the court to grant relief from the codebtor stay to the extent that "such creditor's interest would be irreparably harmed by such stay." The running of a state statute of limitations is not a basis for relief under section 1301(c)(3). Section 108(c) guarantees the creditor at least 30 days after the termination of the stay to file a state collection action against the codebtor.

C. TRUSTEES

There will be a trustee appointed in every Chapter 13 case, section 1302(a). In many districts, the bankruptcy judge appoints a standing trustee who serves as trustee in every Chapter 13 case, section 1302(d).

Remember that in a number of pilot districts, trustees are appointed by United States trustees, section 1501.* In such a district, the United States trustee appoints the standing trustee, section 151302. In such a district, the United States trustee serves as trustee in Chapter 13 cases if there is no standing trustee.

---

* The United States trustee is considered at pages 141–143 supra.

The trustee in a Chapter 13 case is an active trustee. S/he has all of the avoidance powers discussed supra at pages 175–232. Section 1302 imposes a number of duties on a trustee in a Chapter 13 case. Operation of the debtor's business is *not* one of the duties there enumerated. If a debtor engaged in business files a Chapter 13 petition, section 1304(b), contemplates that the business will be operated by the debtor, not by the trustee, "unless the court orders otherwise."

D. PREPARATION OF THE CHAPTER 13 PLAN

Only a debtor may file a Chapter 13 plan, section 1321. The court may dismiss a Chapter 13 proceeding or convert it to Chapter 7 for "failure to file a plan *timely* under section 1321 of this title," section 1307(c)(3).* The Act leaves the question of the meaning of "timely"—of how many days the debtor has to file such a plan—to the rules.

Section 1322 governs the contents of a Chapter 13 plan. Subsection (a) of section 1322 specifies what the plan must provide; subsection (b) specifies what the plan may provide. A Chapter 13 must provide for full payment in cash of all claims entitled to priority under section 507 ** unless the holder of the claim otherwise agrees, sec-

---

* Conversion and dismissal is considered infra at pages 149–150.

** The priority rules of section 507 are considered supra at pages 272–276.

tion 1322(a)(2). A Chapter 13 plan may provide for less than full payment to other unsecured claims. It may not, however, arbitrarily pay some holders of unsecured claims less than others. Rather, the plan must either treat all unsecured claims the same or classify claims and provide for the same treatment of each unsecured claim within a particular class, sections 1322(a)(3), 1322(b)(4).

A Chapter 13 plan may also modify the rights of most holders of secured claims. It may modify the rights of creditor *A* who has a security interest on the Chapter 13 debtor's car. It may modify the rights of Creditor *B* who has a mortgage on the Chapter 13 debtor's store. It may not, however, modify the rights of Creditor *C* who has mortgage *only* † on the Chapter 13 debtor's principal residence, section 1322(b)(2).

In the typical Chapter 13 proceeding, the source of the payments proposed by the plan will be the debtor's wages. This is not, however, a statutory requirement. Section 1322(a)(1) only requires that the plan provide for submission of "such portion of future earnings * * * of the debtor to the supervision and control of the trustee as is necessary for the execution of the plan." Payments under the plan may also be funded by sale of property of the estate, section 1322(b)(8).

---

† Note the word "only" in section 1322(b)(2). If C loaned D $100,000 and obtained a mortgage on both D's residence and D's store, it would seem that the plan could modify D's rights.

Section 1322(c) limits the payment period under a Chapter 13 plan to three years except that the court may approve a payment period of as long as five years.

E. CONFIRMATION OF THE CHAPTER 13 PLAN

In Chapter 13, creditors do not vote on the plan. Chapter 13 requires only court approval. The standards for judicial confirmation of a Chapter 13 plan are set out in section 1325.

Section 1325(a)(1) requires that the plan satisfy the provisions of Chapter 13 and other applicable bankruptcy law requirements. Section 1325(a)(2) conditions confirmation on payment of the $60 filing fee. Section 1325(a)(3) sets out a "good faith" standard.

Section 1325(a)(4) protects the holders of unsecured claims by imposing a "best interests of creditors" test: the present value of the proposed payments to a holder of an unsecured claim must be at least equal to the amount that the creditor would have received in a Chapter 7 liquidation.*

---

* The following hypothetical illustrates the practical significance of the "present value" language in section 1325(a)(4). Assume these facts:

    D owes C $1,000;

    D files a Chapter 13 petition;

    If D had filed a Chapter 7 petition, the sale of the property of the estate would have yielded a sufficient sum to pay all priority creditors in full and pay general creditors like C 36¢ on the dollar;

    D's Chapter 13 petition proposes to pay C $100 a month for 36 months.

Section 1325(a)(4) protects the holders of secured claims "provided for by the plan" by requiring one of the following:

> (A) acceptance of the plan by such a creditor; *or*

> (B) continuation of the lien and proposed payments to such a creditor of a present value that at least equals the value of the collateral; *or*

> (C) surrender of the collateral to the creditor.

Section 1325(a)(6) requires a determination of ability to perform; it requires that the debtor "will be able to make all payments under the plan and to comply with the plan."

A confirmed Chapter 13 plan is binding on the debtor and all of his creditors, section 1327(a). Unless the plan or the order confirming the plan otherwise provides, confirmation of a plan vests all of the "property of the estate" in the debtor free and clear of "any claim or interest of any creditor provided for by the plan," section 1327(c).

After confirmation, the plan is put into effect with the debtor generally making the payments

This plan does not satisfy the requirement of section 1325(a)(4). Payment of $360 over a thirty-six month period does not have a "present value" of $360.

This hypothetical is probably somewhat unrealistic. In the typical Chapter 7 case, a general creditor would receive little if anything. Accordingly, in the typical Chapter 13 case, section 1325(a)(4) will be easily satisfied.

provided in the plan to a Chapter 13 trustee who acts as a disbursing agent.

F. DISCHARGE

After completion of the payments provided for in the Chapter 13, the debtor receives a discharge, section 1328(a). A section 1328(a) discharge is *not* subject to all of the exceptions from discharge set out in section 523. The only debts excepted from a section 1328(a) discharge are:

(1) allowed claims not provided for by the plan,

(2) certain long-term obligations specifically provided for by the plan,* and

(3) claims for alimony and child support.

The bankruptcy court may grant a discharge in a Chapter 13 case even though the debtor has not completed payments called for by the plan. Section 1328(b) empowers the bankruptcy court to grant a "hardship" discharge if:

(1) the debtor's failure to complete the plan was due to circumstances for which

---

* A Chapter 13 plan may not provide for a payment period of more than five years, section 1322(c). Some of the debtor's debts may have a longer payment period. Assume, for example, that D buys a new car on January 10, 1980. She obtains new car financing from B Bank; the note provides for payments of $100 a month for 60 months. On March 30, 1981, D files a Chapter 13 petition. Her Chapter 13 plan provides for payments of $100 a month to B Bank for the 36 months of the plan, cf. section 1322(b)(5). On completion of the plan, D's obligation to B Bank for the remaining payments is excepted from discharge by section 1328(a)(1).

s/he "should not justly be held accountable; " *and*

(2) the value of the payments made under the plan to each creditor at least equals what that creditor would have received under Chapter 7; *and*

(3) modification of the plan is not "practicable."

A section 1328(b) "hardship" discharge is not as comprehensive as a section 1328(a) discharge. A "hardship" discharge is limited by all of the section 523(a) exceptions to discharge, section 1328(c).

If a debtor receives a discharge under either section 1328(a) or section 1328(b), s/he may not receive a discharge in a Chapter 7 case filed within six years of the date that the Chapter 13 case was filed unless payments under the plan totalled at least 70% of the allowed unsecured claims, and the plan was the "debtor's best effort," section 727(a)(9). A discharge under section 1328(a) or section 1328(b) does not affect the debtor's right to future Chapter 13 relief.

G. DISMISSAL AND CONVERSION

A debtor who files a Chapter 13 petition may change his mind. He may at any time request the bankruptcy court to dismiss the case or convert it to a case under Chapter 7, section 1307(a), (b).

The bankruptcy court may also dismiss a Chapter 13 case or convert it to a case under Chapter 7 on request of a creditor. The statutory standard for such creditor-requested conversion or dismissal is "for cause." Section 1307(c) sets out seven examples of "cause."

If a Chapter 13 case is converted to a Chapter 7 case, "property of the estate" will include property acquired in the period between filing of the Chapter 13 petition and conversion to Chapter 7, section 1306. Similarly, section 1305 makes the claims arising in period between filing of the Chapter 13 petition and conversion to Chapter 7 "allowable" claims.

Section 1307(d) gives a bankruptcy court the power to convert from Chapter 13 to Chapter 11 before confirmation of the plan on request of a party in interest and after notice and hearing. Section 1307(e) protects farmers from creditor-requested conversions from Chapter 13 to Chapter 7 or Chapter 11.

H. COMPARISON OF CHAPTERS 7 AND 13

Only a debtor may file a Chapter 13 petition. Each debtor who files a Chapter 13 petition could instead have filed a Chapter 7 petition. Before filing, the debtor's attorney should carefully compare Chapters 7 and 13. The following chart provides such a comparison:

CHAPTER 13

	Chapter 7	Chapter 13
1. Automatic Stay	Automatic stay of section 362 protects the debtor from creditors' collection efforts	Automatic stay of section 362 protects the debtor from creditor's collection efforts. Automatic stay of section 1301 protects co-debtors
2. Loss of Property	"Property of the estate" as described in section 541 is distributed to creditors	Except as provided in the plan or in the order of confirmation, debtor keeps "property of the estate"
3. Availability of Discharge	Section 727(a) lists ten grounds for objection to discharge	Section 727 is inapplicable. Discharge depends on completion of payments required by the plan, section 1328(a). Section 1328(b) provides for a "hardship" discharge to a debtor who makes some but not all payments required by the plan
4. Debts Discharged	Section 523(a) excepts nine classes of claims from the operation of a discharge	A section 1328(a) discharge is only subject to the exception for alimony and child support. A section 1328(b) discharge is subject to all of section 523(a)'s exceptions to discharge
5. Effect on Future Chapter 7 Relief	A debtor who receives a discharge in a Chapter 7 case may not obtain a discharge in another Chapter 7 case for six years	A Chapter 13 discharge does not affect the availability of discharge in a future Chapter 7 proceeding if the Chapter 13 plan was the debtor's "best effort" and paid 70% of all general claims

[C517]

[314]

I. COMPARISON OF CHAPTERS 11 AND 13

Any debtor who files a Chapter 13 petition could instead have filed a Chapter 11 petition. Accordingly, before filing, the debtor's attorney should carefully compare Chapters 11 and 13. Chapter 13 would seem to offer an eligible debtor * the following advantages:

1. Codebtors are protected by the automatic stay, section 1301.

2. A business debtor desiring to continue operating his or her business is probably less likely to be replaced by a trustee in Chapter 13 than in Chapter 11.**

3. Only the debtor may file a plan in Chapter 13.

4. Chapter 13 makes no provision for creditors' committees.

5. Chapter 13 does not require creditor acceptance of a plan of rehabilitation.

---

* Remember that Chapter 13 is not available to all debtors. Corporations and partnerships are not eligible for Chapter 13, and individuals have to meet the $100,000/$350,000 debt limits of section 109(e).

** Section 1303 sets out the duties of a Chapter 13 trustee. It does not mention operating the business. The phrase "Unless the court orders otherwise" in section 1304(b) is, however, statutory authority for the court turning over the operation of the debtor's business to the Chapter 13 trustee.

*

INDEX

References are to Pages

INDEX

References are to Pages

INDEX

References are to Pages

[*319*]

INDEX

INDEX

References are to Pages

INDEX

†